THE BASEBALL TRUST

THE BASEBALL TRUST

A HISTORY OF BASEBALL'S
ANTITRUST EXEMPTION

STUART BANNER

OXFORD
UNIVERSITY PRESS

OXFORD
UNIVERSITY PRESS

Oxford University Press is a department of the University of Oxford.
It furthers the University's objective of excellence in research,
scholarship, and education by publishing worldwide.

Oxford   New York

Auckland   Cape Town   Dar es Salaam   Hong Kong   Karachi
Kuala Lumpur   Madrid   Melbourne   Mexico City   Nairobi
New Delhi   Shanghai   Taipei   Toronto

With offices in

Argentina   Austria   Brazil   Chile   Czech Republic   France   Greece
Guatemala   Hungary   Italy   Japan   Poland   Portugal   Singapore
South Korea   Switzerland   Thailand   Turkey   Ukraine   Vietnam

Oxford is a registered trade mark of Oxford University Press
in the UK and in certain other countries.

Published in the United States of America by
Oxford University Press
198 Madison Avenue, New York, NY 10016

Library of Congress Cataloging-in-Publication Data
Banner, Stuart, 1963–
The baseball trust : a history of baseball's antitrust exemption / Stuart Banner.
p.   cm.
Includes bibliographical references and index.
ISBN 978-0-19-993029-6 (hardback : alk. paper)
1. Baseball—Law and legislation—United States.
2. Antitrust law—United States. I. Title.
KF3989.B36   2013
343.7307'21—dc23   2012028136

1 3 5 7 9 8 6 4 2

Printed in the United States of America
on acid-free paper

TABLE OF CONTENTS

ACKNOWLEDGMENTS

For help with the research, thanks to Freddy Berowski at the Baseball Hall of Fame, Jon Kendle at the Pro Football Hall of Fame, Glenn Longacre at the National Archives in Chicago, Charles Miller at the National Archives in San Francisco, Lesley Schoenfeld at Harvard Law School, Mary Huth at the University of Rochester, Jeff Suchanek at the University of Kentucky, Erika Gottfried at New York University, Patrizia Sione at Cornell University, Gabe Juarez at UCLA, and the archivists at the University of Wisconsin-Milwaukee and the Library of Congress.

Baseball statistics are from the indispensable Baseball Reference website, at www.baseball-reference.com.

For advice on drafts of chapters, I am grateful to participants in workshops at Boston University, the University of Iowa, and UCLA.

For advice on the manuscript as a whole, thanks to Dave McBride, Chris Schmidt, and Brad Snyder.

For financial support, I am indebted to the UCLA School of Law and the UCLA Faculty Senate.

ABBREVIATIONS

ABC	Albert B. Chandler papers, Margaret I. King Library, University of Kentucky, Lexington, Ky.
AH	August Herrmann papers, BHF.
AJG	Arthur J. Goldberg papers, LC.
BB	Bert Bell clipping file, PFHF.
BHF	A. Bartlett Giamatti Research Center, National Baseball Hall of Fame, Cooperstown, N.Y.
BR	Branch Rickey papers, LC.
CAH	Celler Antitrust Hearings, BHF.
Chicago Case	*Federal League of Professional Baseball Clubs v. National League of Professional Baseball Clubs* (N.D. Ill. 1915), Equity Case 373, RG21, NA-C.
EC	Emanuel Celler papers, LC.
FF	*The Felix Frankfurter Papers* (Frederick, Md.: University Publications of America, 1986) (microfilm).
FLS	Papers of the Federal League Suit, BHF.
HAB	Harry A. Blackmun papers, LC.
HHB	Harold H. Burton papers, LC.
HLB	Hugo L. Black papers, LC.
KBK	Kenneth B. Keating papers, Rush Rhees Library, University of Rochester, Rochester, N.Y.

LC	Manuscript Division, Library of Congress, Washington, D.C.
LH	Learned Hand papers, Harvard Law School Library, Cambridge, Mass.
MM	Marvin Miller papers, Tamiment Library, New York University, New York, N.Y.
NA-C	National Archives, Great Lakes Region, Chicago, Ill.
NA-SF	National Archives, Pacific Region, San Francisco, Calif.
PFHF	Pro Football Hall of Fame, Canton, Ohio.
PS	Peter Seitz papers, Kheel Center, Cornell University, Ithaca, N.Y.
RHJ	Robert H. Jackson papers, LC.
SRRH	Stafford, Rosenbaum, Rieser and Hansen: *State of Wisconsin vs. Milwaukee Braves et al.* records, WHS.
WHS	Wisconsin Historical Society Archives, Golda Meir Library, University of Wisconsin–Milwaukee, Milwaukee, Wisc.
WJB	William J. Brennan, Jr., papers, LC.
WOD	William O. Douglas papers, LC.

INTRODUCTION

This book is about one of the oddest features of our legal system, the near-complete exemption of baseball from antitrust law. Every other sport—like virtually every sort of business—is governed by the antitrust laws, but not baseball. In a legal system with no shortage of quirks, this one may be the most famous, because it is frequently discussed in the sports media. Most sports fans may have only the vaguest sense of what antitrust law is, but if they know one thing about it, it is that baseball is exempt.

Scarcely anyone believes that baseball's exemption makes any sense. The antitrust laws prohibit business competitors from colluding in ways that harm consumers—for example, by fixing prices or reducing output. Applying antitrust law to sports can raise some difficult questions, but they are the same questions in every sport. There is nothing unique about baseball that would justify an exemption denied to the other sports.

Each team in the major American sports league is a separately owned business. The teams compete in their games, of course, and they are also business competitors in many respects. The Mets and the Yankees both sell tickets to baseball games, for example, and while there are some customers so loyal to one team that they would not be interested in attending the other's games, there are also customers who choose whether to see the Mets or the Yankees based on factors like the price of the tickets and the quality of the product on the field. All major league baseball teams compete with one another to hire players and coaches. In these respects, sports teams differ little from grocery stores or auto manufacturers. They are engaged in a competition to offer the best products at the lowest prices, and consumers benefit from that competition.

In other respects, however, sports are very different from other industries, because a sports league cannot long survive without some degree of equality among its teams. In most markets, if there is one firm that can make a better product than its competitors, or sell at a lower price than its competitors, the firm will succeed at its competitors' expense, and consumers will be the beneficiaries. Not so in sports. If the Yankees become so much better than all the other teams that baseball games lose their suspense, baseball will cease to be an entertaining product, and all teams, including the Yankees, will suffer. A grocery store or an auto manufacturer will strive to do so well that its competitors are driven out of business, but if the Yankees' competitors are driven out of business, the Yankees will be out of business too. Meanwhile, sports teams have to cooperate on matters like playing rules and schedules. Agreements among competitors in most industries are harmful to consumers, but in sports, consumers would be harmed by the absence of such agreements. If the Mets play by a rule requiring three strikes for an out but the Yankees insist on four, or if the Mets and Yankees both show up in Cleveland to play the Indians on the same day, the fans would not benefit.

These differences between sports and other industries raise some difficult antitrust questions. To ensure that players are allocated roughly evenly among teams, for instance, is it lawful for a league to have a player draft? In most industries, a draft for entry-level employees would be a clear violation of antitrust law. A computer programmer just out of college can work for whichever company offers her the best package of salary, location, and so on. If the software companies colluded to institute a draft of computer programmers, so that a programmer drafted by Microsoft had to work at a salary and in a city of Microsoft's choosing, there would be little doubt of the scheme's illegality. Are conditions in sports sufficiently different to have a different rule? The same question could be asked about any number of aspects of the sports business, including the location of teams, the licensing of merchandise, the sale of television rights, and so on. Grocery stores cannot collude to allow only one company per city. Can sports teams? Movie studios cannot collude to sell a single package of broadcast rights to television networks. Can sports teams? These are genuinely hard questions.

The important point is that these difficult antitrust questions are exactly the same in baseball as in any other sport. There is no reason that antitrust law should treat a draft of baseball players differently from a draft of football players. An agreement to restrict the location of baseball teams raises the same antitrust issue as an agreement to restrict the location of basketball teams. Whatever antitrust concerns are implicated by the sale of broadcast rights to baseball games are equally implicated by the sale of broadcast rights to hockey games. If baseball should have an antitrust exemption, so should other sports, and if other sports should be governed by the antitrust laws, so should baseball. On this point there is virtually no disagreement. As one law professor summarizes the near consensus, "baseball's unique antitrust status . . . has been a favorite whipping boy for scholars and journalists alike. . . . It has enjoyed almost no support except from the baseball hierarchy itself."[1]

How is it, then, that baseball came to be the only sport exempt from the antitrust laws? The exemption's origin is a 1922 Supreme Court case called *Federal Baseball Club of Baltimore v. National League,* in which the Court held that the federal antitrust laws did not apply to baseball, because these laws only governed interstate commerce, and baseball was not a form of interstate commerce. The issue returned to the Supreme Court again in 1953 and once more in 1972, and on both occasions the Court declined to overrule *Federal Baseball Club.* In the 1972 case, *Flood v. Kuhn,* the Court even expanded the exemption by declaring that baseball is exempt not just from federal antitrust laws but from state antitrust laws as well. Meanwhile, in two cases from the 1950s, one involving boxing and the other football, the Court made clear that the exemption is only for baseball, not for sports generally. All other sports are governed by the antitrust laws, just like any other business. Congress has had the power, all the while, to amend the antitrust laws to treat sports equally, but it has done so only to a very limited extent. The outcome of this combination of activity and inactivity is an exemption just for baseball, one that is now nearly a century old.

How can we explain the persistence of such a weird state of affairs?[2] The most common explanation emphasizes the unique position of baseball in American culture. The exemption is "explicable as one more example of the 'peculiar' status of baseball as an American enterprise," concludes one distinguished legal historian. Neither the Court nor Congress has been willing to subject baseball to the antitrust laws, another argues, because to do so "would imply that the national pastime—the national game—is not a game at all." As one commentator sums up this view, baseball's special treatment "has been difficult to explain from a purely legal analysis. Rather it may reflect baseball's truly unique status in American culture. Courts and

Congress historically have left this aberration untouched, perhaps even as an implicit recognition of baseball as the national pastime."[3]

This account rests on two observations that are indisputably true. First, baseball *does* have a unique status in American culture. Baseball is much more than a business, and indeed much more than simply a sport. Baseball has a history and social meaning that set it apart from the other sports. A. Bartlett Giamatti, the Renaissance scholar who briefly served as commissioner of baseball, may have put it best. Baseball, he wrote, is "the most strenuously nostalgic of all our sports, the most traditionally conscious of tradition, the most intent on enshrining its rural origins." This has been true for a very long time. The closest study of the history of federal regulation of professional sports observes that in 1951 baseball already "maintained an image in the hearts and minds of Americans as the pastoral, innocent, and noble national pastime," quite unlike the popular image of other professional sports.[4]

And second, baseball's cultural meaning has given rise to considerable sentimentality over the years, especially among older men, some of whom have been judges and legislators. As we will see, one can find starry-eyed judges professing their love for baseball as far back as 1915, when baseball confronted its first antitrust crisis. In more recent times, Harry Blackmun's opinion for the Supreme Court in *Flood v. Kuhn* is famous for its lengthy ode to the lore of the game, in a section of the opinion so embarrassing that two of Blackmun's colleagues refused to join it even though they agreed with Blackmun's legal reasoning. Members of Congress, meanwhile, have always recognized the political value of being seen as supporters of the national pastime. It is not difficult to collect examples of judges and politicians making sentimental statements about baseball.

The argument of this book, however, is that baseball's cultural status is neither the primary reason it originally gained its exemption nor the primary reason the exemption has persisted for nearly a century. Beyond a simple tale of policy preferences, in which powerful judges and legislators expressed their passion for baseball by insulating it from antitrust attack, the history of baseball's antitrust exemption is something more interesting. It is a story in which a sophisticated business organization has been able to work the levers of the legal system to achieve a result favored by almost no one else. For all the well-documented foibles of the owners of major league baseball teams, baseball has consistently received and followed smart antitrust advice from sharp lawyers, going all the way back to the 1910s. At the same time, it is a story that serves as an arresting reminder of the path-dependent nature of the legal system. At each step, judges and legislators made decisions that were perfectly sensible when considered one at a time, but this series of decisions yielded an outcome that makes no sense at all.

THE BASEBALL TRUST

THE RESERVE CLAUSE

Between 1912 and 1922, professional baseball would be barraged with antitrust claims—in the press, in Congress, and, most ominously, in the courts. By locking up all the best players with perpetual contracts, critics would charge, the National and American Leagues had formed a monopoly that suppressed competition from other leagues and prevented players from earning salaries that reflected the true value of their labor. For ten years, there was a significant chance that either Congress or the courts would force baseball to reorganize in a fundamental way. The threat would not dissipate until 1922, when the Supreme Court held that the Sherman Antitrust Act did not apply to professional baseball.

Perhaps the most curious thing about this episode is that it took so long to begin. The labor practices that formed the core of baseball's monopoly were hardly new in the 1910s. They date to 1879, when the owners of the National League teams first agreed on what would come to be called the reserve clause—the term in player contracts that effectively bound a player to his team for his entire career. Nothing changed in the 1910s. Nor were there any new developments in the law in the 1910s. The Sherman Antitrust Act had been on the books since 1890, and there was a plausible argument, even before then, that baseball was a kind of monopoly prohibited by the common law. The structure of the baseball business and the relevant law had both been in place for more than twenty years before the antitrust crisis of 1912–1922. Why were there no antitrust investigations in Congress and no antitrust suits filed before the 1910s? Trust-busting was in the headlines for many other sorts of businesses around the turn of the century; why not baseball? Certainly, one might think, the players had every incentive to press antitrust claims against baseball, as did the various competing leagues that sprung up from time to time. Why didn't they?

To answer this question, we need to look closely at the origins and the early use of the reserve clause, and particularly at the many court decisions between 1890 and 1914 involving the clause. The reserve clause was a source of considerable controversy in its early years, in the courts and within baseball itself. Players, owners, and outside observers disagreed, not just about the clause's merits, but about whether it could be enforced at all.

The bugbear of baseball

The reserve clause would be a standard term in player contracts for nearly a century, but it did not start that way. It began instead as an agreement among the National League clubs. By the end of the 1879 season, the league's fourth, the teams' owners could look back on some difficult times. In its first season, seven of the eight clubs had lost money, and Philadelphia and New York were even expelled for failing to play all their games. The second year was even worse: the clubs in Hartford, St. Louis, and Louisville all folded at the end of the season. Of the eight original teams only three were left, in Boston, Chicago, and Cincinnati. The league added three new teams for 1878, in Indianapolis, Milwaukee, and Providence, but Indianapolis and Milwaukee lasted only a single season. Four new clubs joined in 1879 to restore an eight-team league—Buffalo, Syracuse, Troy, and Cleveland—but they were in a precarious position as well. Professional baseball was just not a profitable business.[1]

The financial situation was so bleak that representatives of only six of the eight clubs showed up at the end-of-year meeting in Buffalo in 1879. Syracuse and Cincinnati did not attend: the Syracuse club would go out of business before the next season began, and Cincinnati would be expelled the year after for supplementing its income by selling beer at games in violation of a league rule. The six clubs that did attend were eager to find some way to control their costs. "The financial results of the past season prove that salaries must come down," declared league president William Hulbert, the president of the Chicago White Stockings. "The expenses of many of the clubs have far exceeded their receipts, attributable wholly to high salaries." The teams first considered establishing limits on salaries, but they decided that it would be easier if they simply ceased competing with each other to hire the best players. Each club was accordingly allowed to reserve five of its players for the ensuing season. These five men would "not be allowed to sign with any other club without permission," Hulbert explained. "This would prevent unhealthy competition."[2] Once a club reserved a player, the other clubs would treat him as if he were already under contract for the 1880 season.

The players the clubs reserved in the fall of 1879 were, unsurprisingly, the best and most highly paid of the era. They included Cap Anson of the White Stockings, early in a career in which he would become the first player with 3,000 hits; Paul Hines of the Providence Grays, the league leader in batting average and total bases in both 1878 and 1879; and Tommy Bond of the Boston Red Caps, who had the league's lowest earned run average in 1877 and 1879.[3]

This agreement proved successful in reducing the costs of running a baseball team. It "kept salaries within money-making bounds," explained Alfred Spink, founder of The Sporting News, in his 1911 history of the game. Tommy Bond, for example, who had earned $2,200 in 1879, received only $1,500 in 1880. Second baseman Jack Burdock and shortstop Ezra Sutton, Boston's highest paid players after Bond in 1879, saw their 1880 salaries drop from $1,800 to $1,500 and $1,200 respectively. In 1881, for the first time, most of the clubs made a profit. Club owners were so pleased that they expanded the reserve list to eleven players in 1883, twelve in 1885, and fourteen—an entire team—in 1887. Before 1887, the reserve system was included in player contracts only indirectly, in a clause that required players to comply with league rules, one of which was the reserve rule. Beginning in 1887, it was included in contracts explicitly, as a club option to renew the contract for the following year. The most successful of the competing leagues also adopted the reserve clause. The American Association, which existed from 1882 to 1891, reached an 1883 agreement with the National League that both leagues would respect the other's reserve list.[4] The American League, so named in 1899 after several years as a minor league called the Western League, reached a similar agreement with the National League in 1903.

The result was an unusual system of labor relations, in which players were effectively bound for life to the teams that first signed them. Every contract included a clause allowing the club to renew it for the following year. Once renewed, the next year's contract included a similar clause for the year after, and so on, for the remainder of a player's career. Even a player who sat out of baseball for a year or more was still controlled by the team with which he last played. Charles "Pop" Snyder, for instance, one of the best defensive catchers of the period, was on Boston's initial 1879 reserve list. He refused to play in 1880 rather than accept the salary he was offered, but he returned to the team in 1881, at the same salary he earned in 1879, when no other club would offer a contract.[5] The clubs were under no similar obligation binding them to their players. Any player could be sold or traded to another club without his consent. Players could be released at any time with ten days' notice. Even in the late nineteenth century, when workers throughout the economy had few rights enforceable against their employers, baseball stood out as a business in which the rules governing labor were conspicuously one-sided.

The reserve clause had critics from the beginning, including many players, who saw all too clearly its effect in reducing their salaries. "A baseball player may double and treble in professional skill and value," Life magazine remarked in 1887, "and the principal profit will accrue, not to the player himself, but to the club that has the right to reserve him," who could sell the player to another club. "Such a system is rotten." Under the reserve clause, charged the labor leader Charles Lichtman, "it is possible practically to condemn a man to perpetual slavery." The system of annually renewing contracts "would be about as near perpetual employment as you could get."[6]

The most well known critic of the reserve clause was John Montgomery Ward (figure 1.1), the star pitcher, shortstop, and manager for the New York Giants in the 1880s and early 1890s. Ward possessed a remarkable combination of talents and interests. He began his career as a pitcher, and led the National League in wins and strikeouts in 1879. When pitching wore out his arm—he pitched 587 innings in 1879 and 595 innings in 1880—he switched to shortstop and was one of the best hitters in the league. When the Providence Grays sold him to the Giants in 1883, Ward enrolled at Columbia Law School. He graduated in 1885, and used his legal training to organize and lead the first labor union in sports, the Brotherhood of Professional Base Ball Players, as well as the short-lived Players' League, which broke away

John M. Ward, Capt. New York B. B. Club.

Newsboy   NEW YORK.

Figure 1.1: John Montgomery Ward of the Giants, one of the stars of the 1880s and a graduate of Columbia Law School, was an eloquent critic of the reserve clause. Ward organized the first players' union and led the Players' League, which broke away from the National League in 1890. The Giants' lawsuit against Ward was the first to test whether the reserve clause was enforceable in court. B-276.59, National Baseball Hall of Fame.

from the National League in 1890 but lasted only one season. As we will see shortly, his litigation against the Giants yielded the first important court opinion on the enforceability of the reserve clause. After he retired in 1894, Ward remained active in baseball as a lawyer for players and then as president and part owner of the Boston Braves.[7]

In the middle of the 1887 season, while batting .338 and leading the league with 111 stolen bases, Ward published an article titled "Is the Base-Ball Player a Chattel?" in *Lippincott's Magazine*, a widely read literary monthly. He argued that the reserve clause indeed turned players into property. "Like a fugitive-slave law, the reserve-rule denies him a harbor or a livelihood, and carries him back, bound and shackled, to the club from which he attempted to escape," Ward charged. "We have, then, the curious result of a contract which on its face is for seven months being binding for life, and when the player's name is once attached thereto his professional liberty is gone forever." The reserve clause "inaugurated a species of serfdom which gave one set of men a life-estate in the labor of another," and gave rise to "the manipulation of a traffic in players, a sort of speculation in live stock, by which they are bought, sold, and transferred like so many sheep." Ward argued that baseball could instead be run like any other business, without treating its employees as property.[8]

Ward was not the first to compare the reserve clause with slavery, and he would not be the last. A system in which players were controlled for life, and in which they could be bought and sold, did resemble slavery, which had been abolished only a few decades earlier. For all their travails, however, baseball players earned considerably more than the average American worker. They were hardly wealthy by later standards, but they were comfortable enough to make complaints of slavery seem a bit incongruous. Their work, meanwhile, did not seem particularly grueling. "Ward simply demanded a pitiful $5,000 to play baseball for the New-York Club this year," one local paper mocked, at a time when the average annual wage for non-farm employees was only around $460. "The labor consists in playing for about two hours six times a week, for about six months." If this was slavery, it was a form of slavery most workers would have been happy to accept. By the 1880s, the notion that baseball players were enslaved was already being satirized in the press. "It would not be a bad idea for the clubs to establish a slave-market," smirked *Puck*, the leading humor magazine of the period. "Baseball players today are nothing more than slaves," the *Los Angeles Times* joked, slaves like Johnny Evers, "who just bought a dandy new car the other day," and Joe Tinker, who "makes about $5000 for five months' work in baseball and $350 a week for his vaudeville sketch of baseball in the winter." Recurring allegations of slavery were enough, though, to make club officials circumspect about how they described their transactions. "You have doubtless seen, as I have," A. G. Mills advised Thomas Lynch, "talk about the 'sale and slavery' of players." Mills was a former president of the National League; Lynch was the current president. "While I would be the last to advocate any relaxation of the rules of reservation," Mills explained, "yet it has seemed to me that the terms 'purchase' and 'sale,' as applied to the transfer of players, might wisely be avoided in newspaper talk and eliminated from the rules."[9]

The original purpose of the reserve clause, and one clear effect of it, was to reduce the salaries of players by preventing them from offering their services to the highest bidder. Club officials knew, however, that for public relations purposes it would be better to rely on other justifications. Perhaps the most common defense of the reserve clause was that it was necessary to prevent the richest clubs from signing all the best players. In an era before games were broadcast on radio or television, revenue came almost entirely from ticket sales, so clubs in bigger cities had an advantage. The National League played in cities with widely disparate populations, ranging from New York (1.2 million in the 1880 census) and Philadelphia (850,000) all the way down to Hartford (42,000). "The reserve clause was placed in contracts to prevent the wrecking of leagues by competitive bidding," explained the sportswriter Hugh Fullerton, "whereby the richest club could always win." August Herrmann, president of the Cincinnati Reds and longtime president of the National Commission (a precursor to the present-day position of commissioner of baseball), shared this view, at least in public. "The chief factor in its adoption," he testified in one of the antitrust suits of the 1910s, "was the resentment by press and patrons in smaller cities at [the] annual loss of favorite players" to richer clubs in bigger cities.[10] A commercially successful league required a minimum level of competitive balance among the teams. From the perspective of club officials, the reserve clause was an essential means of preserving that balance.

Even apart from competitive balance, baseball officials added, there was commercial value in preventing teams from raiding other teams for players. In his autobiography, Cap Anson recalled this as the primary purpose of the reserve clause. The earliest years of professional baseball were marred by instances of players jumping from one club to another in the middle of the season, a practice called "revolving," which on occasion caused teams to disband without completing their schedules. By the turn of the century, revolving was a distant memory, and many, including A. G. Mills and the influential sportswriter Francis Richter, gave the credit to the reserve clause.[11]

The reserve clause was also necessary, some argued, to protect the clubs' investments in the players. Players were usually signed when they were young and inexperienced. "Thousands of dollars and years of care and attention are expended by a club in an endeavor to convert a recruit into a finished player," explained the Arkansas lawyer Charles Jacobson. "This would have to be abandoned if, after this expense, the services of the player could not be reserved by that club." The novelist and baseball fan Charles Stewart compared the training of a baseball player with the training of a soldier. As a nation claimed the labor of its army, he argued, a club had a similar right in the services of its players, as recompense for its investment in their skills. "Each of the big clubs is taken in the winter to some favorable clime,— possibly Florida or California,—and trained in preparation for the base-ball campaign," Stewart reasoned. "This development of a good player consti- tutes a sort of governmental right in him, and this right is jealously guarded. In every way, the handling of the base-ball player, the observation of a prop- erty right in him, and the expectation of 'loyalty,' is comparable to the way of a nation with a soldier."[12]

None of these arguments was very persuasive. The reserve clause was not the only way, and was likely not the best way, to assure competitive balance. The reserve clause permitted the poorer clubs to sell players to the richer; the only effect of the clause was to ensure that the proceeds went to the club's owners rather than to the players themselves. The league might instead have pooled ticket revenue or used a salary cap, as in many sports today. Another option would have been to locate teams only in the largest cities, so revenue would have been roughly equivalent for each team. Even with the reserve clause, meanwhile, there were usually very large disparities among the teams. In 1890, for instance, Pittsburgh won 23 games and lost 113, while Brooklyn was 86–43; in 1895, Louisville was 35–96 while Brooklyn went 87–43. In later years, when the composition of the two major leagues remained fixed for long stretches, despite the reserve clause there would be some teams (like the New York Yankees) who were nearly always among the best and others (like the Washington Senators) who were virtually always among the worst.

The problems of "revolving" and of recouping investments in players could likewise have been handled by other methods. Players could not jump to other teams mid-season unless club owners were willing to ignore year-long contracts already signed, so a simple agreement to respect exist- ing contracts would have put an end to revolving. There was no need to make contracts perpetual. The sums clubs actually invested in early-career players—to the extent such "investments" can be disentangled from pay for services already at a sufficiently high level of skill—were probably never very large. Such investments, in any event, could have been recouped by using multi-year contracts.

On the other hand, it was equally clear that baseball was much more stable and profitable under the reserve clause than it had been before and that to some extent the players were sharing in this success. "The reserve rule has proven to be one of the fundamentals of successful Base Ball control," concluded Albert Spalding, the player turned equipment manufacturer. "It is now conceded by all familiar with management to be a requisite of professional ball." F. C. Lane, the editor of *Baseball Magazine*, conceded that the reserve clause brought hardship in individual cases, but considered that on balance "the so-called ownership of the player by the magnate has injured the few for the greater good of the many. For it has enabled baseball to develop into a huge industry employing thousands of men and paying much larger salaries than would otherwise be possible." "The Reserve Clause is the bugbear of baseball," Lane concluded on another occasion. "Criticised without measure, and deserving of criticism, it still remains the foundation of all permanent prosperity, the sole dependable source of stability and organization in the modern game."[13]

Even many of the players were ambivalent. Johnny Evers, the second baseman for the Chicago Cubs, was certain that the reserve clause was illegal, and even "directly in defiance of the Constitution and of the Rights of Man," but he reluctantly concluded that it was necessary, "because of the nature of the peculiar business" of baseball. "Legally, the baseball player is a slave held in bondage," Evers declared, "but he is the best treated, most pampered slave of history." David Fultz (figure 1.2), a lawyer and former player who in 1912 founded the Fraternity of Professional Baseball Players of America, a short-lived labor union, summed up the players' dilemma in his monthly column in *Baseball Magazine*. "We have given this situation a great deal of thought for a number of years," Fultz explained, "and although realizing the individual hardships brought about by the reserve rule, we have never yet been able to formulate any substitute for it."[14] The reserve clause reduced the share of the pie enjoyed by the players, but many were certain that it also increased the overall size of the pie, so its net effect on the welfare of players was ambiguous.

INVALID AND UNENFORCEABLE

Was the reserve clause permissible under the law of contracts? The question arose in many court cases between 1890 and 1914. These early cases were not antitrust challenges. Rather, they were suits by National League clubs

Figure 1.2: The lawyer David Fultz, shown here in his playing days with the New York Highlanders (later the Yankees), founded the short-lived Fraternity of Professional Baseball Players in 1912. "Although realizing the individual hardships brought about by the reserve rule," Fultz admitted, "we have never yet been able to formulate any substitute for it." BL-4022.99, National Baseball Hall of Fame.

(and later, American League clubs as well) against their players for breach of contract, in which the players responded by claiming that the reserve clause was unenforceable under the common law. Litigation came in waves, each wave corresponding to the birth of a competing league that tried to sign away players bound by the reserve clause. Without a competing league to offer an alternative job, there could be no occasion for asserting that the reserve clause was inconsistent with the law of contracts, because a player could not sue one of the other National League clubs for failing to make a competing offer. "The courts possess no power to compel a person to hire another," as one editorialist explained, so a player who hoped to earn more with another National League club had no recourse under contract law. Only when job opportunities arise outside of the existing structure of baseball could the reserve clause come under judicial scrutiny. Until then, "baseball law is a law unto itself," the same writer continued, "a collection of arbitrary customs, adopted by the baseball men, that are not in accordance with common law."[15]

A few competing leagues arose between 1890 and 1914, however, so by the end of this period there was an elaborate jurisprudence of baseball contracts. The cases were not all consistent, but by and large the players won. The reserve clause was held to be unenforceable more often than it was enforced.

The first wave of reserve clause litigation took place in the winter of 1889–1890, when many of the leading players, led by John Montgomery Ward, announced their plans to form the Players' League for the 1890 season.[16] The Players' League would have eight teams, all composed mostly of players who had spent 1889 under contract with a National League team and were thus subject to the reserve clause. Of the fourteen players reserved by the second-place Boston Beaneaters (the team that would later be called the Braves), for example, ten left for the Players' League, including the team's stars, first baseman Dan Brouthers, outfielder Michael "King" Kelly, and pitcher Charley "Old Hoss" Radbourn. This "secession movement," worried the sportswriter Henry Chadwick, threatened "to substitute a chaotic condition of things in the professional arena in the place of law and order."[17] The National League prepared to fight back in the courts.

At the November 1889 National League meeting, John Rogers, owner of the Philadelphia Phillies, reported that "it is a notorious fact that a number of players reserved by League Clubs have declared their intention to violate said reserve" to join the Players' League. Rogers declared that he had obtained "the opinions of eminent counsel" that the National League clubs had the rights to these players in 1890. The owners accordingly resolved that the National League would provide financial assistance to each club in filing suits against defectors, and that the League would form a committee to provide each club with legal advice.[18]

From the perspective of the National League clubs, there was little point in suing the players for money. "Such suits would amount to nothing," confided Arthur Soden, owner of the Boston Beaneaters, "because there would be no property to attach." Few players were wealthy enough to pay damages. The only remedy worth the cost of a suit would be an injunction ordering the players back to their National League clubs. Here, though, the owners faced an obstacle. American courts, following longstanding English practice, consistently refused to order employees to work for their employers. In legal jargon, courts did not award specific performance of employment contracts. Money damages were the only available remedy. "The reason of this is obvious," explained Frederic Jessup Stimson in his treatise on labor law. "The contract of service is by its nature indefinite in its terms, and deals not with goods or commodities in the ordinary sense, but with a man's self, his abilities or his person. To enforce such a contract against a person's will would be too much like enforcing a contract of slavery."[19] The reserve clause thus could not be enforced by compelling players to return to their clubs.

There was only one way around this obstacle. While courts would not order employees to work for the employer with whom they were under contract, in certain cases courts *would* order employees *not* to work for other employers. These were exceptional cases, in which the service provided by the employee was so unique and specialized that money damages would not be an adequate remedy. The most famous example at the time was an English case from 1852 called *Lumley v. Wagner*, in which a famous opera singer (Johanna Wagner, the composer's niece) under contract with one theater was enjoined from singing at another theater during the term of the contract. A similar case, involving the actress Fanny Morant Smith, had been decided in New York in the 1870s. National League club owners were confident that professional baseball players fell within the same principle, and that even if they couldn't force the players back to their clubs directly, they could do so indirectly, by securing injunctions barring the players from taking the field for the Players' League. "The most eminent lawyers in New York, Chicago and Indianapolis have written opinions on the case," Arthur Soden declared. "I read one very lengthy one, in which cases were cited bearing on our point, of actors and actresses." The National League was planning to file one such suit. It would be a highly symbolic suit against the ringleader of the players' revolt: the New York Giants, Soden explained, "will sue John M. Ward as a test case."[20]

The players and the owners of the new Players' League clubs were equally certain that they would prevail. "What shall we do?" asked John Vanderslice, the lawyer for the Philadelphia Athletics of the Players' League. "Why, fight them in court, of course. And we don't want any delay about the matter, either. The quicker it comes the better it will suit us." The players had consulted counsel too—men "of world-wide reputation," Vanderslice insisted—who had bolstered their confidence. "When we submitted a [National] League contract to a certain leading lawyer at the Philadelphia bar, and explained matters to him," Vanderslice reported, "he snapped his fingers and said it was not worth the paper it was printed on. 'Why,' said he, 'where is the equivalent? Where is the consideration? This contract is all one sided.... Do you suppose any court will ever uphold such a contract? Never!'" Francis Richter thought this argument doomed the reserve clause to extinction. "It is inconceivable that the courts will recognize any other interpretation of the clause than the one put on it by the players," he predicted in the pages of *Sporting Life*. "If the [National] League's position were sustained it would introduce and legalize another form of chattel slavery in the United States. The same clause could be introduced into contracts in other forms of business, and the result might be, could be, as far as the law would be concerned, a complete sale of employees to employers."[21]

National League clubs filed three suits against defecting players in December 1889 and January 1890. Two were brought by the Giants, one, as promised, against John Montgomery Ward, and the other against star catcher Buck Ewing, who was then at the peak of his career. Ward had signed on to be the shortstop and manager for the Players' League's Brooklyn team, to be called the Ward's Wonders; Ewing had signed with the New York team, which the Players' League defiantly called the Giants, the same name as the existing National League club in New York. The third suit was filed by the Philadelphia Phillies against young shortstop Bill Hallman, a veteran of only one full season, who had left for Philadelphia's Players' League club, the Athletics. All three suits alleged that the players had been under contract for the 1889 season and were thus, because of the reserve clause, bound to their clubs for the 1890 season as well. In all three, the National League clubs sought injunctions prohibiting the players from participating in games for the Players' League clubs.

Ward's case was decided first, in January 1890, because it was the only one of the three in which the National League club sought a preliminary injunction, a temporary order barring Ward from playing for the Players' League until a trial could be held. New York Judge Morgan O'Brien agreed with the National League that Ward was a talented enough player to fit within the doctrine of *Lumley v. Wagner*. "Between an actor of great histrionic ability and a professional base-ball player, of peculiar fitness and skill to fill a particular position, no substantial distinction" could be made, O'Brien held. If an enforceable contract existed between Ward and the Giants, therefore, O'Brien would have been willing to enjoin Ward from jumping to the Players' League. But was there an enforceable contract for the 1890 season? Ward's 1889 contract included the usual reserve clause, which provided that the Giants had the right to reserve Ward for 1890, but said nothing about what his 1890 salary would be. In a supplemental agreement signed the same day, the Giants promised that if they reserved Ward for 1890, his salary would be at least $3,000. These were the only terms to which Ward and the Giants had agreed.

Judge O'Brien concluded that this was not enough to make an enforceable contract for the 1890 season, for two reasons. First, the contract was too indefinite to be enforced. "What does the defendant, Ward, agree to do?" the judge asked. "What salary is to be paid him?" Ward was to be paid at least $3,000, "but how much more is he to receive? And in case of a dispute between the parties, how is the amount of salary to be determined?" Because it lacked definite terms, O'Brien held, the reserve clause did not create a contract between Ward and the Giants for 1890, but was merely a preliminary agreement to make a contract at a later time. Alternatively, the judge continued, one could assume that a player's salary in one year would remain the same indefinitely. That assumption would remove the ambiguity as to salary, O'Brien concluded, but it would only make the reserve clause unenforceable for a different reason—lack of mutuality. Under this principle of equity jurisprudence, a plaintiff could not secure an injunction ordering a defendant to comply with a contract if, under the terms of the contract, the defendant lacked the power to secure a comparable injunction against the plaintiff. "We have the spectacle presented of a contract which binds one party for a series of years and the other party for 10 days," he remarked, "and of the party who is itself bound for 10 days coming into a court of equity to enforce its claims against the party bound for years." In practical terms, the contract bound the player to the club, but it did not bind the club to the player. Such a contract, O'Brien determined, was too one-sided to be enforced with an injunction. "A party not bound by the agreement itself has no right to call upon a court of equity to enforce specific performance against the other contracting party," the judge concluded, quoting a recent treatise on the specific performance of contracts. O'Brien accordingly refused to grant a preliminary injunction barring Ward from playing for the Players' League.[22]

"Ward Wins His Fight," read the headline in the next day's newspaper. The players proclaimed victory. The decision "unmistakably and plainly shows on what slippery ground base ball, as now organized, stands," *Sporting Life* declared. "The League must be blind or willfully perverse if it fails to realize the futility of its efforts." The National League owners made the best of a bad situation; they emphasized that Judge O'Brien had only denied a preliminary injunction, not a final one, and that they would still have the opportunity to prove their case at a trial. At a special meeting the day after O'Brien issued his decision, they resolved not only to continue with the New York and Philadelphia suits, but to file similar suits "in every State and Federal Court in the United States" if necessary to stop players from jumping to the new league.[23] They must have realized, however, that they had little hope of persuading Judge O'Brien to change his view. They never did set Ward's case for trial. Ward spent the 1890 season in the Players' League. The players had won the first battle.

They won the second battle six weeks later, when Judge Martin Russell Thayer reached precisely the same conclusions in the Philadelphia case. Bill Hallman's contract was similar to John Montgomery Ward's: his 1889 salary was $1,400, and the Phillies had the right to reserve Hallman for the 1890 season at a salary no less than that. "A careful reading of the agreement," Judge Thayer reasoned, "discloses the fact that there is not a word in it binding Hallman to renew that contract for another season, upon the same terms." Because the reserve clause failed to specify what Hallman's 1890 salary would be, Thayer continued, "it does not make any definite contract whatever between the parties, in 1890, but only reserves the defendant, subject to a contract thereafter to be made setting out the particular terms and provisions upon which he should be engaged." The reserve clause was thus too indefinite to be enforced. On the other hand, if one were to assume that Hallman's 1890 salary was to be identical to his 1889 salary, "then it follows of course that he must thereby bind himself afresh" in each subsequent year, "so long as it may suit the pleasure of the plaintiffs to insist upon the reservation clause and its annual renewal." So interpreted, however, the reserve clause would be unenforceable for lack of mutuality. "He is absolutely at their mercy," Thayer remarked, "and may be sent adrift at the beginning or in the middle of a season, at home or two thousand miles from it, sick or well, at the mere arbitrary discretion of the plaintiffs." Where one side was bound for life, and the other could terminate the agreement at any time, "it is perfectly apparent that such a contract is so wanting in mutuality that no court of equity would lend its aid to compel compliance with it."[24] Hallman was free to join the Philadelphia Athletics of the Players' League.

The reserve clause seemed on the verge of extinction. "The decision of Judge Thayer of Philadelphia that the 'reserve' clause in the contracts of ball players is null and cannot be enforced, simply puts in the form of a judicial ruling what every reasoning man outside the ranks of professional ball players has always assumed," the *New York Times* editorialized soon after the opinion was published. "Henceforth a player will be worth just what he can get for his services." The "slave system of the League" had now twice been declared unenforceable. "I have nothing further to say," acknowledged the Phillies' owner, John Rogers, "except that in Philadelphia our 'reserve' clause will have to be rewritten, or it must disappear from all future contracts."[25]

In late March, just as the 1890 season was about to begin, the players won the third case too. "What is this right to 'reserve' the defendant?" asked the federal judge William Wallace. "In a legal sense, it is merely a contract to make a contract if the parties can agree." Because Buck Ewing had never made any such contract with the National League Giants for the 1890 season, they had no right to prevent him from signing a contract with the Players' League Giants.[26] Ewing would be one of the stars of the Players' League, finishing the 1890 season with the league's sixth-best batting average and second-best slugging percentage.

The Players' League was not a commercial success. It folded after the 1890 season. Four of the eight teams merged with the National League clubs in their cities, two merged with clubs in the American Association, and two ceased to exist. The best players returned to the National League. But if the players' challenge to organized baseball had failed as a business matter, it had yielded what looked to be an important legal victory. Every time the National League clubs had tried to enforce the reserve clause, they had been told, unambiguously, that the clause was unenforceable and that they had no legal remedy against players who disregarded it.

Indeed, the owners' legal position was even shakier than that. In two other cases from 1890 and 1891, courts in Pennsylvania and Ohio refused to grant injunctions barring players from signing with other teams—not in the period covered by the reserve clause, but during the very term of the contract itself. The second baseman Frank Grant signed a contract with one minor league team in Harrisburg and then jumped to another, but a local judge declined to enjoin Grant from playing with the second team, because he disagreed with the doctrine of *Lumley v. Wagner* and thought injunctions were never appropriate in employment cases. (Grant, generally considered the best African-American player of the nineteenth century, had a career that began before baseball was segregated. In the second part of his career he would be one of the stars of the early Negro Leagues, and he would be inducted into the Baseball Hall of Fame in 2006.) Charlie Reilly, the third baseman for the Columbus Solons of the American Association, signed a contract with Columbus for the 1891 season but then jumped to the National League's Pittsburgh Pirates. A judge in Ohio refused to enjoin Reilly from playing for the Pirates. He accepted that injunctions could be granted in employment cases, but decided that Reilly was not an exceptional enough player to justify one. The Solons, he held, could find another third baseman who would be comparable, and if they couldn't, they could always sue Reilly for damages. (The judge turned out to be right: Reilly hit only .219 for the Pirates, while his replacements in Columbus were collectively slightly better.) The clubs did win one case in 1890, when a Philadelphia judge enjoined John Pickett, who was under contract with the Kansas City Cowboys of the American Association, from playing with the Philadelphia Athletics of the Players' League.[27] It was a short-lived victory: the Cowboys folded before the 1890 season began, so Pickett ended up with the Athletics anyway. The year had not been a good one for the owners, at least not in the courtroom. By the end of the 1890 season, there was considerable doubt as to whether player contracts could be enforced at all and near certainty that the reserve clause could not be enforced.

With the demise of the Players' League, however, the National League shed its primary competitor. Competition diminished even more after the 1891 season, when the American Association also folded. The National League was the only one left with a plausible claim to be a major league. Even though the reserve clause lacked any legal effect, the league continued to require it in player contracts, and the players had no recourse. So long as National League club owners refrained from trying to sign players reserved by other clubs, a National League player had nowhere to go if he chose to leave his team. In the absence of a competing league, the owners did not need the courts to enforce the reserve clause. They could enforce it themselves, simply by agreeing to it. Despite the legal defeats of 1890, baseball went back to business as usual—that is, until another major league surfaced, and National League players once again had alternative sources of employment.

The National League contracted from twelve teams to eight in 1900. Seizing the opportunity, the American League declared itself a major league in 1901 and began signing National League players. Another wave of litigation followed, as National League clubs once again sued to enjoin players from leaving. The players again won most of the cases. A judge in St. Louis refused to bar the pitcher Jack Harper from leaving the St. Louis Cardinals of the National League for the St. Louis Browns of the American League, on the grounds that Harper's contract lacked mutuality and that Harper was not a sufficiently exceptional player to warrant an injunctive remedy. For the same reasons, a federal judge in Philadelphia refused to prevent Deacon McGuire, the catcher for the Brooklyn Superbas (later renamed the Dodgers), from jumping to the American League's Detroit Tigers.[28] If the law was reckoned by counting cases, the players were the winners once again.

This time, however, the owners did win one case, and it was the biggest one, decided by a court higher than any of the others and, unlike the others, involving one of the star players of the era. Napoleon Lajoie (figure 1.3) of the Phillies was still early in his career, but he was already known as one of the best hitters in baseball after leading the National League in runs batted in and doubles in 1898. He would retire in 1916 with 3,242 hits, still the four-teenth most in the history of the game. Lajoie's contract with the Phillies for the 1900 season included the reserve clause for 1901 in an unusual form. Reserve clauses in other contracts typically did not place any limit on the number of times a contract could be renewed by the reserving club. They simply provided that the contract would be renewable for the following year. Lajoie's contract, by contrast, was expressly renewable only for 1901 and "two successive years thereafter." The reserve clause in his 1900 contract would expire, at least on paper, after the 1903 season.[29] Before the 1901 season began, however, Lajoie signed with the Athletics, Philadelphia's American League team. The Phillies brought the usual lawsuit, seeking to enjoin Lajoie from playing for the Athletics. The trial judge, quoting the opinions in the prior reserve clause cases, ruled in Lajoie's favor. The reserve clause lacked mutuality, he held, and thus could not be enforced by the Phillies.[30] Lajoie went on to win the American League triple crown in 1901 for the Athletics, with 14 home runs, 125 runs batted in, and a batting average of .426, which would be the highest ever achieved in the twentieth century.

Figure 1.3: Napoleon Lajoie, perhaps the best hitter of his era, jumped from the Philadelphia Phillies of the National League to the Philadelphia Athletics of the upstart American League in 1901. In the Phillies' suit against Lajoie for breach of contract, the Pennsylvania Supreme Court became the first court in the nation to find the reserve clause enforceable. BL-1402.92, National Baseball Hall of Fame.

The previous reserve clause cases had all ended at the trial court, but the Phillies appealed, and a year later the Pennsylvania Supreme Court became the first court in the nation to find the reserve clause enforceable. If any ballplayer was exceptional enough to be irreplaceable under *Lumley v. Wagner* it was Napoleon Lajoie. "Lajoie is well known, and has great reputation among the patrons of the sport," the Supreme Court determined, "and was thus a most attractive drawing card for the public. He may not be the sun in the baseball firmament, but he is certainly a bright, particular star." An injunction barring Lajoie from playing for another team would thus be an appropriate remedy, if the reserve clause was an enforceable contract for seasons after 1900.

On this point, the Pennsylvania Supreme Court disagreed with all the prior courts that had considered the reserve clause. Lajoie was bound to the Phillies for three years, the court acknowledged, while the Phillies could terminate Lajoie with ten days' notice at any moment. But this imbalance, the court held, did not amount to a lack of mutuality. Lajoie was receiving a "large salary" in exchange for binding himself to the Phillies, and that was enough to supply the necessary mutuality. "We cannot agree that mutuality of remedy requires that each party should have precisely the same remedy," the court held. "The defendant [Lajoie] sold to the plaintiff [the Phillies] for a valuable consideration the exclusive right to his professional services for a stipulated period, unless sooner surrendered by the plaintiff," the court concluded. "Why should not a court of equity protect such an agreement?"[31]

The decision was "the talk of fans everywhere," as a headline in the *Washington Evening Times* put it. The reserve clause had been upheld in court for the first time. The National League owners and management rejoiced. "This decision brings back to the National League over two dozen players who jumped to the American League," declared Jim Hart, the president of the Chicago Orphans (later the Cubs). "I cannot see it in any other light than a fatal blow to the rival league." The American League saw the case very differently. The opinion "applies only to Lajoie, and has no reference to any other player," insisted Benjamin Shibe, the Athletics' president. "Lajoie is an extraordinary player, whose services cannot be replaced, and it is because of the extraordinary character of his abilities that the decision . . . has been reversed." As it happened, the decision would not even apply to Lajoie. Ban Johnson, the American League president, hastily arranged a trade that sent Lajoie outside the boundaries of Pennsylvania, to the Cleveland Bronchos, who promptly changed their name to the Cleveland Naps to capitalize on Lajoie's popularity. (In 1915, after Lajoie left, they would become the Indians.) The Phillies sued Lajoie in Ohio to enforce the Pennsylvania injunction, but a Cleveland trial judge refused, on the ground that the injunction only prohibited Lajoie from playing for other teams in Pennsylvania, but had no application to other states. For the rest of the season, when his teammates traveled to Philadelphia to play the Athletics, Lajoie passed the time in Atlantic City, New Jersey.[32]

Some contemporaries suspected that Justice William Potter, the author of the Pennsylvania Supreme Court's opinion upholding the reserve clause, had been influenced by his own interest in baseball and perhaps even a desire to keep Lajoie with his hometown Phillies. "From his fervent description of

Lajoie's prowess as a player," one lawyer remarked, "it may be inferred that he not only attended the games in Philadelphia, but that he was an ardent and consistent supporter of the home team." As another lawyer put it, after quoting Potter's description of Lajoie as a "bright particular star" in the base-ball firmament, "surely this is a voice from 'the bleachers.'" They could easily have said the same of Theodore Strimple, the Cleveland judge whose legally dubious refusal to enforce the Pennsylvania injunction kept Lajoie in Cleve-land. Judges were members of their communities, and many were known to be baseball fans, so it would not be surprising if their views as to the best interests of the game colored their decisions. "We have no established church," remarked one Columbia law student (who may well have been a classmate of John Montgomery Ward) in 1885, "but base ball is an institu-tion whose welfare our courts will jealously guard."[33]

Had the rivalry between the American and National League continued, there would have been more reserve clause cases in the years after 1902, and the implications of the *Lajoie* decision would have been more fully explored. As of 1902, the reserve clause had been found unenforceable under the common law of contracts by lower courts in New York and Missouri, but it had been held to be enforceable by a much more influential court in Penn-sylvania. Later judges might have tried to distinguish *Lajoie* from the others by emphasizing the difference in Lajoie's contract, on the theory that a con-tract with a perpetual reserve clause is more one-sided than a contract with a reserve clause ostensibly lasting only three years. Or they might simply have chosen sides, either with the Pennsylvania Supreme Court or with the others. But matters never progressed that far. The two leagues reached an agreement before the 1903 season, as part of which the clubs in each league pledged to respect the reserve clause in the contracts of the other league's clubs. Once again, the players had nowhere else to go. Without an alterna-tive major league to offer employment, the players had no opportunity to challenge the lawfulness of the reserve clause.

That opportunity finally came in the fall of 1913. The Federal League had begun play in 1913 as a six-team independent minor league, but its club owners declared at the season's end that it would become an eight-team major league in 1914. The result was a third wave of contract litigation. Both sides began preparing early. To be a true major league, the Federal League would have to attract players from the American and National Leagues. In November 1913, the owners of the Federal League clubs announced that while they would refrain from signing players who were under contract for 1914 with an American or National League club, they intended to sign players covered only by the reserve clause for 1914, because they did not think the reserve clause would be enforced in court. Only in Pennsylvania had the reserve clause been enforced, and only one of the eight Federal League clubs, the Pittsburgh Rebels, was in Pennsylvania. (Three of the Federal League clubs—Brooklyn, Buffalo, and St. Louis—were in the two states whose courts had refused to enforce the reserve clause.) The two established leagues responded by threatening to bring lawsuits against any players who jumped to the Federal League. These promised suits "will take their cases into the courts and force the players to remain idle until decisions are handed down," warned August Herrmann. "They will never be employed again." The Federal League in turn promised to furnish a legal defense to any player who needed it.[34] Before any of the Federal League clubs even signed any players, the stakes were already growing high.

The American and National League clubs, aware that their player contracts would soon be scrutinized by judges, took care to modify the contracts in order to strengthen the argument for enforceability. They had already taken one step in this direction before the 1913 season. The reserve clause in the standard contract had previously been separate from the clause specifying a player's salary, but now the two were combined, so that the salary was apportioned 75 percent for playing in the current year and 25 percent for agreeing to the reserve clause. The purpose of the change was to provide explicit compensation to the player in exchange for the reserve clause, in the hope that judges would perceive the clause to be equitable. "In former years there existed a doubt with reference to the reservation clause in the player's contract, it being contended and probably correctly so, that it was not an equitable arrangement," August Herrmann declared. "This condition has now been changed. A player signing a contract containing a reservation clause is compensated for his action." Less partisan observers recognized that "such apportionment is a subterfuge," as one of them put it, in that a player's total pay was no greater than it had been before. The players were not really receiving any additional compensation for the reserve clause. The change, one critic suggested, "seems to have a moral rather than a substantial legal effect."[35]

As competition from the Federal League loomed on the horizon, organized baseball made a more serious change to player contracts for the 1914 season. One of the main problems with the reserve clause in the two prior rounds of litigation had been the lack of any definite salary in the reserve year. Baseball's lawyers unanimously advised that contracts should instead set a definite salary for the reserve year. The most prominent was John Cromwell Bell, the attorney general of Pennsylvania, who also happened to be the personal attorney of John Tener, who was simultaneously governor of Pennsylvania and president of the National League. By leaving the salary open, Bell explained, "the clause is merely an agreement to make a new or second agreement," one that a court would not enforce, as experience had shown. The lawyers hoped that specifying the salary would solve this problem. "The reservation clause in the old contract was unenforceable," agreed Ellis Kinkead and John Galvin, the Cincinnati Reds' lawyers, but with a clear salary in the reserve year, "the reservation clause as framed in the new contract is valid." There were still other questions as to whether the contract as a whole would be enforceable, cautioned Paul Moody, counsel to the Detroit Tigers, questions that had been aired in the prior cases, but Moody agreed that if the contract as a whole was enforceable, the new improved reserve clause would be too. The American and National League clubs were confident that they had shored up the primary weakness in their legal position.[36]

Organized baseball faced a dilemma as to where to litigate, a problem its lawyers understood well. To pick one example, Grover Land, an occasional backup catcher for the Cleveland Naps of the American League since 1908, signed for 1914 with the Brooklyn Tiptops of the Federal League. As the season was about to begin, Land was on his way from Sioux City, Iowa, to Brooklyn. His train was scheduled to stop in Pittsburgh. In light of the *Lajoie* decision, Pennsylvania was the state in which organized baseball was most likely to secure an injunction barring a player from jumping to the Federal League. It would be possible to serve a summons on Land when he reached Pittsburgh, which would be enough to force him into a Pennsylvania court. The problem, Kinkead and Galvin worried, was that an injunction issued by a Pennsylvania court would be useful only to bar Land from playing for the Tiptops in Pittsburgh, something Land would do only a few times a year. "To make an injunction against a man like Land really effective," they explained, "it ought to be obtained in the courts of Brooklyn, New York, where he is under contract to play, because an injunction there would effectually stop him from playing at Brooklyn." But that only raised another obstacle, which was that the cases most unfavorable to organized baseball,

Ward and *Ewing*, had been decided in New York. "In view of the decisions in New York," the lawyers noted, "it would be much more difficult to get an injunction there than it would be in Pennsylvania."[37] There was no solution to this dilemma. The American and National League clubs would have to sue in Federal League home states, even where the courts of those states had rendered adverse decisions in the past.

Apart from suing individual players, the established leagues also considered suing the Federal League as a whole for conspiring to interfere with the contracts between organized baseball and the players. "We have not found any close precedent" for such a suit, Kinkead and Galvin reported, "but on principle," they advised, it was certainly possible. "Our theory of this action is that every club of the League suffers an injury when a player is stolen from any one club of that League," because "the maintenance of the contests requires the integrity of each club and a substantial balance of playing ability among the several clubs." Organized baseball refrained from filing a conspiracy lawsuit during the 1914 season, but in late 1914, when Brooklyn's Federal League team threatened to lure away the New York Giants' star pitcher Rube Marquard, Harry Hempstead, the Giants' owner, was so angry that he raised the issue once again.[38] Cooler heads again prevailed: organized baseball would file suits against players for jumping their contracts, but not against the Federal League or its clubs.

Meanwhile, the players were bracing for litigation too. The veteran shortstop Joe Tinker became a player-manager for Chicago's Federal League team, the Chi-Feds, for a substantial raise over his National League salary, plus stock in the club. "If I believed that the reserve clause of organized ball was binding I could not honorably ignore it," Tinker declared. "But I do not think that any court in the United States at the present time would uphold anything that prevents a man from bettering his condition, regardless of the *Lajoie* precedent." Many of the players were members of a new labor union, the Fraternity of Professional Baseball Players of America, which had been organized in 1912 by the lawyer and former player David Fultz. Fultz advised Fraternity members that they were not bound by the reserve clause in their contracts. The clause was "unquestionably unenforceable," Fultz told the press shortly before the 1914 season began. "If this very troublesome clause is tested, as now seems likely, we believe the result will prove that we have been wise in the stand we have taken."[39]

In the end, 81 players left American and National League clubs for the Federal League. Eighteen of them jumped during their contract year, the other 63 during the year covered by the reserve clause. The American and National League clubs prudently shied away from putting the reserve clause to the test. They did not file suits against any of the players under reserve, but only sued players who had broken their 1914 contracts. Even so, the players were, on balance, the winners once again. Of the three resulting court decisions, the clubs won only one. The Cuban outfielder Armando Marsans, under contract with the Cincinnati Reds, had jumped to the St. Louis Terriers of the Federal League. The Reds filed their suit in the federal trial court in St. Louis, but somehow the case came before Judge Walter Sanborn, a Court of Appeals judge from St. Paul, Minnesota. Sanborn, who was presumably free of any sympathy for the Terriers, enjoined Marsans from playing for any team other than the Reds.[40]

The other two cases were won by the players. The Reds filed another suit against the pitcher George "Chief" Johnson ("Chief" was a common nickname for Native American players during the period). Johnson, who had jumped to the Kansas City Packers, was pitching in Chicago when he was served with a complaint between innings. A trial judge ruled in the Reds' favor, but that decision was quickly reversed by the Illinois Court of Appeals, which held that the standard player contract was unenforceable by injunction, even during the contract year, for lack of mutuality. Nearly simultaneously, in the most closely followed of the 1914 cases, a judge in New York refused to enforce the American League contract of Hal Chase, perhaps the best first baseman of the era, who in mid-season had jumped from the Chicago White Sox to the Buffalo Buff-Feds. "The *quasi* peonage of baseball players," declared Justice Herbert Bissell, "is contrary to the spirit of American institutions."[41] Chase remained with the Buff-Feds and Johnson with the Packers for the 1914 and 1915 seasons, after which the Federal League ceased to exist.

In choosing Marsans, Johnson, and Chase as defendants in these suits, the Reds and the White Sox may have been acting strategically, because all three players were outcasts of one kind or another. Armando Marsans would likely have been excluded from organized baseball due to the color of his skin had he been born in the United States rather than Cuba. Like several other dark-skinned Cuban players who came after him but before Jackie Robinson, Marsans was eligible only because the Reds could characterize him as "Castilian and not Negro." George Johnson suffered the same anti-Indian hostility leveled at all Indian players of the era. Hal Chase, finally, was notorious for throwing games. In an era when players associated freely with gamblers, salaries were low enough for players to seek supplements to their incomes, and accusations of game-fixing were frequent, Chase stood out as the most corrupt player of all.[42] Yet even though organized baseball chose the easiest targets, baseball lost two out of its three efforts to enforce player contracts.

The reserve clause was tested in only one of the 1914 cases, and that suit was filed by the Federal League. Bill Killefer (figure 1.4) had played catcher for the Philadelphia Phillies since 1911. In January 1914, while still reserved by the Phillies, Killefer signed a three-year contract with the Chicago Chi-Feds, at an annual salary of $5,833. This must have prompted the Phillies to raise his

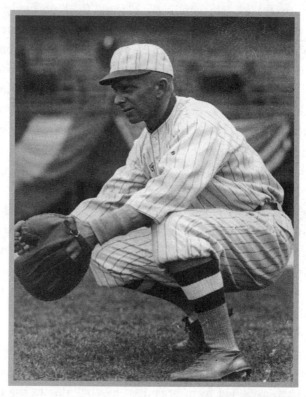

Figure 1.4: The catcher Bill Killefer signed two contracts for 1914, one with the Philadelphia Phillies and the other with Chicago's Federal League club. In the ensuing litigation, two federal courts found the reserve clause unenforceable. BL-1280.2002, National Baseball Hall of Fame.

salary, because two weeks later Killefer signed another contract with the Phillies, also for three years, at $6,500 per year. The Chi-Feds promptly sued Killefer, seeking an injunction barring him from playing for any other team. Killefer was "a catcher of unique and extraordinary skill and expertness," the Chi-Feds' owners alleged, whose "loss cannot be substantially compensated for by the services of some other baseball catcher." Killefer did not deny it. His defense—one apparently proffered with a straight face despite its evident irony—was that he belonged to the Phillies by virtue of the reserve clause, and that the Chi-Feds were the ones at fault for enticing him to leave the Phillies.[43]

Killefer's 1913 Phillies contract included one of the old-style reserve clauses that did not specify a salary for 1914, and that was enough for the trial court to find it unenforceable. "It is wholly uncertain and indefinite with respect to salary and also with respect to terms and conditions of the proposed employment," the judge held. "It is nothing more than a contract to enter into a contract, in the future." The Chi-Feds nevertheless lost the case, because they ran afoul of the "clean hands" doctrine, according to which parties cannot avail themselves of equitable remedies (like an injunction) if they are guilty of wrongdoing themselves. The Chi-Feds had wronged the Phillies, the judge concluded, by offering Killefer a contract when they knew that he "was under a moral, if not a legal, obligation to furnish his services to the Philadelphia Club for the season of 1914." The decision was affirmed by the Court of Appeals two months later, in the middle of the 1914 season.[44]

Both sides claimed to have won the *Killefer* case. "I regard this as a victory for the Federal League," its lawyer proclaimed, "in that it sustains our contention in regard to the reserve clause." On the other hand, when the case was over Killefer was entitled to remain with the Phillies. "We naturally feel much gratified at the decision," declared the Phillies' lawyers, "because the contention of the Philadelphia club is sustained in every particular." In private, however, the lawyers were more worried. The *Killefer* decision "definitely settles" the law as to the reserve clause, Ellis Kinkead remarked to August Herrmann. The clause, at least in its 1913 version, was "invalid and unenforceable."[45]

When players and officials of the Federal League took stock of the 1914 litigation, they could not help but feel vindicated. "We won nearly every court case which we had with organized baseball," chortled Charles Weeghman, owner of the Chi-Feds (figure 1.5). "We knew all along," insisted James Gilmore, the Federal League's president, "that the reserve clause was a joke."[46]

Figure 1.5: James Gilmore, president of the Federal League, and Charles Weeghman, owner of Chicago's Federal League club, defeated organized baseball in most of the reserve clause litigation of 1914. LC-B2-3275-12, Prints and Photographs Division, Library of Congress.

Had they taken a longer look back, they would have felt just the same. Between 1890 and 1914, in three waves of litigation, five courts had been asked to enforce the reserve clause, and four of them had found the clause unenforceable. Napoleon Lajoie's case was the only one in which a court had been willing to enforce it. In eight other cases, courts had been asked to enforce the standard player contract—not the reserve clause but the heart of the contract, during the player's actual contract year—and six of them had refused. The contract had been enforced in only two of the eight cases. The lawyers involved with organized baseball must have realized that the business side of the game rested on some very shaky legal foundations.

GRASPING MONOPOLY

Yet the business of baseball proceeded as usual. Despite all the rulings finding the reserve clause unenforceable, it continued to be a standard term in player contracts. And despite all the decisions that contracts lacked mutuality where players could be dropped on ten days' notice, the ten-day clause likewise continued as a standard term. Club owners and their lawyers knew that so long as the players lacked an alternative source of employment, the clubs had the leverage to force the players to agree to these terms. When the Federal League went out of business after the 1915 season, the American and National Leagues were once again the only ones with a claim to major league status. The players had nowhere else to go. Because there would be no competing major leagues for the rest of the twentieth century, there would be no more contract-law challenges to the reserve clause. The reserve clause may have been unenforceable in court, at least outside Pennsylvania, but it would nevertheless be a fundamental part of baseball for decades to come.

In practice, the reserve clause had teeth, not because it was part of player contracts, but because the owners of American and National League clubs agreed among themselves to abide by it. Had the reserve clause remained as it was between 1879 and 1887, a league rule rather than a contract term, its force would have been just the same. To attack the reserve clause in a meaningful way, therefore, one could not simply try to strike it from player contracts. One would have to establish that it was an illegal rule for a baseball league to adopt. One would have to prove that the agreement *among the owners*, not the agreement between a club and a player, was unlawful.

Antitrust law already provided the vocabulary and the conceptual structure for such a claim, even in the earliest years of the reserve clause. John Montgomery Ward, who knew more about law than any other baseball player and more about baseball than any other lawyer, argued as early as 1887 that the reserve clause was a means by which the owners "sought to secure a monopoly of the game." Baseball, Ward alleged, was a "trust . . . as compact and effectual as the Standard Oil, the Sugar, or any of the other trusts of which we hear so much." Such claims soon became commonplace. "The baseball men understand the art of forming trusts and pool-making, precisely as practiced in other business enterprises," one newspaper charged. Another called the National League one of "the most highly perfected trusts in the country." *Sporting Life*, the leading sports periodical of the era, was particularly harsh in its condemnation of the economic structure of baseball. "The National League fostered and lived upon a monopoly for years," the journal declared in 1890, at the peak of the battle with the Players' League. "Under this monopoly the player had but a stunted ambition. This grasping monopoly has said, 'so high shall thy ambition soar and no higher.' Around you is bound the iron-clad rule of reservation which makes you mine for life, and you can never hope to rise higher than I and my monopoly choose to allow you to go."[47] The idea that the reserve clause made baseball an unlawful monopoly was aired in the press almost continuously from then on.

Antitrust claims only began to creep into litigation, however, with the emergence of the Federal League in the 1910s. In the first two waves of litigation, sparked by the Players' League in 1890 and the American League in 1901, antitrust law did not figure at all. Why not?

An antitrust claim could have been brought by a player, by a labor organization of players, or by a competing league, but before the 1910s neither the players nor the leagues had much incentive to do so. The players were already successful in defending lawsuits on contract law grounds whenever they jumped to another league. A second defense based on antitrust law would not have put them in any better of a position. In the absence of a competing league offering another job, it would have been possible, in principle, for a player dissatisfied with his salary or with some other term of his contract to sue his club or his league, seeking a declaration that the reserve clause of his contract violated antitrust law, so that he might offer his services to the highest bidder. A player who filed such a suit, however, would have been risking his career. First, of course, there was hardly a guarantee that the player would prevail in court. Whether the business side of baseball was inconsistent with antitrust law was a hotly disputed question, as we will see in the next chapter, with plausible arguments on both sides. Second, and probably more important, regardless of who won an antitrust suit, the player who filed it might well have been blacklisted from major league baseball. Even if he won, he would have been unlikely to enjoy the benefits of his victory. If he hoped to keep playing, he would bring an antitrust claim only when there was a competing major league offering a job, but that was precisely when an antitrust claim was unnecessary.

The players formed a few short-lived labor unions—the Brotherhood of Professional Base Ball Players in 1885, the Players' Protective Association in 1900, and the Fraternity of Professional Baseball Players of America in 1912. These might have been appropriate plaintiffs in an antitrust suit. By banding together, the players would have made it more difficult for the owners to blacklist any particular player or group of players. The owners could not have banished *all* current players without seriously diluting the quality of their product. But the unions never filed any such suit. The Brotherhood chose the more direct strategy of breaking with the National League entirely and forming a league of its own, the Players' League. The Protective Association briefly bargained with the National League but was never very strong. It disbanded shortly after it was formed. The Fraternity, finally, was always ambivalent about the reserve clause, on the theory that while it occasionally harmed individual players it was good for the game as a whole. David Fultz, the Fraternity's president, tried only to limit the reserve period to five years rather than abolish the clause entirely. Although the players repeatedly tried to organize, their unions were never simultaneously able and willing to test the lawfulness of the reserve clause in court.[48]

Competing leagues might also have brought antitrust suits against organized baseball. The purpose of invoking antitrust law would not have been to free individual players from the reserve clauses of their contracts—the players were already doing that themselves, one by one, under contract law. The goal of an antitrust suit filed by a league would have been to free all the players at a single stroke and thus to compress the expensive and time-consuming process of case-by-case litigation into a single court decision. The Players' League did not need to take this course, because it was already full of players who had jumped from the National League. The American League did not need to file suit either, because it was already so successful that it forced the National League to capitulate and admit it as an equal partner in organized baseball. Before the 1910s, then, neither of the National League's main competitors had a reason to file an antitrust suit.

The Federal League was in a different position. It succeeded in luring some players away from organized baseball, but not so many that it lost the incentive to acquire more. It was successful enough to spend time and money litigating, but not so successful that it lost the reason to litigate. The Federal League was the first of the competing leagues with a significant motive to challenge the reserve clause on antitrust grounds. And it did. The result would be a decade of congressional threats and court cases, all on the question of whether baseball was an illegal monopoly.

THE BASEBALL TRUST

The National League "is a sort of baseball trust," one newspaper alleged in 1892, "for no player can be employed who does not knuckle down to the rules." By the first decade of the twentieth century, the idea that baseball was an unlawful trust or monopoly was already a cliché. "The sport of baseball has become as closely knit a trust as ever defied the Sherman Act," declared the popular *Munsey's Magazine*. "The 'baseball trust,'" one small-town newspaper claimed, "is stronger in its field than the Standard Oil company or the beef trust or the tobacco combine." Attacks like these prompted baseball officials to defend the game in the sporting press. "Those who assail the present system of base ball government, calling it a trust, do not know what they are talking about," insisted National League president Harry Pulliam. "Conditions were never so good for the ball player as they are at the present time." But such defenses did little to dispel the idea that baseball was an illegal monopoly, an idea that could be put to use whenever a writer wished to criticize the game. When a Washington paper was angry that the American League's Senators would not play preseason exhibitions against local clubs, for example, the paper blamed "orders from the old-time monopolists of baseball."[1]

THE MOST AUDACIOUS AND AUTOCRATIC TRUST

What was the law that these critics claimed was being violated? Anglo-American common law had long contained an ambiguous prohibition of certain kinds of agreements among merchants that would harm consumers. "People of the same trade seldom meet together," Adam Smith observed in the late eighteenth century, "but the conversation ends in a conspiracy against the public, or in some contrivance to raise prices." In William Blackstone's ubiquitous summary of English law, he explained that "monopolists are punished with the forfeiture of treble [that is, triple] damages." The nineteenth-century law of many states included similar provisions, although they seem not to have been used very often.[2] Toward the end of the nineteenth century, as firms in many industries attained unprecedented size, concern about the power of "trusts" became a salient national political issue for the first time.[3]

The result was the Sherman Antitrust Act of 1890, which prohibited "every contract, combination . . . or conspiracy, in restraint of trade or commerce among the several States" and authorized the Justice Department and victims alike to bring suits against violators. The Sherman Act threw the formidable weight of the federal government behind the ban on monopolies, but the new law was just as ambiguous as the common law and state statutes it largely supplanted. Not all combinations and conspiracies were prohibited by the Sherman Act—just the ones "in restraint of trade or commerce among the several States." But what exactly did that mean? It would take a few decades for the courts to devise rules for distinguishing the lawful monopolies from the unlawful, and difficult questions still arise today.[4] In the years immediately after 1890, there was considerable disagreement about the implications of the Sherman Act for all sorts of businesses.

One of them was baseball. The economic structure of baseball rested on a detailed agreement among the clubs, a contract called the "National Agreement" after the 1903 settlement between the American and National Leagues. The National Agreement included a few provisions that could plausibly be said to restrain trade, including most obviously the reserve clause, as well as an article that required the approval of a majority of the clubs in each league before any of them could change cities and the permission of the clubs in any given city before any minor league team could locate there. These were the provisions critics had in mind when they alleged that baseball was an illegal trust.

The National Agreement was no doubt a contract, but was it a contract in restraint of trade? Baseball's defenders argued that it was not. "Many monopolies have their good as well as their evil features," reasoned a columnist for *Sporting Life*. "There is no greater monopoly in this country than the Associated Press, and yet to it publishers and the public alike are indebted for the best, most reliable and freshest news." Baseball, in this view, was a kind of monopoly that *promoted* trade. John Montgomery Ward acknowledged that baseball was a monopoly, "but even a monopoly is better than the squabbling and discord which came very near killing the sport" before the club owners instituted the reserve clause. "Base ball under a monopoly," Ward concluded, "is better than no base ball at all." If baseball could not profitably exist without its trust-like features, those features could hardly be called restraints of trade. Baseball "has a business side," the Brooklyn sportswriter John B. Foster explained, "but there isn't any more business to it than there is to buying soap bubbles." A baseball club's assets would be nearly worthless "if you couldn't control the players by such methods as are in effect at the present time." That was enough, in Foster's opinion, to rebut "the monopoly cry which is occasionally raised against base ball."[5]

In their private moments, even baseball insiders admitted that the legality of baseball's business structure was unclear. "I wrote the Rule several years before the Sherman Law was enacted," A. G. Mills recalled, referring to the reserve clause, which was eleven years older than the Sherman Act. There had been no reason, back in 1879, to worry about being called into federal court on antitrust grounds. At the time, the reserve clause "was believed to be in harmony with the principles of the 'common law,'" Mills explained, and while he doubted that the Sherman Act had changed those principles in any meaningful way, "especially in view of the peculiar characteristics of the baseball industry," no one could be sure what the courts would say.[6]

The earliest antitrust attacks against baseball were easy to brush aside. The first appears to have taken place in 1902, as part of the pitcher Jack Harper's defense against the St. Louis Cardinals' effort (described briefly in chapter 1) to prevent Harper from leaving the Cardinals for the St. Louis Browns of the American League. The Cardinals lost for the usual reasons: a state trial judge found that the standard player contract lacked mutuality and that Harper was not a unique enough player for the Cardinals to be entitled to an injunction. Harper had an additional defense, however; he argued that the contract was contrary to public policy, because baseball amounted to an unlawful conspiracy. The judge sounded sympathetic. "Even if it does not come within the prohibition of the anti trust statute," he declared, "the evidence shows that the plaintiff [the Cardinals] was, during the life of the contract in suit, in league or combination with other clubs to fix and control the salary of players." Harper's contract, like that of every other player, "was made in furtherance of this combination, and if, as urged by defendants, it was an unlawful one, it is against public policy, and bars plaintiff from obtaining the relief sought in a court of equity."[7] The judge was careful not to say explicitly that baseball's structure was illegal under either the Sherman Act or the common law, because the Cardinals had already lost the case on other grounds. But his tone certainly suggested that he would have found baseball in violation of at least the common law if he had the opportunity.

A few years later, when the White Sox fired their manager Jimmy Callahan, Callahan sued to recover damages. His lawyer told the press that he intended to prove that baseball "is as much a trust as the Standard Oil Company." Callahan himself claimed that "the Standard Oil trust is a home for widows and orphans as compared with the baseball octopus." These comments turned out to be bluster. Callahan's suit simply alleged a breach of contract. It did not include any antitrust claims. For a few days, though, baseball officials were nervous, at least according to *Sporting Life*, which reported that "it is generally admitted that the structure of organized base ball would not stand the test of an attack in the courts in many particulars."[8]

Similar episodes soon began occurring more frequently. In 1907, when a group of promoters in Pennsylvania, New Jersey, Maryland, and the District of Columbia announced plans for a new league to be called the Union League, one of their first actions was to threaten an antitrust suit against the American and National Leagues. "In our opinion, neither god nor President Roosevelt intended that the United States should be owned by the few gentlemen who compose the body politic of the baseball trust, with authority to close the door of opportunity to all others who do not belong to the charmed circle," declared Alfred Lawson, the Union League's president. "We believe in the inalienable right of every man to enter whatever business he may choose, whether it be the baseball or the oil business." Lawson's threat brought the usual response from Harry Pulliam, the National League's president. "I do not consider organized baseball a trust," Pulliam explained.

"A trust, as I understand it, is a combination for controlling the necessities of life or public utilities, and has for its main object the despoiling of the producer and the wage-earner," but baseball was nothing of the kind. The Union League collapsed before finishing a single season. Alfred Lawson was one of the great zealots of the period, with so many other interests—he founded his own religion, and there is still a University of Lawsonomy in Wisconsin that teaches its tenets—that he never actually filed an antitrust suit.[9] Once again, the day of reckoning had been postponed.

Another threat arose in 1910, when a California state senator named Gus Hartman promised, during his reelection campaign, to introduce a bill that would amend the state penal code to make it a misdemeanor for a baseball club to transfer a player to another club without the player's consent. "I am against organized baseball," Hartman declared, "because it denies a man engaged in that profession the liberties he is given by the constitution." Hartman was a former player himself, and he also complained, in the same speech, about the lack of a major league team in California, so his proposed bill was likely intended as a bargaining chip in an effort to bring a team to the West Coast, or at least as a public gesture in that direction for the benefit of Hartman's campaign. "That's a joke," responded Charles Comiskey, owner of the Chicago White Sox.[10] In the era before air travel, it would have been impractical to locate teams any farther west than Chicago and St. Louis, the westernmost big league cities. In the end, Hartman apparently never introduced any such bill.

In Cincinnati, meanwhile, the would-be promoter of an all-star barnstorming team, deprived of his players when organized baseball would not let them participate, announced that he would sue the American and National Leagues for violating the Sherman Act. In St. Louis, the organizers of a new league, the Columbian League, scheduled to begin play in 1912, declared that they would bring suit under the Sherman Act if the established leagues interfered. John Powers, the Columbian League's president, told reporters that "we have the statutory right to exist and compete with the 'baseball trust.'"[11] Neither of these suits was ever filed. The Columbian League never got past the organizational stage.

These were not serious threats, but they were enough to keep the antitrust question in the public eye for years. The sporting press even began to pay attention to developments in antitrust law. In 1909, when a federal judge ordered the dissolution of Standard Oil of New Jersey, *Sporting Life* closely examined the judge's opinion and found a good omen for baseball. The judge had distinguished between "incidental" and "direct" restraints of trade and had found Standard Oil guilty of the latter. Baseball, *Sporting Life* concluded, was restraining trade only incidentally, and so could not be violating the Sherman Act. A few years later, when New York's Jockey Club was accused of monopolizing horse racing, the press thoroughly weighed the implications for baseball.[12] Antitrust law was almost becoming a regular feature of the sports pages.

Baseball's decade-long antitrust crisis began shortly before the 1912 season, when Representative Thomas Gallagher of Chicago introduced a resolution in Congress to investigate the baseball trust. "This Congress is desirous of investigating and securing information to dissolve trusts or illegal combinations in restraint of trade and liberties of the American people," the resolution began. Baseball, Gallagher had determined, would be a fat target. "The most audacious and autocratic trust in the country is the one which presumes to control the game of baseball," his resolution read; "its officials announcing daily through the press of the country the dictates of a governing commission; how competition is stifled, how territory and games are apportioned, how the prices are fixed which millions must pay to witness the sport, [and] how men are enslaved and forced to accept salaries and terms or be forever barred from playing." Gallagher accordingly requested the appointment of a special congressional committee to hear testimony about "the Baseball Trust" and to inquire of the Justice Department why it had failed to take action.[13]

Gallagher's resolution caught baseball officials by surprise, but they quickly took to the newspapers with the usual bravado. "We would be glad to have an investigation," said Ban Johnson, the president of the American League. "There is no baseball trust and competition is not stifled. Any one who desires is welcome to get in the game." National League president Thomas Lynch pointed out that some of the players earned higher salaries than members of Congress, so baseball could hardly be accused of exploiting its workers. "I don't know what he means," said August Herrmann of Gallagher's resolution, "unless it is a joke. There is no baseball trust, and from the nature of the game, there never can be." Hugh Jennings, the manager of the Detroit Tigers, was a member of the Pennsylvania bar, so he was able to offer a nuanced defense of the game. "Organized ball is not a trust in that it does not prevent competition by illegal means," Jennings explained. "The organization keeps out rivals by offering a better grade of ball than any one else can offer, it is true, but there is nothing to prevent any individual or

corporation from doing this." Connie Mack, the manager of the Philadelphia Athletics, had no education beyond the eighth grade, but he had a
strong opinion as well. "The author of that resolution cannot know a great
deal about base ball," Mack reasoned. "If some one would take him aside and
tell him for about five minutes what base ball really is, he would open his
eyes. You do not hear many of the players complain of being bought and
sold, do you? They seem pretty happy in their so-called slavery."[14]

When baseball officials made discreet inquiries with friendly members of
Congress, they learned that Gallagher's resolution had little chance of even
reaching a vote. Nicholas Longworth was a Republican congressman from
Cincinnati, still early in a career that would culminate in several years as
Speaker of the House. He was an associate of August Herrmann, who was
simultaneously president of the Reds and president of the National Commission, baseball's governing body. "Don't think baseball resolution need be
taken seriously," Longworth promptly cabled Herrmann. "Will advise you
later." He had a fuller picture a few days later. "I have made a quiet investigation of the whole matter and have asked friends of mine on the Rules Committee, to which the resolution was referred, as to whether it was being taken
seriously," Longworth reported. "These gentlemen don't want to be quoted,
and neither do I, but I think I can tell you for your own information that it is
regarded as more or less of a joke, and about all they have been asked to do
is not to laugh at it." Longworth's concluding piece of advice was "don't lose
any sleep over this." Meanwhile, Gallagher's resolution was being mocked in
the press. "The Western newspapers have ridiculed Gallagher," Herrmann
heard from Chicago. If the press's reaction was any guide, "we will hear
nothing more of this Congressional move."[15]

Observers both inside and outside of baseball were baffled by Gallagher's
motive. What political gain could there be in bringing down the national
pastime? "I do not know much about Gallagher although he is a Chicago
man," remarked Charles Murphy, the owner of the Cubs. "He certainly can't
be a very wise proposition when he thinks it's good policy to attack baseball." Murphy suspected that Gallagher was speaking on behalf of "persons
who had attempted an entrance into baseball circles and had failed. It is only
reasonable to suppose that if the same individuals had attempted to build
and maintain a new railroad and had failed, they would want all the railroads
abolished." The *Wall Street Journal* joked that the threat of an investigation
was really intended to get members of Congress free passes to games.

Gallagher may have been representing organizers of the United States League, a would-be league that never completed a season. The only evidence of such a connection that came to light was Gallagher's friendship with Hugh McKinnon, who owned a share of the United States League's Washington club, but that was enough to start rumors flying.[16] Whatever Gallagher's motive was, it was not shared by anyone else in Congress. The House Rules Committee never voted on his resolution.

Some drew the lesson that baseball was in no danger of being found an unlawful monopoly. Gallagher's resolution "got about ten times as many people acutely interested in the Sherman Law as had ever before concerned themselves about it," *Munsey's Magazine* noted. "But let's see. A Kansas farm boy with three curves and extraordinary speed gets seventy-five hundred dollars a year for pitching about forty games, instead of forty dollars a month as a farm-hand. The public gets better, squarer, more satisfactory ball." The economic structure of the game did not seem to be causing anyone any harm. "We venture to say," the magazine concluded, "that if it were left to a referendum of baseball patrons to decide whether the baseball trust should be 'busted,' the majority would be overwhelmingly opposed." The *New York Times* agreed that "there cannot be any political capital at present in investigating baseball. Therefore it is safe to say that baseball will not be investigated." Others were less confident. "In these days of high finance," worried *Baseball Magazine*, "the baseball magnates will probably soon be called before the Bar of Public Opinion. They, as promoters in a business which stifles competition, will have to take their turn along with the beef barons and the heads of the steel trust and show cause to the Supreme Court why they should any longer defy the provisions of the Sherman Anti-Trust Law."[17]

It was the pessimists who were right. Well before the 1913 season opened, there were rumors that the Justice Department would investigate baseball as soon as President William Howard Taft—a mild baseball fan but a lame duck in office—was replaced by Woodrow Wilson. When Wilson threw out the first ball at the Senators' opening-day game in April, joined by several members of his cabinet, the sporting press interpreted it as a good sign. "The most important fact," one writer insisted, "is this: *The heads of the present administration would certainly not have been the guests of the American League if they considered organized base ball an unlawful trust.*"[18] But the first month of the 1913 season saw not one but two threatened congressional investigations, one in the Senate and one in the House.

The Senate's was the less worrisome of the two. Ty Cobb (figure 2.1), the Detroit Tigers' star center fielder, had earned a salary of $10,000 in 1912, when he batted .409 and won his sixth consecutive batting title.[19] Before the 1913 season, Cobb demanded a raise to $15,000, but when Tigers' owner Frank Navin refused, Cobb held out. He announced that he would quit baseball unless he was paid appropriately. As the season began without Cobb, he received a telegram from Senator Hoke Smith of Cobb's native Georgia. "Send me a copy of your contract with Detroit including reserve clause," Smith wired. "Wish to investigate it to see if illegal contract violating federal statutes has been made." Smith explained to the press that he suspected the reserve clause violated the Sherman Act. "What I understand exists," he said, "cannot exist legally." Representative Thomas Hardwick, also of Georgia, began making plans for a similar investigation in the House. Charles Comiskey, owner of the White Sox, urged Navin to hold firm. "We have absolutely nothing to fear from any legislative body," he argued.

Figure 2.1: Ty Cobb's holdout at the beginning of the 1913 season prompted members of Congress from Cobb's home state of Georgia to threaten an antitrust investigation. When Cobb signed a contract and resumed playing, the threat disappeared. BL-2553.2001, National Baseball Hall of Fame.

"Organized base ball of today is conducted open and above board." But Comiskey had his doubts about Navin's resolve. "I am afraid Navin will not show enough back bone in the handling of this young fellow," he confided to August Herrmann. Within a few days, Cobb and Navin settled on a salary of $12,000. Cobb resumed playing, and Smith and Hardwick lost their interest in the antitrust implications of Cobb's contract.[20]

Baseball officials laughed off what in retrospect had obviously been a political stunt. Georgia's congressional delegation had been so busy supporting one of its best-paid citizens, *Life* magazine scoffed, that "they might not know that few States in the Union have more child labor than Georgia." *Outing* magazine joked that the next congressional investigations would be "with reference to charges of child labor made by Christy Mathewson and a loud demand for a minimum wage law emitted by Ty Cobb, Frank Chance, Honus Wagner, Joe Wood *et al.*" Careful observers recognized, however, that baseball might be vulnerable to a more determined opponent. The Sherman Act "is so vague in its terms," one sportswriter worried. Baseball, like other successful enterprises, had developed "a position with regard to the anti-trust law whose uncertainty is becoming annoying and harassing, if not intolerable."[21]

The more disturbing threat arose in the House, where Thomas Gallagher, seizing the opportunity offered by the intense interest in Cobb's holdout, once again introduced a resolution calling for an investigation of the "audacious and autocratic" baseball trust. Gallagher's second resolution drew initial skepticism from all quarters, in light of the outcome of his first. "There's no such thing as a baseball trust," Connie Mack insisted. "All of us are out for ourselves only. That is absolute. We help each other no more than one shoemaker helps his competing neighbor shoemaker." There was another round of jokes in the press. "The Base-ball Trust catches its prey when young and unsuspicious," *Puck* magazine snickered. "It offers them what appear to be attractive inducements, and then, after they have signed up, it puts the screws on them. It makes them work in the hottest weather, sometimes as much as two hours a day. Pitchers especially have a hard time, frequently being called upon to work two days, or four hours, a week. Sometimes a ball-player has the sun directly in his eyes, possibly to the permanent injury of his vision."[22] Gallagher's second resolution seemed at the start to be no more worrisome than his first.

Gallagher, however, now had more powerful backing than before. One backer was Horace Fogel, the former president and part owner of the Phillies, who had been banished from baseball the previous year for repeatedly complaining about the umpires and about National League president Thomas Lynch. A few days after Gallagher introduced his resolution, Fogel was seen in Washington conferring with members of the House Rules Committee and with Attorney General James McReynolds, who was acquiring a reputation as a vigorous trust-buster. Fogel was evidently plotting revenge. He told the press that he had informed Representative Robert Lee Henry, the chair of the Rules Committee, that he could produce several hundred witnesses with knowledge of baseball's monopolistic practices.[23] By himself, Fogel probably would not have had much clout, but soon he was joined by a group of people who did.

The Federal League was formed before the 1913 season as an independent minor league, with clubs in six large midwestern cities. In its first season, the Federal League had no pretensions of competing with the American and National Leagues. Its only well-known names were a few of its managers who were former players, including Cy Young, who managed in Cleveland. But the clubs had some substantial investors, including Otto Stifel, the owner of a St. Louis beer company, and J. Edward Krause, who owned hotels in Pittsburgh. These were men who were not accustomed to being pushed around. Five of the Federal League's clubs were in major league cities, however, and there were inevitable clashes with organized baseball. The biggest took place early in the 1913 season when Western Union, which carried American and National League scores on its telegraph ticker, refused to do the same for Federal League scores, despite the Federal League's offer of payment, apparently because of pressure from organized baseball. The Federal League began preparing to fight back. Edward Gates, the league's general counsel, traveled to Washington to meet with Thomas Gallagher and James McReynolds. The Federal League even planned—at least according to Francis Richter, the editor of *Sporting Life*—to offer its presidency to Horace Fogel.[24] The Gallagher resolution was no longer a laughing matter.

Organized baseball had already jumped into action. Benjamin Minor, the owner of the Washington Senators, urged his colleagues to contact their representatives in Congress, to exert what influence they had and to gather inside information about the likely success of Gallagher's resolution. Alfred Allen, whose congressional district included part of Cincinnati, reported to the Reds that the House Rules Committee was so occupied with tariff legislation that it could not move on to baseball for at least a few weeks. Even then, Allen noted "it may be possible that Mr. Gallagher will be satisfied with the publicity which he would get out of the matter by having a public hearing before the Rules Committee, and that after that the matter would be allowed to drop." William Alden Smith, one of Michigan's senators, and Frank Doremus, a representative from Detroit, both advised the Tigers' Frank Navin that the matter would not get on to the committee's agenda at all before the summer recess. ("My keen interest in the 'Tigers' continues," Smith added, "and I am hopeful that they will strike their 'winning gait' soon.") Congressman James Curley, who would go on to fame as the flamboyantly corrupt mayor of Boston, had even better news for the Braves. "The Gallagher Resolution," he predicted, "is buried in the Committee on Rules and beyond hope of resurrection."[25]

Baseball's leaders recognized that the game had a formidable lobbying army in the hundreds of minor league clubs, which were scattered throughout congressional districts all across the country. The National Commission sent a letter to the owner and president of each minor league team, urging them to contact their representatives. Telegrams and letters reached Congress from the Birmingham Barons and the Chattanooga Lookouts of the Southern Association, from the Indianapolis Indians of the American Association, from the San Francisco Seals of the Pacific Coast League, and from a host of other clubs in states and districts that lacked major league teams.[26] Baseball used what connections it could. A. H. Woodward, the iron magnate who owned the Barons, was the brother-in-law of Oscar Underwood, the House majority leader. O. B. Andrews, president of the Lookouts, was an old friend of Chattanooga's representative, John Austin Moon. The responses to these pleas suggested that baseball had little to fear. "Most of the Members of Congress are Base Ball Fans," explained Charles Curry, who represented San Francisco. "I don't think they would stand for the enactment of a Law that would kill the game." John Austin Moon advised: "I do not think there is a single Representative here who would injure the national game if he could."[27] From the perspective of organized baseball, the game appeared to be in safe hands.

The Washington Senators, who played in then-brand-new National Park, only about three miles from the Capitol, helped smooth relations by handing out free season passes to members of Congress (figure 2.2). This was not a new practice. "This being a political town, everybody was after a season pass," Senators manager (and future owner) Clark Griffith complained shortly before Gallagher introduced his second resolution. The presence of

Figure 2.2: The Washington Senators helped smooth relations with the federal government by giving out free passes to games. In the first two rows at this 1913 game are Secretary of War Lindley M. Garrison, Secretary of the Navy Josephus Daniels, Senator Charles Culberson, and Vice President Thomas Marshall. LC-H261-6720, Prints and Photographs Division, Library of Congress.

pressing business in Congress made the question a delicate one, because as the passes became all the more important, so too did the need to avoid the appearance of graft. The Senators accordingly delayed presenting a pass to Speaker of the House Champ Clark until they could learn, "through some friends" as the team's owner put it, that Clark would not object. "The Speaker was apparently very glad to receive it," a relieved Benjamin Minor reported, "and while he says he does not have an opportunity to go very often, he will go as often as he can." It was widely acknowledged that members of Congress enjoyed baseball. Only a few months later, in the course of scheduling debate in the House, Oscar Underwood proposed meeting at night, because "with a baseball game running in the afternoon, my experience is there is a much better attendance at night." ("That has been my observation, too," agreed John Langley of Kentucky, "especially during the baseball season.") In 1912, just after Gallagher introduced his first resolution, the *Saturday Evening Post* ran a cartoon that showed five top-hatted cigar-smoking congressmen sitting in a "congressional committee private box" in the front row of a baseball stadium. The caption read: "Investigating the Baseball Trust."[28]

Players were ambivalent about Gallagher's resolution, for the same reason they had long been ambivalent about the reserve clause. The business structure of the game undoubtedly caused the best players to earn less than they would have in a competitive market. But baseball had never been more stable or profitable, and player salaries as a whole had never been higher. "Many of the players think that organized baseball amounts to a trust," said David Fultz, the president of the Fraternity of Baseball Players of America. "But it is an open question whether legislative action will better the ball players' condition."[29]

By the summer, it was clear that Gallagher's second resolution would die in the Rules Committee just like his first. There was still no political gain in staging an investigation of baseball. One more threat had been averted. "But that does not alter the fact," *Sporting Life* reminded its readers, "that the Sherman law is so vague in its terms and so prone to mischievous and harassing interpretation that it constitutes a menace."[30] Congress was not the only branch of government with the power to determine that baseball was an unlawful monopoly. It would not be long before the game would have to defend itself in court.

Ready for trial

In late 1913, the Federal League's club owners determined to become a third major league. They knew they had to attract players from the American and National Leagues, and they knew that the two established leagues would fight back. Some of the players who jumped to the Federal League would be under contract with an American or National League club, while the rest would be covered by the reserve clause. The Federal League owners expected, correctly, that they and their players would be sued. One way to defend those suits was to argue that American and National League player contracts were unenforceable under the common law of contracts, and, as discussed in chapter 1, Federal League players were successful in doing so more often than not. But that was not the only available strategy. With all the attention in 1912 and 1913 to baseball's status under the antitrust law, it was not hard to see that the Sherman Act could be a useful weapon for the Federal League.

One way to wield that weapon would be as a defense against suits for injunctions brought by American and National League clubs. In late December 1913, just a few days after Joe Tinker of the Cubs became the first star player to sign with the Federal League, the league announced that it would do just that. Edward Gates, the Federal League's general counsel, issued a clear warning. "Any baseball club that attempts to secure an injunction," Gates promised, "will be immediately confronted" with the question of whether baseball is "a trust within the meaning of the Sherman Anti-Trust act." The Sherman Act could also be an offensive weapon. Rather than waiting to be sued, the Federal League could file an antitrust suit of its own against the American and National Leagues. "We won't wait for the major leagues to start the fight," threatened Charles Weeghman, the president of Chicago's Federal League team. "We are going to fire the first gun and we are going to make it hot for organized base ball. The fact is, we have the goods on them, and, what's more, they know it. The major leagues are infringing on the Sherman Anti-Trust law and it is about time they stopped it. We have hired competent lawyers who know how to handle a case of this importance."[31] Antitrust accusations had thus far been a problem for baseball primarily in the press and in Congress, but they were about to move into the courts.

Organized baseball responded, in public, with the normal assertions of confidence. "If the Federals carry out this plan," Giants' owner Harry Hempstead told the newspapers, "it will be the best thing that could happen to the major leagues." In private, they were far less sure of what to do. Most of the National League owners wanted to litigate as soon as possible to put the issue to rest. The American League owners wanted to stay out of court for fear that a defeat would have disastrous consequences.[32] The one thing they could all agree on was the need to consult their lawyers as soon as possible for advice as to what would happen in an antitrust suit.

Some of the lawyers were confident that organized baseball would win. Baseball could not be violating the Sherman Act, argued John Cromwell Bell, counsel to National League president John Tener. "The exhibition of the game of baseball," Bell explained, "cannot properly be deemed to be 'trade' or 'commerce' within the purview of the Act." The Sherman Act prohibited only agreements "in restraint of trade or commerce among the several states," but if baseball was neither trade nor commerce, then the law would have no application to it. Ellis Kinkead and John Galvin, the Reds' lawyers, agreed. But Paul Moody, the Tigers' lawyer, was less certain.

Whether or not baseball was a form of commerce, in his view, it was prob-ably not a form of *interstate* commerce, the only kind the Sherman Act covered. "While interstate commerce—to wit: the transportation of players—incidentally enters into the business of the different clubs in the league," Moody reasoned, "yet such business is not primarily interstate in its character as the thing produced and sold, to wit: the baseball game, is pro-duced and manufactured in the nature of the case in the same locality where it is sold." Moody admitted, however, that this was only his opinion, and that one could never know whether a judge would see matters differently. "I have heretofore come to the conclusion," he lamented, "that the law upon the extent and meaning of the phrase 'Interstate Commerce' and the meaning and effect of the Sherman Anti-Trust Act, depends very largely upon what the Supreme Court of the United States is going to say next."[33] The law was simply too ambiguous to make any confident predictions.

While both sides plotted their next moves, the usual run of smaller anti-trust controversies continued to pile up. Jack "Peach Pie" O'Connor, the former manager of the St. Louis Browns, had been fired after the 1910 sea-son when, in a season-ending doubleheader, he ordered his team to allow Napoleon Lajoie to reach base safely every time he came to bat, so that Lajoie would edge out Ty Cobb for the batting title. O'Connor was infor-mally blacklisted from organized baseball thereafter. In 1913 he retained a lawyer who vowed to bring an antitrust suit against the eight clubs of the American League for conspiring to keep him out of the game. If the suit was ever filed, however, it appears not to have been litigated to a conclusion. Not long after, while the Pittsburgh Pirates were holding spring training in Hot Springs, Arkansas, the Pirates sued Pittsburgh's Federal League club, the Re-bels, for attempting to lure away second baseman Jimmy Viox and pitcher George McQuillan. The Rebels promptly countersued, alleging that the Pirates were violating the Sherman Act by playing in the National League. The antitrust claim never received a hearing, as the local Hot Springs judge announced that he would limit his consideration to issues of contract law. Before he could reach a decision, in any event, Viox and McQuillan decided to stick with the Pirates, and the suit was dropped. A few months later, when the Reds sued Armando Marsans to enjoin him from jumping his contract to play with the St. Louis Terriers of the Federal League, one of Marsans's defenses was that organized baseball violated the Sherman Act. Marsans lost, but the court did not address his antitrust argument. Meanwhile, at the end of the 1914 season, the United States Attorney in San Francisco announced plans to investigate the Pacific Coast League, the leading minor league in the West, for antitrust violations.[34] The steady drip of antitrust attacks never let up.

The first fully litigated baseball antitrust case took place in the middle of the 1914 season. In June, the first baseman Hal Chase (figure 2.3) jumped from the Chicago White Sox of the American League to the Buffalo Buff-Feds of the Federal League. In July, lawyers for both sides were in court, before Judge Herbert P. Bissell of Buffalo, in a courtroom packed with baseball fans. The White Sox presented the usual argument for an injunction barring Chase from playing for the Buff-Feds, but Chase's lawyer, Keene Addington, was ready. "The only thing new in the hearing was the elaborate and forceful argument made by Mr. Addington on the Sherman Act," an alarmed Ellis Kinkead reported back to August Herrmann. "Mr. Addington spoke for five hours on this subject, and had the good attention of the judge,

Figure 2.3: The first fully litigated baseball antitrust case involved Hal Chase, one of the best first basemen of the period, who jumped from the Chicago White Sox to the Federal League's Buffalo club in the middle of the 1914 season. Chase's victory allowed him to finish 1914 and play the full 1915 season in Buffalo, where he would lead the Federal League in home runs. BL-2626.89, National Baseball Hall of Fame.

who made frequent and copious notes." Addington summed up with a scarcely concealed threat. "There is more at stake here than Chase's individual case," he warned the judge. "Before many weeks have passed we may see the standing of Organized Ball tested under Section 4 of the Sherman Act," the section that authorizes U.S. Attorneys to bring suits to enforce the act. Baseball's lawyers hastily put together and submitted a brief, in which they argued that baseball was not a form of interstate commerce and was therefore not covered by the Sherman Act.[35]

The judge sided with Chase. "It is apparent," he concluded, "that a monopoly of baseball as a business has been ingeniously devised and created." He did not think baseball was in violation of the Sherman Act, he explained, because "I cannot agree to the proposition that the business of baseball for profit is interstate trade or commerce." Baseball, in his view, "is an amusement, a sport, a game that comes clearly within the civil and criminal law of the state, and it is not a commodity or an article of merchandise subject to the regulation of congress on the theory that it is interstate commerce." But Judge Bissell held that the baseball monopoly *was* a violation of the common law of New York. "A combination of forty leagues, major and minor, has been formed," he determined, a conspiracy "controlling for profit the services of 10,000 players of professional baseball, practically all the good or skillful players in the country." As a result, "'organized baseball' is now as complete a monopoly of the baseball business for profit as any monopoly can be made. It is in contravention of the common law." The judge noted that he had not been asked to dissolve this illegal combination, although his tone suggested he would have been willing. He concluded, however, that "the court will not assist in enforcing an agreement which is part of a general plan having for its object the maintenance of a monopoly."[36] Chase was free to play for the Federal League. He would finish 1914 and play the full 1915 season in Buffalo, where he would lead the Federal League in home runs.

All concerned recognized that the importance of the *Chase* case was not limited to Chase himself. Baseball, for the first time, had been held to be an unlawful monopoly. Some were not surprised. "There is nothing new or novel about this declaration," *Sporting Life* editorialized. "Every lawyer who knows something about base ball knows that it is a species of trust." Organized baseball quickly changed the wording of its standard player contract. The old contract included a line stating that the contract's form had been prescribed by the National Commission, baseball's governing body. The new contract eliminated that line, in light of Judge Bissell's decision that the agreement establishing the National Commission was illegal.[37]

When the 1914 season ended, the Federal League had lost money, as had half the teams in the American and National Leagues, whose attendance dropped by nearly a third.[38] The two sides made some unsuccessful efforts at compromise in the fall of 1914, but when these failed, the only weapon left to the Federal League was its long-promised antitrust suit.

The Federal League finally filed its suit in federal court in Chicago in early January 1915. Named as defendants were the National and American Leagues, all sixteen clubs in the two leagues, National League president John Tener, American League president Ban Johnson, and August Herrmann, the chairman of the National Commission. The Federal League's complaint alleged that organized baseball was a combination in violation of federal antitrust law as well as the law of each of the states in which its teams were located, and that organized baseball had conspired to destroy the Federal League's business by suing and threatening to sue the Federal League's players. The complaint concluded by asking for the dissolution of all of the American and National Leagues' player contracts, and for a declaration that organized baseball was an illegal monopoly.[39]

The suit could have been filed in any city where an American or National League club was located. The Federal League chose Chicago. Both Federal League president James Gilmore and American League president Ban Johnson lived in Chicago, and Chicago was one of only three cities where all three leagues had clubs (the others were New York and St. Louis), so Chicago was as likely a choice as any. The Federal League may also have been influenced by the fact that the senior of the two federal district judges in Chicago was Kenesaw Mountain Landis, who had something of a reputation as a trust-buster. To the extent Landis was known outside the community of Chicago lawyers, it was for a 1907 case in which he imposed a fine of over $29 million on Standard Oil, or around $700 million in today's money, the largest fine in the history of the United States to that time.[40] Landis had shown that he had no fear of imposing draconian sanctions on commercial wrongdoers. The Federal League's lawyers hoped he would do so again.

Landis, however, was not just a trust-buster. "Both Judge Landis and Judge Carpenter of the U.S. Court here are dyed-in-the-wool fans and doubtless read all that is published about baseball," Charles Thomas, the president of the Cubs, reported to August Herrmann. Landis had once even written a letter to the Senators' star pitcher Walter Johnson, a fact that Senators' owner Benjamin Minor was careful not to disclose to the Federal League or to the press. "I feel as though our interests are safe in Judge Landis's hands," concluded Clark Griffith, the Senators' manager.[41]

The leaders of the Federal League were just as confident. "We'll break up the baseball trust and the National Commission," James Gilmore predicted. "We'll free every ball player in the United States." Otto Stifel, the owner of the Federal League's St. Louis club, explained that he just wanted to compete on equal terms with the Cardinals and the Browns, the local National and American League clubs. "Baseball is not sacred or different from the rules which apply to any business," Stifel insisted. "There may not be room in a country town for three grocery stores or three meat markets or three churches, for that matter, but that doesn't prevent anyone from investing his money where he thinks he has an opportunity. This is a free country and the law of competition is upheld by the Sherman anti-trust act." Joe Tinker, the shortstop and manager of the Federal League's Chicago club, told the press that the suit was filed in order to give baseball "a good housecleaning."[42] Were the Federal League to prevail, the entire structure of organized baseball would collapse. The National Agreement, the basic contract between the clubs, would be dissolved. The clubs would lose all rights over their players. Baseball would have to reorganize from scratch.

The men who ran organized baseball recognized the extremity of the danger. August Herrmann immediately instructed all sixteen club owners to submit summaries of every instance in which Federal League clubs had attempted to sign away their players, so that organized baseball could present itself as the Federal League's victim rather than vice versa. "This issue has been knocking at our door for a long while and we finally get to meet it," he told John Tener. For reasons of public relations, Herrmann advised, baseball should not raise any technical defenses, like whether the court lacked jurisdiction. "We should place ourselves in position immediately as being ready to establish the falsity of the sensational charges they have made to reiterate that organized baseball is an open book; that its record is clean; that we court a full investigation of all of its acts and for that reason we are going to meet this case on its merits and not on technicality," he declared. "In other words, we should be ready to appear in Court . . . and say *we are ready for trial*."[43]

Both sides wanted the case decided quickly, before the season began. "I think it would be a crime to have constant litigation during the playing season," James Gilmore worried. "It would certainly come very near killing the national pastime." Within a few days of filing its complaint, the Federal League submitted eleven affidavits of witnesses to the monopolistic practices of organized baseball. Joe Tinker recalled how he had been sold from Great Falls to Helena, Montana, and then from Portland to the Chicago Cubs, and then from the Cincinnati Reds to the Brooklyn Dodgers, on each occasion "without at any time being consulted with regard to his sale or his wishes in regard to his place of abode." The second baseman Otto Knabe, who had left the Phillies for the Baltimore Terrapins of the Federal League, stated that organized baseball's ten-day clause, which allowed all players to be fired with ten days' notice, "is unjust to such players and is the source of great dissatisfaction among them." Mordecai "Three Finger" Brown, one of the best pitchers of the previous decade, even testified that the Cardinals had once traded the pitcher Bill Hopper to a minor league club in exchange for a bird dog.[44]

Organized baseball responded a week later with twenty-four affidavits of its own. Most of them recounted how Federal League clubs had tried to induce players to break their American or National League contracts. Clark Griffith, for example, told how Walter Johnson had nearly been lured to the Federal League's Chicago team. The other affidavits were filed to rebut the Federal League's allegations, including one by Roger Bresnahan, manager of the Cardinals, who denied having ever traded any players for dogs. (He insisted that the bird dog he received in exchange for trading Hopper was a gift from the other team's owner.) Professional baseball simply could not exist without the business structure it had developed, swore Charles Ebbets, owner of the Brooklyn Dodgers. "Without a National Agreement," he concluded, "chaos would prevail and conditions would drift back to those of 1871–75."[45]

Both sides were in Judge Landis's Chicago courtroom a few days later for a hearing on the Federal League's motion for a preliminary injunction barring organized baseball from continuing to operate in violation of antitrust law until the case could be decided. Both sides were represented by teams of distinguished lawyers. The Federal League's lead counsel was the prominent Chicago attorney Keene Addington (figure 2.4), who had won the Hal Chase case in Buffalo the previous year. Organized baseball's lawyers were led by George Wharton Pepper of Philadelphia, who would become a U.S. senator a few years later. On the first day of the hearing, the courtroom was

Figure 2.4: After successfully representing Hal Chase in his 1914 antitrust case, the Chicago lawyer Keene Addington was retained by the Federal League in its 1915 antitrust suit against organized baseball. "The most important point," Addington argued, was that the player contracts used by organized baseball "reduce the player to a chattel." LC-B2-3366-6, Prints and Photographs Division, Library of Congress.

filled with baseball fans. There had never been so much popular interest in antitrust law, the *New Republic* noted. Even the prosecution of Standard Oil had not been so closely followed. "Most men," the journal remarked, "would rather be brought to poverty by costly kerosene than be deprived of the best baseball that can be provided." The fans were disappointed when the entire proceeding consisted of legal argument, with no players anywhere to be found. Attendance dropped sharply on the second day.[46]

"The most important point," Keene Addington told Judge Landis, was that the rules of organized baseball "reduce the player to a chattel." New leagues could not enter the marketplace, because "all of this skilled labor is under the domination and control of organized baseball." George Wharton Pepper had several responses. He began by emphasizing how long baseball had been in business, and how major a disruption would be caused by granting the Federal League's motion. He next retold the organizational history of baseball, to make the point that the National Agreement among the clubs had not been intended to suppress competition from rival third leagues, but was rather for the purpose of facilitating competition among the American and National Leagues' members.[47]

Pepper then turned to his legal arguments. He quoted the Clayton Act of 1914, which provided that the labor of human beings was not an article of commerce for purposes of the antitrust laws. This provision was due to the lobbying of labor unions, some of which had been prosecuted for antitrust violations for organizing their members. Pepper put the Clayton Act to a purpose unlikely to have been envisioned by its proponents: he argued that organized baseball could not be found liable under the antitrust laws for the way it treated its employees, because they were human beings, after all, and so their labor was not commerce. Finally, Pepper argued that the federal antitrust laws simply could not apply to baseball. Baseball was not *commerce*, he declared, quoting the words of Judge Bissell from the *Chase* case, but was rather "an amusement; it is a sport; it is a game." The players were paid, to be sure, but "the fact still remains that the thing in which the parties are concerned is the furnishing of amusement to the public." The federal government had power to regulate interstate commerce, in statutes like the Sherman Act, but amusements "are essentially matters of local concern," governed by the states and not the federal government.[48]

The Federal League responded to this last point after the hearing, in a lengthy brief devoted to the proposition that baseball *was* interstate commerce. The sport had gross revenues of several million dollars per year, the brief pointed out. It paid its employees hundreds of thousands of dollars annually. It regularly transported players and equipment across state lines. "The sport of a boy of yesterday has become the commercialized amusement of the nation of today," the Federal League concluded. "It is subject to the power of Congress to regulate commerce among the states."[49]

The hearing lasted four days. On two occasions, Judge Landis made comments that revealed his fondness for baseball. When Pepper was discussing the Clayton Act's exemption of labor from the antitrust laws, Landis interrupted him. "As the result of thirty years' observation" of baseball, Landis remarked, "I am somewhat shocked to hear you call it labor." He may simply have been expressing his skepticism that Congress had meant to extend the Clayton Act to skilled workers like baseball players, but it is also likely that

Landis was thinking of baseball as leisure rather than work. Pepper quickly recovered. If the service performed by a baseball player was not labor, he argued, then it was even less an article of commerce than labor was. An even more revealing exchange took place on the hearing's third day, when Pepper, in the midst of his closing argument, began to rhapsodize about how much he loved the game. "Well, we will have to keep affection, love and affection, out of this lawsuit," Landis snapped. Pepper tried to apologize, but Landis cut him off. "I think you gentlemen here all understand that a blow at this thing called baseball—both sides understand this perfectly—will be regarded by this court as a blow at a national institution," Landis declared. "Therefore you need not spend any time on that phase of this subject."[50] The lawyers for the Federal League could not have been heartened.

When the hearing was over, the men who ran organized baseball were cautiously confident of a favorable outcome. "If this is the only thing that will cause organized base ball to be broke up," cracked Samuel Lichtenstein, the president of the International League's Montreal Royals, "it certainly has been hanging on a very thin thread." The Federal League's suit encountered considerable skepticism in the press. "We are in somewhat of a pickle regarding one or two phases of the trust idea," confessed the sportswriter Grantland Rice. It did seem unfair to Rice that players could not sell their services to the highest bidder. "But as long as a city of 400,000 is forced to compete with a city of 3,000,000 or 5,000,000 and keen competition is the basis of the sport," Rice asked, "what is to be done about it?" The *Sporting News* complained that for all the Federal League's accusations, "they have given no hint as to the remedy they would offer to better the existing conditions." The *Chicago Tribune* concluded that if the Federal League won the suit, "it will have a great deal to answer for to the present generation of baseball fans."[51]

Both sides had proceeded very quickly because they hoped for a decision before the 1915 season began, but when April arrived, there was still no word from Judge Landis. Both sides "must perforce undergo a period of depression and anxiety until that decision is rendered," *Baseball Magazine* noted. As the season went on, the parties waited in vain for a ruling. Every so often the rumor would circulate that a decision was imminent, but each time it proved incorrect. By September, the sporting press was accusing Landis of laying down on the job. The Red Sox beat the Phillies in the World Series in October, and Landis had still not taken any action on the case. "I do hope some of these days Judge Landis may hand down his decision," August Herrmann lamented. "Until that is done, baseball conditions are certainly in chaotic shape."[52]

Landis's failure to decide the case grew particularly frustrating to baseball officials when the season ended. The Federal League had lost so much money in 1915 that a third season was out of the question. In October, a group of Federal League owners quietly began negotiating a settlement with August Herrmann and John Tener under which the more financially sound Federal League clubs would be merged into the American and National Leagues. But Herrmann and Tener were afraid to reach any such settlement before Landis decided the case. "It would, in my judgment, be most injudicious to form any combination while the case is still in the hands of the Court," George Wharton Pepper warned. If Landis were to find that organized baseball was an illegal monopoly, "it would follow that any arrangement would be illegal which involved the elimination of competition between so-called Organized Baseball and the Federal League." Herrmann and Tener reluctantly agreed to call a halt to the negotiations, but they looked for ways around the problem. What if the Federal League were simply to go out of business on its own accord, Tener asked Pepper, and then the former owners of Federal League teams were to purchase stock in some of the clubs in organized baseball? "Would that transaction," he wondered, "be dangerous or embarrassing to us pending the decision of Judge Landis?" Pepper replied that the judge would see right through any such scheme. If the Federal League dissolved, and "the individuals who had composed the Federal League were then to purchase stock interests in Major League clubs, this would be strong evidence that the dissolution of the Federal League and such subsequent purchases of Major League stock were steps taken in pursuance of an understanding or agreement reached between all parties in interest." There was simply no way to reach a settlement without the risk of having the settlement look like one more monopolistic act. "With the decision in the present suit pending," Pirates president Barney Dreyfuss concluded, "we cannot make haste too *slowly* for our own good." Landis's delay was the only thing preventing organized baseball from reaching a settlement that would put the Federal League out of business. August Herrmann agreed that "the unfortunate part of the whole baseball controversy at this time is the holding up by Judge Landis of the case presented for his consideration last winter."[53]

By January 1916, an entire year had elapsed since the hearing, and Landis had not taken any action on the case. "Judge Landis, for reasons best known to himself, has elected to delay the rendering of his classic decision to a point where all interest in that decision has expired of old age," *Baseball Magazine* complained. After three weeks of furious activity on the part of the lawyers, Landis had sat on the case for a full year. Herrmann decided to stop waiting. The two sides announced a complex agreement, under which the Federal League and its clubs would cease to exist. The Federal League would drop the antitrust suit before Judge Landis. In return, organized baseball in effect absorbed the five Federal League clubs located in metropolitan areas with major league teams. Charles Weeghman, owner of the Federal League's Chicago club, bought the Chicago Cubs of the National League, with $50,000 of the purchase price paid by the National League. The rosters of the two clubs were merged, and the Cubs moved into Weeghman Park, the Federal League's new stadium on the north side of Chicago. (The park would later be renamed Wrigley Field, after Weeghman sold the team to the chewing gum tycoon William Wrigley.) The St. Louis Terriers of the Federal League purchased the St. Louis Browns of the American League. The owners of the Federal League's Brooklyn club received $400,000, Newark got $100,000, and Pittsburgh received $50,000, each sum to be paid evenly by the American and National Leagues.[54]

Three Federal League clubs received nothing in the settlement: Kansas City, Buffalo, and Baltimore. Kansas City and Buffalo were nearly bankrupt and thus had no leverage to extract any concessions. The Baltimore club was offered $50,000 as part of the settlement but the club turned it down. Unlike the other Federal League teams, the Baltimore Terrapins were owned not by wealthy individuals but by approximately six hundred local shareholders. Their main objective was to bring major league baseball back to Baltimore, which had been without a top-level team since 1903, when the American League's Baltimore Orioles had moved to New York and become the Highlanders (later the Yankees). At a tense meeting, late at night in New York's Waldorf-Astoria Hotel in December 1915, the Terrapins' lawyer pleaded with the owners of the American and National League clubs. "We are willing to purchase and pay for a franchise in the major leagues, if we can get it," Stuart Janney explained. "We do not ask anything if we could be given the privilege of buying and locating a major league club in Baltimore." Not a single owner agreed. Adding a ninth team to an eight-team league would pose difficult scheduling problems in a sport in which each team was expected to play nearly every day. None of the owners of existing teams was willing to move to Baltimore or sell to a group of Baltimore investors. They all remembered the Orioles, who had lasted only two years in Baltimore because of poor attendance. Baltimore was "a minor league city, and not a hell of a good one at that," smirked Charles Comiskey, owner of the White Sox. "It is one of the worst minor league towns in this country," agreed the Dodgers' owner Charles Ebbets. "You have too many colored population to start with. They are a cheap population when it gets down to paying their money at the gate."[55] The Terrapins remained the lone holdout in the Federal League's settlement with organized baseball.

Lawyers for all concerned filed into Kenesaw Mountain Landis's courtroom in February 1916 for the formal termination of the Federal League's antitrust suit. The only one to object was Janney, on behalf of the Terrapins. The settlement, he complained, was "in a sense the very consummation of the conspiracy alleged in the original bill," in that organized ball had bought off its rivals by incorporating them into its monopoly. He acknowledged, though, that without a Federal League to bring the suit, there was no point in continuing. He asked Landis, when dismissing the suit, to clarify that the Terrapins still had the right to bring an antitrust suit of their own, and the judge did so.[56]

Landis then explained, for the first and only time in public, why he had delayed for so long in deciding the case. It was because his decision would have been in the Federal League's favor, but he did not want to destroy the game of baseball. He had his "own knowledge of the subject matter of your litigation," he told the assembled lawyers, "resulting from thirty years acquaintance with the subject matter of your litigation, before most of you gentlemen who were in that litigation knew anything about any such thing as baseball." Landis's own knowledge of baseball had convinced him that the decision he would have been compelled to reach "would have been if not destructive, vitally injurious to the subject matter of the litigation. That is the plain truth." The judge had accordingly resolved to do nothing. "I decided," Landis explained, "that this court had a right, if not a right a discretion, to postpone the announcement of any such order, and that is the reason that the entry of that order was postponed."[57] Four years later, the grateful leaders of organized baseball would make Landis their first commissioner (figure 2.5).

Figure 2.5: Kenesaw Mountain Landis watches the first game of the 1940 World Series in Cincinnati. Landis became the first commissioner of baseball in 1920. A few years earlier, as a judge in Chicago, he postponed a decision in the Federal League's antitrust suit for over a year, to avoid having to rule in the Federal League's favor. BL-1844.81, National Baseball Hall of Fame.

Baseball had withstood its most dangerous antitrust challenge to date, because it was lucky enough to get a judge who put his love of the game above his professional obligation to follow the law. The Federal League had crumbled, and there were no other rivals on the horizon. The stockholders of the Baltimore Terrapins were still disappointed, however. It would not be long before they would be heard from again.

THE SUPREME COURT STEPS IN

In a 1922 case called *Federal Baseball Club of Baltimore v. National League*, the U.S. Supreme Court decided that the Sherman Antitrust Act did not apply to professional baseball, on the ground that baseball was not a form of interstate commerce. The case would have important long-term consequences: it is the origin of baseball's so-called "antitrust exemption." Few court decisions have been so widely ridiculed. "Most commentators thought the decision was wrong at the time and now consider it ludicrous," according to one typical criticism of Justice Oliver Wendell Holmes's "simple and simplistic opinion." In the view of another representative critic, the decision was "remarkably myopic, almost willfully ignorant of the nature of the enterprise." *Federal Baseball Club*, some contend, can only be understood as evidence that the justices were willing to bend the law to protect baseball's status as the national pastime. The distinguished federal judge Henry Friendly summed up the conventional wisdom: the case "was not one of Mr. Justice Holmes' happiest days."[1]

As we have already seen, however, the question of whether baseball was violating the Sherman Act had already been litigated twice before *Federal Baseball Club*. In the *Chase* case, one judge had decided it was not, while in the Federal League's antitrust suit of 1915, another judge may have privately determined that it was. (Judge Landis declared that he would have ruled against baseball, but he never said whether his decision would have been based on federal or state law.) Judges would reach differing conclusions in *Federal Baseball Club* itself. The one thing we can say with certainty about *Federal Baseball Club* is that the case was not nearly as easy as the critics suggest. The legal system offered plenty of material for both sides to make plausible arguments about whether baseball was governed by federal antitrust law.

Let's go to the mat with them

When the Baltimore Terrapins were left out of the Federal League's settlement with organized baseball, their first move was to try to convince the Justice Department to bring an antitrust suit. Their spokesman was the Baltimore congressman John Charles Linthicum, who urged Attorney General Thomas W. Gregory to consider whether "some Government control could be enforced to prevent such a monopoly." He received a terse response. The elimination of Baltimore as a major league city, one of Gregory's assistants replied, "does not appear to constitute any ground for action by the department."[2] The Terrapins were on their own.

In March 1916, the club filed its own antitrust suit in federal court in Philadelphia. Among those named as defendants were all the defendants from the Federal League's suit of the previous year—the National and American Leagues, all sixteen major league teams, and the three people in charge of organized baseball, National League president John Tener, American League president Ban Johnson, and August Herrmann, the chairman of the National Commission (figure 3.1). The suit also added three new defendants, the men who had led the Federal League's settlement negotiations, league president James Gilmore, Chicago owner Charles Weeghman, and Newark owner Harry Sinclair. The Baltimore club's complaint alleged that all concerned had conspired to monopolize baseball, at a cost to the Terrapins of $300,000 in losses, which, when tripled as the Sherman Act required, yielded a request for $900,000 in damages, or around $18 million in today's dollars.[3] The complaint did not seek the dissolution of organized baseball, as the Federal League had in its Chicago suit the previous year. It was too late for such a remedy to help the Terrapins. As the only club left standing outside of organized baseball, even if they had been able to sign players, they would have had no one to play against.

Figure 3.1: The members of the National Commission attend the 1916 World Series in Boston's Fenway Park. From left to right: Red Sox owner Joseph Lannin, American League president Ban Johnson, National League president John Tener, and National Commission president August Herrmann. At the time, the Baltimore Terrapins' antitrust suit was pending in Philadelphia. LC-USZ62-50112, Prints and Photographs Division, Library of Congress.

Sporadic settlement negotiations led the parties to postpone trial several times, but a trial finally began in June 1917. After four days of trial, the Baltimore club abruptly dropped the suit without explaining why. The lawyers for organized baseball told the press that it was because the Terrapins realized they could not win the case, but in light of subsequent events this explanation seems unlikely.[4] A more likely reason is that the parties believed they were so close to a settlement that further litigation was pointless. On what would have been the fifth day of trial, the Terrapins' lawyer spoke up first thing in the morning to say that "after full consideration of this case last night by counsel for the plaintiff, circumstances have arisen which make us desire to discontinue it." He did not say what those circumstances were, but baseball's lawyer, George Wharton Pepper, seemed to know about them too. "We have no objection," he told the judge. "We feel very great gratification at the decision for the plaintiffs just announced to the Court." If a settlement was imminent, talks broke down, because within a few weeks Pepper received word that the Terrapins intended to file their antitrust suit once again. By midsummer, the press was reporting that the new suit would be filed in Washington, the major league city closest to Baltimore and thus, the Terrapins' lawyers may have hoped, the location where jurors would be most sympathetic. (The suit could not have been filed in Baltimore itself, because none of the defendants was located in Maryland.) After a brief pause for more fruitless settlement negotiations, the Terrapins indeed filed the new antitrust suit in Washington in September.[5] This was the case that would get to the Supreme Court.

The new complaint made the same allegations against all the same defendants. Nearly a year and a half of still more settlement talks followed. At first, organized baseball floated the idea of settling the case by creating a third major league, to be made up of clubs promoted from the highest level of the minors, and letting the Terrapins' owners have the Baltimore franchise. "A new league might benefit the game during the war," Ban Johnson told the newspapers. Johnson had heard from a banker who owned stock in the Terrapins that this kind of a deal was what the club was really after. "The Baltimore Feds have no expectation of getting a favorable decision in their new suit," he informed August Herrmann, "but they hope to compel Organized Baseball to come across with a settlement out of court." Herrmann was not interested in settling the case. "I believe the time has come when we should get to the finish with a case of this kind and ascertain positively whether we are violating the Sherman Law or not," he replied to Johnson. "Unless this is done we will have trouble right along, as soon as an adjustment is made with one party another one will 'pop up.' Therefore I repeat 'Let's go to the mat with them.'"[6] This disagreement would make settling the case nearly impossible.

An additional complication in reaching a settlement was that organized baseball was already under an obligation to make annual payments to most of the other Federal League owners under the settlement of the Federal League's suit before Judge Landis. When the Terrapins filed their own suit, organized baseball stopped making those payments, on the ground that the Federal League was not living up to its end of the bargain. The Terrapins' pending suit was thus not entirely a bad thing from the perspective of organized baseball, because it provided a reason to avoid paying out significant sums, which in turn provided a reason to keep the Terrapins' suit pending for as long as possible. It was not until early 1918, when the other Federal League owners agreed to post bonds indemnifying organized baseball in the event the Terrapins won their suit, in exchange for the resumption of payments under the Landis settlement, that this logjam was finally broken. Even then, however, it took another year for the case to be set for trial, to begin in March 1919.[7]

The men who ran baseball were once again divided. Ban Johnson thought it unnecessary to hire high-priced lawyers, because the suit "to me personally looks like a joke affair, and I am confident it will be swept out of the Washington courts in a jiffey." John Heydler, who had replaced John Tener as president of the National League, was more apprehensive. George Wharton Pepper had advised him that the case was "much more formidable than the law suit which we defended in Philadelphia in 1917." Heydler accordingly urged the owners and presidents of all eight National League clubs to attend the trial. He explained that "the presence of substantial people, representing the big investments in base ball properties, Mr. Pepper believes, is absolutely essential in a trial case of this character."[8]

The trial took place in late March and early April, just before the 1919 season began. The judge, Wendell Phillips Stafford (figure 3.2), had nearly twenty years of experience. He had been a member of the Vermont Supreme Court before Theodore Roosevelt appointed him to the District of Columbia bench in 1904. Stafford was perhaps best known as a poet and a sought-after speaker on ceremonial occasions. *Dorian Days*, his 1909 book of verse,

Figure 3.2: Judge Wendell Stafford determined in 1919 that organized baseball was an illegal monopoly under the Sherman Antitrust Act. His decision would be reversed on appeal. LC-H25-105830-G, Prints and Photographs Division, Library of Congress.

reminded at least one lawyer of Keats, while his collected speeches, published in 1913, covered topics ranging from Abraham Lincoln to the history of his native Vermont.[9] If he had any views on antitrust law, however, Judge Stafford had not put them on record. Unlike Kenesaw Mountain Landis, he was an unknown quantity.

After the first week of testimony, John Heydler was even more nervous than he had been before trial. "The Baltimore Federals are presenting a stronger front and are building up a more formidable case than in the 1917 trial at Philadelphia," he reported to the National League club presidents who had not been in attendance. The Terrapins' main lawyer, William Marbury, was "rated as the leading Maryland attorney," Heydler explained, and his performance justified the reputation. Marbury's most effective witnesses had been the marginal players Jimmy "Runt" Walsh, John Priest, and George Maisel, all of whom testified about how "for a period of years they were shunted around from Club to Club, or from coast to coast, as in Maisel's case." Heydler worried that all this evidence of players being bought and sold had "made the most unfavorable impression on the Court." Pepper tried to argue that much of the evidence Marbury had introduced was beside the point. "This is not a suit by a player claiming that he has been damaged," Pepper told the jury, "and if you were of the opinion that various players had received a raw deal from organized baseball, that would not be a ground for finding a verdict for the plaintiff." Baseball had not tried to deprive the Federal League of players, he argued. "Organized baseball has never yet signed up players beyond the actual needs of its own clubs," he claimed. "It has never yet signed up players and held them on reserve for the purpose of preventing them from going into the service of competitors." In any event, he pointed out, the Terrapins hardly had the right to complain that organized baseball was an unlawful monopoly, when after all they had tried desperately to join it. "A combination is either a thing from which you stay out or it is a thing you go in," Pepper argued. "You cannot try to get in and then, if you are refused permission, say, 'I have suddenly discovered this is a den of iniquity and a combination of conspirators, and I want damages for having such a thing on the face of the earth.'" But he felt all along, he recalled later, that "the atmosphere of the Washington courtroom was unfriendly" to organized baseball.[10]

When the testimony ended and Judge Stafford instructed the jury, Heydler's and Pepper's fears were proven accurate. "The acts of the defendants, alleged and proved, by way of maintaining the system of organized baseball, constituted in law an attempt to monopolize the business of competitive baseball exhibitions for profit," the judge stated. As an "inseparable part" of those acts, he continued, organized baseball had attempted "to monopolize commerce between the States." Much of the defense case had rested on the asserted benefits of the reserve clause for the stability and profitability of the game, but Stafford told the jury to ignore that aspect of the case. "The law forbids monopolizing or attempting to monopolize any part of Interstate Commerce and no monopoly or attempt at monopoly can be justified on the ground that it is beneficial to any body," the judge instructed. The jury was accordingly to pay no mind to any testimony showing "that players are generously treated by Organized Ball, or that their salaries are high, or that they are well-disciplined, they are better behaved, less disposed to rowdyism, or that they are prevented from violating their contracts, or that better games are played." In Stafford's view, none of that mattered. The only question was whether baseball was a monopoly, and that, he held, had been decisively proven. All that was left for the jury to decide was how much the Terrapins had lost as a result of baseball's actions.[11] The jury determined that the Terrapins had lost $80,000, so the outcome of the trial was an award of three times that much, or $240,000. The award was only a bit more than a quarter of what the Terrapins had requested, but the amount was less important than the judge's ruling. After years of anticipation, organized baseball had finally been held to constitute an illegal monopoly.

"I was thunderstruck," August Herrmann acknowledged. Baseball immediately announced that it would appeal and that the game would go on as usual while the appeal was pending. Behind the scenes, the men who ran the game engaged in their usual squabbling. Ban Johnson blamed George Wharton Pepper and his team of lawyers. "I was not at all satisfied with the manner in which our lawyers handled the case," he complained. "There was a lack of 'team work.'" Johnson wanted to fire them and hire new ones. Heydler thought that "Mr. Pepper most ably and brilliantly presented our side" and that the blame lay only with the judge. Pepper, for his part, professed certainty that baseball would win on appeal, because it was so clear that baseball was not a form of interstate commerce. "If baseball is interstate commerce," he noted, "the same thing is true of a brotherhood of railway engineers or any other organization composed of persons engaged in interstate activities." Judge Stafford's ruling, if taken to its logical extreme, threatened to include realms of life Pepper was sure no court would find covered by the Sherman Act.[12]

The lawyers for the Baltimore Terrapins must have been worried that Pepper might be right, because when the 1919 season ended, while the appeal was pending, they paid a visit to Pepper's Philadelphia office to discuss settling the case. "They said that the Baltimore Club was anxious to realize on its recovery," Pepper related to Heydler. "While no figures were mentioned I got the impression that they would be willing to scale down the amount of their recovery very considerably." Pepper thought a settlement might be wise. "As you know it is my expectation that we can ultimately win this case on the points of law involved," he advised Heydler, "but you will realize that several of the questions are novel and it may ultimately turn out that my view is mistaken." Pepper recommended that baseball pay the Terrapins the $80,000 the jury determined as damages, which he considered "as a reliable estimate by impartial people of what ought to be paid to Baltimore to give them a square deal." If baseball paid only the actual $80,000 in damages, but not the extra $160,000 required by the Sherman Act's treble damages provision, Pepper suggested, baseball could maintain the position that it had not violated the act, which would "minimize the danger that the settlement could afterwards be used against us as an admission that we had broken the law." Baseball once again refused to settle. "I wouldn't give fifty cents to settle it," insisted Benjamin Minor, the former Senators' president and one of the lawyers assisting Pepper. "What we want to show is that we are blameless under the law." John Conway Toole, another of baseball's lawyers, reminded Ban Johnson that any settlement would leave Judge Stafford's jury instructions as the final word in the case. "Any zealous Federal official who desired to look on base ball as a trust could point to Judge Stafford's charge to the jury," he noted. Baseball had an interest in obtaining a declaration from a higher court that Stafford was wrong. "The Baltimore judgment is still ringing in my ears" even eight months later, August Herrmann admitted. He told Pepper that the National Commission had determined "to go ahead and fight the case at Washington to the finish."[13]

Pepper had reasons other than the novelty of the legal issue to advise settling the case rather than appealing it. Baseball had litigated three antitrust cases and lost the two that were not settled; baseball would have lost them all had Judge Kenesaw Mountain Landis been more forthcoming. Pepper had no cause to expect any sympathy from the three judges of the District of Columbia Court of Appeals, the court that would hear the appeal from the most recent loss.[14] The court's chief judge, Constantine J. Smyth, had made his name as a foe of big business while serving as Nebraska's attorney general. He was the Smyth in the famous case of *Smyth v. Ames,* in which the Supreme Court invalidated Nebraska's railroad rate regulation. In Woodrow Wilson's first term, Smyth was a special assistant to the U.S. attorney general, with responsibility for representing the government in antitrust cases. The Terrapins could hardly have asked for a judge more likely to be predisposed to rule in their favor. The other two judges, Charles Henry Robb and Josiah Van Orsdel, had no particular antitrust record, but, like Smyth, both had spent significant parts of their careers as government lawyers. Both had worked in the Justice Department during the Roosevelt administration, and Van Orsdel had spent many years as the attorney general of Wyoming.[15] Pepper could not have been optimistic.

The Court of Appeals held oral argument in October 1920. "It was rather a striking coincidence," Pepper noted, that the deciding game of the World Series was being played at the very same time. (Cleveland beat Brooklyn 3–0.) Baseball had experienced extraordinary highs and lows over the past few months. Babe Ruth, who had just been sold from the Red Sox to the Yankees, hit an astonishing 54 home runs, nearly doubling his own record of 29 from the previous year. Ruth's closest competitor in home runs was George Sisler of the Browns, who hit 19, which would have been the most in baseball in almost any prior year. Ruth became a national hero. The Yankees' home attendance doubled. And Ruth was just the hefty tip of an even larger iceberg. The number of runs scored per game increased by 16 percent in 1920, aided by rule changes that banned pitchers from tampering with the ball and required umpires to replace scuffed and dirty balls with new ones. (The ball itself may also have become livelier, although this is still a matter of controversy.) Attendance throughout the American and National Leagues jumped by 40 percent. On one view, the game had never been in better health. But all was not well. In August, the Indians' shortstop Ray Chapman died after being hit in the head by a pitch thrown by Carl Mays of the Yankees, in what is still the only death of its kind in the history of major league baseball. More ominously for the financial health of the game, the Black Sox scandal broke in the fall of 1920. Ever since the previous fall there had been rumors that some of the White Sox had been bribed by gamblers to throw the 1919 World Series. In September and October 1920, as a grand jury began to investigate, those who had knowledge of the scheme started confessing in the press.[16] The antitrust case had been the most significant issue confronting baseball when it began back in 1916, but by 1920 it was just one of several developments competing for the attention of fans and insiders alike.

"By far the most important question" in the case, Pepper argued, "is whether professional baseball is interstate commerce." This was a question of great import to "everybody in the United States," he noted, because if baseball really was an illegal monopoly, "the annual world's series games are the result of a criminal conspiracy." The three judges must have known that the World Series was taking place at that very moment and that millions were waiting anxiously for the outcome. If baseball was interstate commerce, Pepper implied, the 1920 World Series might be the last one. "The organization alleged to be unlawful has been in existence for nearly twenty years," he continued. "During all that time all the details of its organization have been matters of public knowledge. Its operations have been of the keenest personal interest to millions of people. If there was any public wrong to right there has been superabundant opportunity for the Department of Justice to act." Yet the Justice Department—which, as the judges knew well, had filed lawsuits against alleged monopolies in all sorts of industries, some filed by Judge Smyth himself—had never gone after baseball.[17] The reason for the department's inaction, Pepper argued, was that baseball was not governed by the Sherman Act, because baseball was not a form of interstate commerce.

The Court of Appeals issued its decision in December 1920—a unanimous opinion in baseball's favor written by, of all people, the former trust-buster, Chief Judge Constantine Smyth. Baseball, the court held, was not a form of "trade or commerce," and thus the Sherman Act had no application to it. "Trade and commerce require the transfer of something, whether it be persons, commodities, or intelligence, from one place or person to another," Smyth reasoned. "A game of baseball is not susceptible of being transferred." Of course, the players and their equipment traveled from place to place, Smyth acknowledged, "but they are not the game. Not until they come into contact with their opponents on the baseball field and the contest opens does the game come into existence. It is local in its beginning and in its end. Nothing is transferred in the process to those who patronize it. The exertions of skill and agility which they witness may excite in them pleasurable emotions, just as might a view of a beautiful picture or a masterly performance of some drama; but the game effects no exchange of things." A display or a performance was something different from commerce. There were commercial transactions connected with the game, to be sure, like the sale of tickets to spectators, but again, these were not baseball itself. "Baseball is not commerce," Smyth concluded, "though some of its incidents may be."[18]

Smyth then provided a set of analogies to clarify the conception of commerce he had just elucidated. "Suppose a law firm in the city of Washington sends its members to points in different states to try lawsuits," he posited. "They would travel, and probably carry briefs and records, in interstate commerce. Could it be correctly said that the firm, in the trial of the lawsuits, was engaged in trade or commerce?" Smyth did not answer his own question, but his implication was that no one would use the word *commerce* to refer to the practice of law. "Or, take the case of a lecture bureau, which employs persons to deliver lectures before Chautauqua gatherings at points in different states," he continued. "It would be necessary for the lecturers to travel in interstate commerce, in order that they might fulfill their engagements; but would it not be an unreasonable stretch of the ordinary meaning of the words to say that the bureau was engaged in trade or commerce?" Again, he did not answer the question, but again his implication was that no reasonable person would call lecturing a form of commerce. "If a game of baseball, before a concourse of people who pay for the privilege of witnessing it, is trade or commerce," Smyth explained, "then the college teams, who play football where an admission fee is charged, engage in an act of trade or commerce." But such a result, in Smyth's view, flowed from confusing the act itself with the commercial transactions surrounding it. "The act is not trade or commerce; it is sport," he concluded. "The fact that the appellants produce baseball games as a source of profit, large or small, cannot change the character of the games. They are still sport, not trade."[19]

After years of litigation and threatened congressional investigations, baseball finally had a court decision immunizing the game from the Sherman Act. The decision met with a mixed reception in the legal community. Some lawyers thought it was clearly right. As one put it, "in baseball, the game's the thing, not the transportation incidental thereto." Others thought the Court of Appeals had made a mistake. "The players' contracts contemplated that they be transported around the different states to the various cities of the league," one argued. "The interstate travel of the ball players is so 'essential' an element of their contract as to make it interstate commerce." Still others took the view that right or wrong, the decision was a happy occasion, because baseball could not function well without the reserve clause, and a contrary ruling would have led to the clause's demise.[20] There was just as much disagreement outside the courtroom as inside.

At the end of Judge Smyth's opinion, he ordered the case returned to Judge Stafford for a new trial. In their complaint, the Terrapins had relied not only on the Sherman Act but also on the common law. This was the same strategy that had been pursued successfully in the Hal Chase case, and perhaps the strategy that would have succeeded in the Federal League's case if Kenesaw Mountain Landis had announced any ruling. Neither Judge Stafford nor the jury had reached a decision on the Terrapins' common law claim because a decision had not been necessary at the time. Smyth seems to have meant to give the Terrapins a chance to argue before Judge Stafford that they should prevail under the common law. Rather than take this opportunity for a new trial, however, the Terrapins informed the Court of Appeals that they would prefer to go directly to the Supreme Court. They asked the Court of Appeals to change its order granting a new trial into an order simply reversing the decision of the trial court and entering judgment in favor of organized baseball. The Court of Appeals agreed to do so.[21] The Terrapins had given up their chance to win in the trial court on the common law in order to get to the Supreme Court faster.

Why were the Terrapins in such a hurry? The most likely explanation is that they were running out of money. The club had not earned any revenue in more than five years, since the Federal League played its last games in October 1915. All it had done in the interim was pay lawyers. Even if the Terrapins prevailed at a new trial before Judge Stafford, baseball was sure to appeal, and the club could be tied up in litigation for several more years. The Terrapins seem to have decided to gamble everything on one last throw of the dice, an effort to persuade the Supreme Court to reverse the decision of the Court of Appeals. If they won, the jury verdict would be reinstated, and the club's shareholders would finally receive the award of $240,000. If they lost, the case would be over.

INTERSTATE COMMERCE

The question before the Supreme Court—whether baseball was a kind of interstate commerce—depended, of course, on what interstate commerce was understood to mean. By the early twentieth century, that was already a very old question, with a great deal of history behind it.

Congress possesses only the powers the Constitution gives it, one of which—the most important one when it comes to economic regulation—is the power to regulate interstate commerce. Today that power is interpreted very broadly, to allow Congress to enact statutes governing virtually any sort of economic activity, but for most of American history lawyers and judges understood the Constitution's commerce clause as an important limit on the federal government's power. In an era when most transactions did not cross state lines, and when state and local governments were still the primary regulators of economic life, the commerce clause was the major boundary between the realms of state and federal power. Most of the economy was a local matter for the states to govern. When interstate commerce was at issue, by contrast, a state might find it impossible to regulate transactions spilling over its borders, or the interests of two states might come into conflict. In such cases, but only in such cases, did the federal government have the power to regulate.

This was why the Sherman Act was limited in application to interstate commerce. A statute without that limitation would almost certainly have been found unconstitutional by the courts, as exceeding the power of Congress. When a court had to decide whether any given activity, like baseball, was or was not a kind of interstate commerce, the court was not merely trying to discern what the words of the statute meant or what was intended by the legislators who enacted it. The court was also necessarily considering the limits of the federal government's power under the Constitution. Even if Congress intended to regulate that activity, if it was not a form of interstate commerce, Congress lacked the power to do so. Whether the Sherman Act covered baseball was thus very nearly the same question as whether the Sherman Act even *could* cover baseball. Both turned on whether baseball was a form of interstate commerce.

The Supreme Court had already considered whether many other industries were engaged in interstate commerce. There was a long line of cases, for example, holding that insurance was not a form of commerce, and thus that state regulation of the insurance business, though it might limit or even prohibit interstate transactions, did not encroach on the federal government's power over interstate commerce. "Issuing a policy of insurance is not a transaction of commerce," Justice Stephen Field explained in 1869. "These contracts are not articles of commerce in any proper meaning of the word. They are not subjects of trade and barter, offered in the market as something having an existence and value independent of the parties to them." Insurance policies no doubt related to commerce and might even profoundly influence commerce, Justice Edward White reasoned in a similar 1895 case, but that was not enough to call the insurance business itself a form of commerce. "If the power to regulate interstate commerce applied to all the incidents to which said commerce might give rise and to all contracts which might be made in the course of its transaction," White cautioned, "that power would embrace the entire sphere of mercantile activity in any way connected with trade between the States," which would make the federal government the supreme regulator of the economy, a result almost unthinkable at the time.[22] For there to be a firm line between state and federal authority, insurance could not be a form of commerce.

In another group of cases, the Court had drawn a sharp line between manufacturing and commerce. Perhaps the most famous of these was *United States v. E. C. Knight Company*, from 1895, in which the Court held that the Sugar Trust, a combination controlling 98 percent of the nation's sugar refining business, could not be prosecuted under the Sherman Act. The *production of* sugar, the Court reasoned, was something different from *commerce in* sugar, and monopolies only in the latter fell within the proscription of the Sherman Act. "Doubtless the power to control the manufacture of a given thing involves in a certain sense the control of its disposition," Chief Justice Melville Fuller acknowledged, "but this is a secondary and not the primary sense." Commerce and production were two different things. "Commerce succeeds to manufacture, and is not a part of it," Fuller explained. "The fact that an article is manufactured for export to another State does not of itself make it an article of interstate commerce." The purpose of insisting on this distinction was, again, to police the boundary between the proper areas of state and federal control. "If it be held that the term [commerce] includes the regulation of all such manufactures as are intended to be the subject of commercial transactions in the future," Justice Lucius Lamar warned in 1888, "the result would be that Congress would be invested, to the exclusion of the States, with the power to regulate, not only manufactures, but also agriculture, horticulture, stock raising, domestic fisheries, mining—in short, every branch of human industry."[23]

Interstate commerce was thus a much narrower concept in the early twentieth century than it would later become. Perhaps it was too narrow to include baseball. The business of organized baseball was the production of baseball games. The games themselves took place in one location at a time, just like the manufacture of anything else. There was a great deal of interstate travel to get from one game to another, but that was not the main point of the enterprise. Organized baseball wasn't shipping bats or balls from one state in order to sell them to customers in another. Insurance agents sometimes traveled to meet their customers in other states, and presumably sugar refiners did too. But if that didn't make insurance or sugar refining a kind of interstate commerce, why should it for baseball?

The concept of interstate commerce was not so narrow, however, that one could not make a plausible case for including baseball within the category. There were other cases on the books that made the question more complicated. In the years just before *Federal Baseball Club*, the Supreme Court had determined that several potentially analogous industries *were* forms of interstate commerce.

In 1911, for example, the Court found that both Standard Oil and the American Tobacco Company were combinations in violation of the Sherman Act. Both companies had argued that they were engaged in manufacture—oil refining and tobacco production—rather than commerce, but the Court scarcely paid these arguments any attention, because the monopolies in the two cases involved both manufacture and interstate shipping, and that was enough to bring the enterprises as a whole within the Sherman Act. A few years earlier, the Court had allowed the federal government to break up the Beef Trust, a combination of the country's largest meatpackers, even though each packed meat only in a single state. Justice Oliver Wendell Holmes drew a distinction between the *E. C. Knight* case, "where the subject matter of the combination was manufacture," and the prosecution of the Beef Trust. "Here the subject matter is sales," Holmes concluded, "and the very point of the combination is to restrain and monopolize commerce among the States in respect of such sales."[24] These were fine distinctions between commerce and production, so fine that they allowed room for argument on both sides with respect to a wide range of industries, including baseball. Perhaps the business of organized baseball was best understood, not merely as the presentation of games in a single location, but as the organization and transportation, across a national network, of a traveling troupe of baseball-playing performers. Maybe baseball was an amalgam of production and commerce. Maybe it was more like oil, or tobacco, or meatpacking, than it was like insurance or sugar.

Other recent cases must have made organized baseball's lawyers worry. The Court had held that a correspondence school was engaged in interstate commerce when it sent books and papers from one state to students in another. On one view, the actual business of the school was its teaching, and that took place locally, wherever any given student happened to live. The defendant was a school, after all, not a book distributor. The circumstance that it mailed books to other states, on this view, was only incidental to the main thrust of its business, and was thus not enough to constitute interstate commerce. This may well have been the view of Chief Justice Fuller and Justice Joseph McKenna, who dissented without writing opinions. But the rest of the Court was willing to say that the school was engaged in interstate commerce.[25] If a game of baseball was analogous to teaching, and the travel of the players analogous to the shipment of books, then organized baseball was engaged in interstate commerce too.

Even more recently, the Court had upheld the Mann Act against constitutional challenge. The Mann Act was a federal statute that prohibited the transportation of a woman or girl across state lines "for the purpose of prostitution or debauchery, or for any other immoral purpose." A defendant convicted under the statute argued that human beings could not be objects of commerce and that the transportation of people across state lines thus could not amount to interstate commerce. The Court unanimously rejected this argument, with language that could be understood to have direct application to baseball. Commerce, the Court held, "includes the transportation of persons and property. There may be, therefore, a movement of persons as well as of property; that is, a person may move or be moved in interstate commerce."[26] What was baseball but the movement of players in interstate commerce?

The Supreme Court's precedents thus supported reasonable arguments on both sides of *Federal Baseball Club*. None of those precedents, however, involved show business, the industry that seemed most similar to baseball. Like baseball players, actors and singers traveled from state to state, carrying the tools of their trade with them. As with baseball, the purpose of the travel was to present exhibitions in a single location. For all the fine distinctions involved in defining interstate commerce, it would have been odd for baseball and show business to fall on different sides of the line. There were no Supreme Court cases addressing whether show business was a form of interstate commerce, but there were two lower court opinions on the topic, decided within a few months of each other in 1914. One court decided that show business was not covered by the Sherman Act because it was not a kind of interstate commerce, the other that it *was* interstate commerce and thus that it *was* covered by the Sherman Act.

The first case was a dispute between the Metropolitan Opera and the opera impresario Oscar Hammerstein, grandfather of the Broadway lyricist. When Hammerstein sold his own opera company to the Metropolitan, he agreed not to produce any competing operas for ten years, but he reneged on that promise, and the Metropolitan sued. One of Hammerstein's defenses was that his agreement with the Metropolitan was void because it violated the Sherman Act, a claim that raised the question whether opera was a form of commerce. The court relied on the distinction between manufacture and commerce to decide that opera was not commerce. "The production of opera or other theatrical exhibitions before an audience in exchange for the price of the tickets involves none of the elements of trade or commerce as commonly understood," explained Justice Francis Key Pendleton, who also came from a musical family—his grandfather was Francis Scott Key, composer of "The Star-Spangled Banner." Opera was production, not trade. It was like the manufacture of sugar or the provision of insurance. "The holder of the ticket pays a certain price as a consideration for the privilege of experiencing the gratification of an artistic sense," Pendleton continued. "Such a transaction is as far removed as possible from the commonly accepted meaning of trade or commerce." If opera was commerce, Pendleton worried, so would be many other realms of activity not normally placed in that category. "It would seem to follow," he shuddered, "that every museum which exhibits pictures, every university which gives courses of instruction or lectures, every lawyer who prepares a brief, every surgeon who performs an operation, every circus, moving picture show, exhibiting pugilist, actor or performer is engaged in commerce." The notion that the federal government rather than the states would have primary regulatory authority over all these activities was simply too absurd to contemplate. And if opera wasn't commerce, interstate opera wasn't interstate commerce. The Metropolitan sometimes went on tour to different states, but the singers' travel and the shipment of stage sets were "neither an essential part of opera nor a necessary incident thereto." The production of opera was a local matter, one to be regulated by the states rather than the federal government.[27]

The other case was decided by Learned Hand, then only a few years into what would be a distinguished 52-year career as a federal judge. Hand had what his biographer calls "a broad view of the national commerce power," in the sense that he was more willing than many of his fellow judges to classify particular activities as interstate commerce in order to find constitutional support for congressional regulation of the national economy. The case before Hand was a Sherman Act suit against a group of theater owners alleged to have monopolized the vaudeville circuit, in which performers would travel from theater to theater, often crossing state lines. Was vaudeville a form of interstate commerce? Hand decided that it was. "Undeniably certain aspects of the business are interstate commerce," he began. "The performers must go from state to state, throughout the circuit, acting here and there, and fulfilling their contracts as much by the travel as the acting." They carried their props with them, and the theaters themselves sent scenery and advertising across state lines. "In respect of all these details," Hand determined, "the business, therefore, consists of interstate commerce." But that was not enough to make vaudeville as a whole interstate commerce, Hand knew. The case turned on how significant these commercial aspects of vaudeville were, as compared with the business as a whole. He concluded that they were significant enough. "Here," he reasoned, "the contracts of hiring involve for their performance the transit quite as much as the performance." Vaudeville actors were, by their nature, interstate travelers. That made vaudeville different from the Metropolitan Opera, which also traveled from state to state on occasion but normally stayed in New York. "Suppose the case of a traveling troupe of players, who were constantly on tour from state to state at short 'stands,' and who had no fixed playhouse," Hand imagined. "Certainly their business would be interstate. On the other hand, a combination of local playhouses might not be in restraint of interstate commerce, though it affected the interstate movement of actors or scenery." Vaudeville was a form of interstate commerce, even if opera was not.[28]

These two opinions were not easy to reconcile. In the opera case, the court focused on whether theatrical productions were *commerce*; in the vaudeville case, the focus was on whether the productions were *interstate*. If theatrical performance was not commerce at all, the first court might have replied to the second, it could not become interstate commerce simply by crossing state lines. In response, the second court might have pointed out that the shipment of people and paraphernalia from one state to another *was* the vaudeville business, or at least a major part of it, so that vaudeville was commerce enough, and that if an opera company traveled as often as vaudeville performers did, then opera would become commerce too. But both sides would have recognized that the difference between the two cases was a product, not of faulty reasoning by one court or another, but of a more fundamental disagreement over the scope and desirability of federal control of the economy. If two courts started with divergent ideas about the appropriate degree of federal power, they would reach divergent conclusions about the nature of interstate commerce.

These two cases provided arguments for both sides of *Federal Baseball Club*. Baseball was like opera, organized baseball could say—even if the performers did travel from one state to another, the travel was only incidental to the exhibitions of their skill, which was a local matter. Baseball was not commerce in the first place, so the movement of players between states could not convert it into interstate commerce. On the other side, the Terrapins could emphasize the similarities between baseball and vaudeville. Both involved traveling groups of performers, whose contracts required them to put on exhibitions in several states in succession. The Terrapins were not alleging a monopoly of stationary baseball clubs who happened to be located in different states; the monopoly was rather of an entire interstate baseball circuit, just like the vaudeville circuit.

In order to determine whether the Sherman Act applied to baseball, the Supreme Court would have to decide whether baseball was a form of interstate commerce. In the early 1920s, that was not an easy question. Under the constitutional law of the era, there were good arguments on both sides.

Purely state affairs

Federal Baseball Club would probably never have reached the Supreme Court if it had taken place a few years later. In 1922 the Court was still required by statute to decide nearly every case appealed to it. The swelling caseload of the late nineteenth and early twentieth centuries reduced the amount of attention the Court could devote to each case and resulted in repeated requests to Congress for relief. Indeed, while the Court was considering *Federal Baseball Club*, Chief Justice William Howard Taft testified before Congress in favor of a bill that would grant the Court the power to choose for itself most of the cases it would hear. These efforts eventually bore fruit in the Judiciary Act of 1925, which in effect transformed the Supreme Court into what it is today, a tribunal that decides only those questions the Court deems to be of national importance.[29]

Had *Federal Baseball Club* arrived at the Court in 1926 rather than 1922, it might not have passed the test. Baseball was a relatively small industry, with its own unique system of labor relations. There were not yet any other significant professional team sports. A decision in the case would have been important within baseball, of course, but any legal principle established in the decision would likely not have been all that important to the world outside. There were only two published lower court opinions addressing whether the Sherman Act applied to baseball, the *Chase* case and *Federal Baseball Club* itself, and both had decided that it did not. There was thus no conflict in the lower courts for the Supreme Court to resolve. The immediate practical consequences of a decision were not particularly pressing. The Federal League was defunct, so there was no longer a competing league to benefit from a decision against organized baseball, and such a decision would not, in the short run, increase the nationwide level of competition among baseball leagues. The only beneficiaries would be the shareholders in the moribund Baltimore Terrapins, who would receive some money. Perhaps baseball's cultural status would have been enough to prompt the Court to hear the case, but it is very likely that had it arisen a few years later, the opinion of the Court of Appeals would have been the final word. In 1922, however, the Court had no choice but to decide the case.

The nine justices had varying degrees of interest in baseball. Oliver Wendell Holmes had none at all. As one of his law clerks later recalled, "there was nothing that did not interest him except athletics." William Howard Taft was only the slightest of baseball fans. As president, Taft prudently made appearances at the first game of each season and was even the first president to throw the ceremonial first pitch. His brother Charles briefly owned the Chicago Cubs, so Taft sometimes attended Cubs games. These visits to ballparks seem to have been mostly a matter of public relations. He stopped going to games when he was no longer president and took up his real passion, golf. Justices Joseph McKenna and Mahlon Pitney were more serious fans, but the Court's most earnest follower of the game was Justice William Day, who routinely attended Senators' games. Each October, when the Court sat during the World Series, Day would have a page slip him inning-by-inning updates.[30]

When the case reached the Supreme Court, George Wharton Pepper reflected, "the situation was similar to the beginning of the deciding game in a World Series." The two sides had each won a game: the Terrapins in the trial court, organized baseball in the Court of Appeals. "There had been an even break and everything depended on what was about to happen." The Terrapins' team of lawyers was once again led by William Marbury, whose argument naturally highlighted the commercial aspects of professional baseball. The defendants in the case "are not baseball players," the argument began. "They are business corporations," whose business "is one of colossal proportions, representing the investment of many millions of dollars, and the profits from which have been enormous." The Terrapins' 202-page brief repeatedly emphasized that "the entire foundation, the primary idea, the vitalizing element in this business of furnishing exhibitions of professional baseball is interstate travel, communication, intercourse and commerce." If players did not travel between states, and if news about the games was not telegraphed across the country, professional baseball could not exist. "Not only is interstate commerce an element in the business of providing exhibitions of professional baseball," the brief declared, "it is the very essence and foundation of it." The *game* of baseball might be a sport, as Judge Smyth had concluded for the Court of Appeals, but the *business* of baseball was a kind of commerce. A major league club "is not engaged in a pastime for its own amusement," Marbury reiterated. "Its players are the employees of a corporation which uses their services for the purpose of transporting them from state to state in order that they may give an exhibition of skill, which people can be charged to witness. Here again the interstate character of the business appears prominently." The baseball business was like the tobacco business. Customers might smoke locally, and smoking was not commerce; it was a leisure pursuit, like watching baseball. But the federal government had been allowed to use the Sherman Act to break up the Tobacco Trust, because the business of supplying consumers with tobacco was a form of interstate commerce. The business of supplying them with baseball games, Marbury argued, was no different.[31]

Baseball, once again led by George Wharton Pepper (figure 3.3), naturally emphasized the game's noncommercial aspects. "Playing baseball, whether for money or not, is a striking instance of human skill exerted for its own sake and with no relation to production," Pepper argued. "In the case of an exhibition of athletic skill, as in the case of dramatic performance, the on-lookers

Figure 3.3: Baseball was represented in the antitrust litigation of 1915–1922 by George Wharton Pepper of Philadelphia. Pepper would go on to serve one term as a U.S. Senator. LC-B2-2634-11, Prints and Photographs Division, Library of Congress.

receive nothing but enjoyment." A skilled performer communicated something to others, "but nothing is involved in the transaction which can properly be regarded as a subject of traffic." He acknowledged that "it is possible, in popular phrase, to speak of 'selling' a sensation to an audience or education to a class, just as it is sometimes said that insurance is 'sold.' But the subject-matter of sale is really absent in all these cases and unless interstate commerce is the distinctive feature of the transaction there can be no interstate commerce." Pepper had to concede that the players and their equipment traveled across state lines. "It is obvious, however, that the transit is not the end in view," he argued. "It is merely the means of getting the players to the point at which the contest is scheduled to take place. The transportation of the paraphernalia is a wholly incidental and subsidiary feature." The gist of the baseball business was the game itself, not the interstate transport between the games.[32]

In order to fit their arguments within the Court's precedents relating to interstate commerce, the lawyers had to present two very different characterizations of professional baseball. In the Terrapins' depiction, baseball consisted of the shipment of players and equipment from one state to another, in order to sell tickets to displays of athletic skill. Once in any given location, baseball games were played, but the real business was in the shipment of players, not the games. In organized baseball's portrayal, by contrast, baseball consisted of games. To get from one game to another, the players and equipment had to cross state lines, but the real business was in the games, not in the shipments. These divergent portrayals were not driven by any genuine differences in how the parties on either side understood the business of baseball. If asked privately for their sincere views, both sides would almost certainly have described the business the same way. These were litigating positions, structured strategically, to squeeze the facts of baseball into the legal doctrines that would determine the outcome of the case.

Pepper then turned to a very different kind of argument, one that rested on the purpose of antitrust law rather than its field of application. "When a court dissolves such a trust-combination as the Standard Oil Company or the American Tobacco Company," he suggested, "the judicial objective in all cases is better and cheaper oil or tobacco. . . . Separate companies can furnish oil and tobacco," and the economic theory underlying the Sherman Act was that "such separate production in the long run results in greater public advantage than is attained by production under conditions of combination and restraint." In baseball, by contrast, the public would not receive better games or cheaper games by requiring each club to operate independently of the others. The situation was just the opposite. "The thing sought to be produced, namely, dramatic and sensational contests between teams playing under precisely the same conditions, is attainable only by combination and restraint."[33] Strictly speaking, this argument had no bearing on whether baseball was a form of interstate commerce governed by the Sherman Act. As a matter of logic it was directed at a question that had not yet been reached—whether, if baseball *was* governed by the Sherman Act, how the act should be applied. Nevertheless, the argument provided some intuitive backing for organized baseball's side of the case. If the financial structure of baseball did not violate the Sherman Act, there would be no harm in declaring that the act did not even apply to baseball in the first place.

When the Supreme Court published its decision six weeks later, organized baseball was the winner, in a short, unanimous opinion written by Oliver Wendell Holmes (figure 3.4). The justices' initial vote had not been unanimous. The elderly Joseph McKenna had sided with the Terrapins, but

Figure 3.4: Justice Oliver Wendell Holmes, Jr., wrote the Supreme Court's short unanimous opinion in *Federal Baseball Club* (1922). The Court held that the Sherman Act did not apply to baseball because baseball was not a form of interstate commerce. LC-F81-33175, Prints and Photographs Division, Library of Congress.

the justices' practice at the time, unlike today, was to register dissents only when they thought it was particularly important to do so. McKenna accordingly told Holmes that "I have resolved on amiability and concession" to join his opinion for the Court.[34]

Holmes agreed with organized baseball's characterization of itself as a local activity, with only incidental interstate travel. "The business is giving exhibitions of base ball, which are purely state affairs," he wrote. "It is true that, in order to attain for these exhibitions the great popularity that they have achieved, competitions must be arranged between clubs from different cities and States. But the fact that in order to give the exhibitions the Leagues must induce free persons to cross state lines and must arrange and pay for their doing so is not enough to change the character of the business." (The "induce free persons" language was Holmes's way of distinguishing the prior decision upholding the Mann Act, in which the Court had determined that *forcing* people to cross state lines *was* a form of interstate commerce.) Holmes cited *Hooper v. California*, the most recent of the major insurance cases, for the proposition that there was no interstate commerce where "the transport is a mere incident, not the essential thing."

Holmes also agreed with baseball's contention that the sale of tickets to watch a display of sporting skill was not "commerce" as the term had been defined in prior cases. The exhibition of baseball games, "although made for money would not be called trade or commerce in the commonly accepted use of those words." That was because "personal effort, not related to production, is not a subject of commerce. That which in its consummation is not commerce does not become commerce among the States because the transportation that we have mentioned takes place." He repeated the analogies Judge Smyth had used in his opinion for the Court of Appeals. "A firm of lawyers sending out a member to argue a case, or the Chautauqua lecture bureau sending out lecturers, does not engage in such commerce because the lawyer or lecturer goes to another State." "We are of the opinion," Holmes concluded, "that the Court of Appeals was right."[35] So ended the Terrapins' suit. Baseball was not covered by the Sherman Act.

Baseball officials felt an enormous weight lifted from their shoulders. After a decade defending the game in the press, in Congress, and in the courts, they had at last won a decisive victory. "I cannot tell you how relieved I feel to finally have this matter out of the way," John Heydler told George Wharton Pepper. "It is a great boon to everyone connected with the game," he confided to another colleague, "to be rid of the constant petty legal attacks." Julian Curtis, the president of the Spalding sporting goods company, joked that "the National League should pass a vote of thanks to the Baltimore Federal League crowd for carrying this matter to a final decision."[36] After losses in several battles, the war had finally been won.

At the end of the year, Heydler tallied up the cost to the National League of all the lawsuits between 1914 and 1922—attorneys fees, court costs, and amounts paid in settlements. He arrived at a figure of $478,595.49. That was just the National League's share. Assuming the American League paid the same amount, baseball had spent nearly a million dollars to fight the Federal League in court, more than a hundred thousand dollars per year for nine years. In the last three of those years, the only ones for which data are available, the combined annual income of all sixteen major league clubs was only around two million dollars.[37] For almost a decade, baseball had to spend roughly 5 percent of its earnings in litigating against the Federal League. It was money well spent.

The legal community's conventional understanding of interstate commerce would begin to change dramatically not long after *Federal Baseball Club*, so Holmes's opinion would come to seem more and more anomalous with the passage of time. Decades later, the outcome would seem so clearly wrong that critics would grasp for explanations by supposing the justices had been overcome by a romantic attachment to the national pastime. In its own day, however, lawyers did not find the opinion anomalous at all. Contemporary accounts of the case in law journals are written in a matter-of-fact tone, without any criticism of the result. Anyone who gave the case much thought must have realized that it involved a difficult judgment, on which reasonable people could have different views, about whether interstate travel was a sufficiently important part of the enterprise. Cases like *Federal Baseball Club*, one lawyer advised, necessarily hinged on "whether the transport is a mere incident or the essential thing."[38] In 1922, no one needed to invoke baseball's iconic cultural status as an explanation, because the decision was easily explained as an unremarkable application of an ambiguous but well-accepted doctrine of constitutional law.

Federal Baseball Club lies at the origin of baseball's "antitrust exemption," so it bears emphasizing that no one involved in the case would have understood *Federal Baseball Club* to have created any sort of exemption. Because of the constitutional limits of Congress's power, the Sherman Act applied only to "interstate commerce." All that *Federal Baseball Club* said was that according to contemporary understandings of that term, baseball—like law practice, or lecturing, or the sale of insurance, or the production of sugar—was not a form of interstate commerce, because the interstate travel involved was not the gist of the business. At the time, no one would have thought that baseball had any special exemption. No one spoke of an "insurance exemption" or a "sugar exemption." Baseball was just one of a great many fields of endeavor that were understood not to fall within the Sherman Act. The idea of an "antitrust exemption" only arose much later, when it would be read, anachronistically, back into *Federal Baseball Club*.

Federal Baseball Club is often misunderstood as having created a distinction between "business" and "sport," and having placed baseball on the "sport" side of the line. Bill Veeck, the maverick owner of three different major league baseball teams, provided a colorful example of this mistake when he recalled "that delightful day in 1922 when the Supreme Court granted us an exemption on the grounds that baseball was 'not a commercial enterprise.' Of course not. Baseball, like loan-sharking, is a humanitarian enterprise." The error is still common today. At a recent congressional hearing, for example, Representative Jim Sensenbrenner complained that in 1922 "the United States Supreme Court held that baseball was not a business and thus not subject to the antitrust laws."[39] This misunderstanding fits neatly with the cultural explanation of the exemption, because one can imagine judges so enthralled with the national pastime that they cannot see its business side. In fact, however, the Court declared no such thing. Judge Smyth of the Court of Appeals did distinguish between sport and commerce—in context, this was his way of explaining why baseball was not interstate commerce, and under the reigning constitutional definition of commerce, it was not a silly thing to say. But the Supreme Court never did.

With the end of the Terrapins' lawsuit, the final vestige of the Federal League was gone. It would be a long time before organized baseball faced another challenger. By then, lawyers would be thinking about interstate commerce very differently.

THE BIRTH OF THE ANTITRUST
EXEMPTION

In *Federal Baseball Club*, the Supreme Court had held that baseball was not governed by the Sherman Act because it was not a form of interstate commerce. The Court had *not* said that Congress intended to exempt baseball from the antitrust laws. Rather, the Court had determined that Congress *could not* apply the antitrust laws to baseball, because it lacked the power to do so.

The transition to the modern version of baseball's antitrust exemption—an exemption said to be intended by Congress, which could have applied the Sherman Act to baseball but chose not to—took place in a 1953 Supreme Court case called *Toolson v. New York Yankees*. *Toolson* is roundly ridiculed today, perhaps not as often as *Federal Baseball Club* (because the case is not as well known), but usually with even more vehemence. "While one could argue that *Federal Baseball* reflected the prevailing limited conception of interstate commerce," one typical commentator suggests, "the Supreme Court's action in *Toolson* is indefensible."[1]

When one places *Toolson* in its context, however, the decision becomes much easier to understand. The late 1940s and early 1950s were a period in which baseball's immunity from the antitrust laws was repeatedly challenged in the courts and in Congress. There were moments when baseball seemed to be on the brink of losing its immunity, and other moments when Congress seemed poised to enact a statute confirming that immunity. At the end of all this activity, baseball emerged with an antitrust exemption, but one that rested on a different basis than before.

AN IMPOTENT ZOMBI

The Supreme Court had declared baseball immune from the antitrust laws in the *Federal Baseball Club* case of 1922, but that decision rested on a particular conception of interstate commerce, one that began to crumble very soon after. Only a year later, the Supreme Court heard an antitrust suit against a group of vaudeville theaters. The theaters' defense relied on *Federal Baseball Club*. Vaudeville was just like baseball, they argued: it consisted of the presentation of performances in a single location. Like baseball players, the performers had to travel across state lines to get from one performance to the next, but, the theaters argued, the travel was merely incidental to the performances, just as the travel of baseball players was incidental to baseball games. To present their argument, the theaters even retained George Wharton Pepper, fresh off his victory in *Federal Baseball Club*. Pepper and his clients must have been astonished when they lost the case, especially because they lost in a unanimous opinion by Oliver Wendell Holmes, the author of the Court's opinion in *Federal Baseball Club*. The plaintiffs in the vaudeville case, Holmes noted, contended that interstate travel was more important in vaudeville than in baseball, indeed so essential to the enterprise that it made vaudeville a form of interstate commerce even though baseball was not, and he concluded that they should be given an opportunity to prove that claim.[2]

The two cases were distinguishable in a technical, lawyerly sense, in that the plaintiffs in *Federal Baseball Club* had already been given the chance to demonstrate the importance of interstate travel, while the vaudeville case had been dismissed for lack of jurisdiction, so the plaintiffs had not yet received that opportunity. It was nevertheless hard to imagine how vaudeville could be interstate commerce without repudiating the logic of *Federal Baseball Club*. (In fact, when the vaudeville case was returned to the trial court, and the plaintiffs were given the opportunity to prove that interstate travel was more important in vaudeville than in baseball, they were unable to, so they lost in the end.)[3] The understanding of interstate commerce underlying *Federal Baseball Club* was beginning to show signs of weakening.

Labor relations within baseball, meanwhile, were just as unusual as they had always been. In a cartoon published in the *New York World* in 1923, soon after the Supreme Court decided the vaudeville case, Alfred Frueh explored the comic possibilities "If Other Things Were Organized Like Baseball." In the first panel, one rich woman offers another: "I'll give you my dressmaker and two butlers and a left-handed-chamber-maid for your cook." In the second, one businessman says to another: "Listen, Mr. Morgan, what do you say to trading that red-headed stenog for three book-keepers and a good cigar?" In the third, one man tells another: "Say, Ed, you've got four sons. I've got four daughters. How 'bout trading two of your sons for two of my daughters?" In the fourth, a Turk offers a Mormon: "I'll swap you a whole string of brunettes for a blonde." In the fifth and final panel, set at the League of Nations, Uncle Sam offers to trade William Jennings Bryan to John Bull, in exchange for the former prime minister David Lloyd George. "Say," John Bull replies, "what did he bat on the Chautauqua circuit last year?" The joke, of course, was that baseball's unique system of labor relations would seem absurd in any other sphere of life.[4]

There would be sporadic calls for federal regulation of baseball all through the 1920s and 1930s, and each time, proponents of federal control argued that the time had come to recognize baseball as interstate commerce. At the end of the 1924 season, Commissioner Kenesaw Mountain Landis permanently banned two members of the Giants, outfielder Jimmy O'Connell and coach Cozy Dolan, for offering a $500 bribe to the Philadelphia shortstop Heinie Sand to throw a game against the Giants. Sol Bloom, a Manhattan representative whose constituents included many angry Giants fans, declared that he would introduce a bill to shift the control of baseball from Landis to a federal commission. "Baseball is a matter of interstate commerce," Bloom insisted while the Giants were playing in the World Series. "Congress has power to regulate the interstate operation of railroads and the interstate movement of foodstuffs, medicines, etc. If Congress can do this it can regulate interstate baseball." A similar episode took place two years later, when Ty Cobb and Tris Speaker, two of the game's biggest stars, both abruptly announced their resignations, in the wake of accusations that they had fixed a game back in 1919. This time it was the Philadelphia congressman Clyde Kelly who argued for a federal commission to take charge of baseball, and an antitrust investigation as well. "The plan would be constitutional," Kelly announced, because baseball was a form of interstate commerce.[5] Neither of these commissions was created, but the fact that they were even proposed—despite the clear holding of *Federal Baseball Club* that baseball was not interstate commerce—suggests that the case was already viewed with some doubt.

It was still the law, however. In 1937, Representative Raymond Cannon of Wisconsin asked the Justice Department to commence antitrust proceedings against baseball, on the ground that the reserve clause violated the Sherman Act. Cannon had long been involved in labor issues on behalf of baseball players. As a lawyer, he had represented some of the players banned from baseball due to the 1919 Black Sox scandal in their suits against Charles Comiskey, the owner of the Chicago White Sox. In the early 1920s, he had led an unsuccessful effort to unionize the players. In response to Cannon's request for an antitrust investigation, Attorney General Homer Cummings referred the question to the Justice Department's Antitrust Division. (This occurred right in the midst of the controversy over Franklin Roosevelt's court-packing plan, which would have allowed Roosevelt to increase the size of the Supreme Court, ostensibly because the nine justices were behind on their work. At a press conference, a reporter jokingly asked Cummings whether the department would have any prejudice against baseball teams, "because they have only nine members." Cummings gave the perfect answer: baseball teams started with nine, but they always had substitutes available in case the starters flagged.) Cummings eventually announced that the Justice Department would not investigate Cannon's charges. In light of *Federal Baseball Club*, he explained, the antitrust laws simply did not apply to baseball. A decade later, when Senator Joseph O'Mahoney of Wyoming urged another federal investigation, Albert "Happy" Chandler, the commissioner of baseball, happened to meet the actor Louis Calhern, who was portraying Oliver Wendell Holmes in the play "The Magnificent Yankee." "Apparently the senator isn't familiar with some of the decisions handed down in the Supreme Court by the justice you play on the stage," Chandler remarked.[6] Despite lingering doubts, *Federal Baseball Club* was still on the books. Baseball was still not interstate commerce.

Questions about the vitality of *Federal Baseball Club* grew much more pressing in the late 1930s and early 1940s, when the Supreme Court decided some high-profile cases that dramatically expanded the professional understanding of interstate commerce. The most striking of these cases was *Wickard v. Filburn*, in which the Court upheld the constitutionality of agricultural quotas over the claim of a small farmer who consumed, on his own farm, all the wheat he grew in excess of his quota. The farmer was engaged in interstate commerce, the Court held, because by growing his own wheat, he was not purchasing wheat from someone else, and that could affect the price and volume of wheat that flowed in interstate commerce. Within a few years, the old distinctions between commerce and manufacture, and between whether interstate transport was incidental or essential, ceased to be relevant. "If I were to be brutally frank," Justice Robert Jackson confided to Sherman Minton, "I suspect what we would say is that in any case where Congress thinks there is an effect on interstate commerce, the Court will accept that judgment. All of the efforts to set up formulae to confine the commerce power have failed." *Federal Baseball Club* had relied in part on an analogy to insurance, which had long been thought not to be interstate commerce, but now the Supreme Court overruled its prior cases, classified insurance as interstate commerce, and allowed antitrust cases to be brought against insurance companies.[7] The entire structure of constitutional thought underpinning *Federal Baseball Club* had collapsed.

By the 1940s, virtually all commentators predicted that *Federal Baseball Club* was ripe for overruling, and that baseball would thus soon come under the antitrust laws. (Perhaps the only commentator to take the contrary view was the Ohio lawyer John Eckler, who happened to be the son-in-law of Dodgers' general manager Branch Rickey.)[8] Even the men who ran organized baseball saw the writing on the wall. In the middle of the 1946 season, the American and National Leagues appointed a joint committee to examine the various issues confronting the game and to make recommendations as to how to handle them. The committee's report covered a wide range of questions, including whether the reserve clause was enforceable in court (the answer: still no) and whether to allow African-American players to join major league teams (the recommendation: not yet, even though Jackie Robinson was already playing for the Dodgers' minor league affiliate in Montreal). The very first issue the report considered was whether baseball amounted to an illegal monopoly. The committee was under no illusions about baseball's status as interstate commerce. "Professional Baseball," the report declared, "is more than a game. It is Big Business—a one hundred million dollar industry." The committee did not even suggest that *Federal Baseball Club* provided any immunity from antitrust suits. "Our counsel do not believe we are an illegal monopoly," the committee concluded, but that was not because antitrust law did not apply. It was, rather, because when antitrust law *was* applied, baseball was not violating it—it was "because our partnership arrangement and cooperative agreements are necessary in the promotion of fair competition and are therefore for the best interests of the public." In litigation, organized baseball continued to invoke *Federal Baseball Club*.[9] In private, baseball's lawyers expected that the game's immunity from antitrust law was unlikely to last very long.

These speculations were soon put to the test. Mexico had long had a baseball league of its own. Americans had occasionally played for Mexican teams. African-American stars like Josh Gibson and Cool Papa Bell played in Mexico in the era before the integration of baseball in the United States. Sometimes players who had retired from American baseball played in Mexico, like Rogers Hornsby, who was in his late forties and had not played in the United States for several years. Salaries in Mexico were not comparable to salaries in the United States, nor was the quality of play, so there was little reason for white players in their prime to go to Mexico. Before the 1946 season, however, Mexican League teams began offering lucrative contracts to American players, most of whom were just returning to baseball after completing their military service during World War II. As Happy Chandler recalled in his memoirs, "all hell broke loose." Johnny Pesky, the shortstop for the Red Sox, earned $4,000 in Boston; he was offered $45,000 to play in Mexico. Phil Rizzuto of the Yankees and Pete Reiser of the Dodgers were both offered $100,000 for three-year contracts. Ted Williams, perhaps the best hitter of the era, was offered a blank check—at least that's the story that was told at the time. None of the game's biggest stars jumped to the Mexican League in 1946, but 23 major league players left for Mexico, including the pitcher Sal Maglie, who had just finished a very successful rookie season with the Giants, and the Dodgers' catcher Mickey Owen, who had played in four all-star games. For the first time since the demise of the Federal League in 1915, organized baseball had a competitor.[10]

Chandler retaliated against the players who jumped to Mexico by banning them from organized baseball for five years. The Mexican League's revenues turned out to be no match for the salaries promised to the players, many of whom were unhappy with the playing conditions in any event. Only a few returned to Mexico for the 1947 season; none did for 1948. Back in the United States, they were unable to earn a living from baseball because of the ban.

Danny Gardella (figure 4.1) had been the first major leaguer to sign with a Mexican team, back in February 1946. Gardella was an outfielder for the New York Giants in 1944 and 1945, when rosters were depleted by the war. With the return of many of the Giants from military service, Gardella was unlikely to make the team. Rather than signing a $5,000 contract with the Giants, he accepted an offer of $8,000, plus a $5,000 bonus, to play for the Veracruz Blues. "Giant Manager Mel Ott was not exactly sleepless" over losing Gardella, *Time* magazine noted, in light of Gardella's "knack of making fly balls look hard to catch." Gardella played the 1946 season in Mexico, where he was one of the better hitters on his team. At the end of the season, with an offer to play again for Veracruz in 1947 but at a reduced salary of $5,000, Gardella returned to New York.[11]

Figure 4.1: Giants' outfielder Danny Gardella was one of many players banned from baseball after leaving for the Mexican League in 1946. When his antitrust suit led Judge Learned Hand to conclude that the sport had become interstate commerce, baseball settled the case to avoid giving the Supreme Court a chance to agree. BL-2085.68, National Baseball Hall of Fame.

Banned from organized baseball and with a family to support, Gardella struggled through 1947, playing semiprofessional baseball once a week on Staten Island. "Finally," he recalled, "a friend of mine sent me to his dentist's brother, who was a lawyer."[12] The lawyer was Frederic Johnson, who filed a suit on Gardella's behalf, claiming that his exclusion from organized baseball was a violation of federal antitrust laws. Organized baseball sought to have the complaint dismissed, unsurprisingly, on the ground that the antitrust laws did not apply to baseball. Judge Henry Goddard, who was nearing the end of a 30-year career on the bench, recognized that the case presented a dilemma. On one hand, there was clear precedent from the Supreme Court. In light of *Federal Baseball Club*, there was no room to argue that baseball was a form of interstate commerce. On the other hand, it was equally clear that interstate commerce was understood very differently in 1948 than it had been back in 1922 when *Federal Baseball Club* was decided. If the question had never arisen in 1922, and the Supreme Court were to consider it for the first time in 1948, there was little doubt that the Court would find that baseball *was* interstate commerce and was therefore governed by the antitrust laws. If Gardella's suit were eventually to reach the Supreme Court, Goddard acknowledged, "it is quite possible that the Supreme Court may not adhere to its earlier decision." Gardella's case thus forced Goddard to confront a difficult question about the role of a lower court within the American legal system. If Goddard's job was to follow the Supreme Court's decided cases, he would have to rule in favor of organized baseball. On the other hand, if his job was to predict how the Supreme Court would decide a case, he would have to rule for Gardella.[13]

Goddard resolved the dilemma by noting that the Court of Appeals for the Second Circuit, the intermediate appellate court that sat above Goddard but below the Supreme Court, had recently cited *Federal Baseball Club* in a case involving the question whether opera was a form of interstate commerce. If the Court of Appeals still considered *Federal Baseball Club* to be authority, Goddard concluded, he had to consider it authority as well. He accordingly granted baseball's motion to dismiss Gardella's suit.

On appeal, the three judges of the Court of Appeals faced the same dilemma, and they resolved it in three different ways. Judge Harrie Chase believed his duty was to follow *Federal Baseball Club*. "If we are not bound by authority and should consider this appeal in the strictly up-to-the-minute conception of what is interstate commerce," he acknowledged in a memorandum to his colleagues, "I should probably come to the conclusion that the anti-trust laws apply to this business of baseball." But *Federal Baseball Club* was the law. "It is for the Supreme Court to overrule it, if it is no longer the law, and not for us to disregard it," Chase insisted. He accordingly voted to affirm the dismissal of Gardella's suit.[14]

Judge Jerome Frank took the opposite view. "There is nothing new about a lower court announcing that a Supreme Court decision is dead," he observed. He mentioned some examples, including a celebrated case from just a few years before, in which a district judge correctly predicted that the Supreme Court would overrule one of its own prior cases and decide that the First Amendment bars a school district from requiring children to salute the flag and say the Pledge of Allegiance. Frank concluded that there was no reason to wait for the Supreme Court to say that baseball was interstate commerce, when the Court of Appeals could say so for itself. He also concluded, however, that there was no need to predict that *Federal Baseball Club* would be overruled. The Court of Appeals could also find *Federal Baseball Club* inapplicable to Gardella's case on the ground that even if baseball was not interstate commerce in 1922, it had become so by 1948. Back in 1922, Frank noted, there had been no broadcasting of baseball games, but in 1948 the games were broadcast on interstate radio networks and were just beginning to be shown on interstate television networks as well. That was enough, in Frank's view, to bring baseball within the definition of interstate commerce. The weakness in this argument, as Frank acknowledged, was that accounts of baseball games had been transmitted by interstate telegraph in 1922. The only difference between the two cases was the presence or absence of a wire. To draw a distinction on that ground, Chase responded, "seems just silly."[15]

The third judge was Learned Hand, and his view was somewhere in the middle. "One of the most embarrassing of our jobs is to know how far to use a shift in the attitude of our Betters as indicating that a particular decision would be overruled if it were to come up again," he confided to his colleagues. He added—in a dig at the most liberal justices—"this is particularly true when four of the nine conceive their function to be to remould this world nearer to the heart's desire." Hand agreed with Frank that "there does come a time when we must no longer wait" to find that a Supreme Court opinion had become obsolete. If he shared Frank's certainty that *Federal Baseball Club* was one such opinion, he explained, he would join him in ruling in Gardella's favor. But one never knew what the Supreme Court would do when it came to interstate commerce. "It is all a game of blind-man's-bluff," Hand complained, "and although, if I had to bet at even odds, I think I should bet that five of the nine would not follow the Federal Base-ball Case, it does not seem to me proper for a lower court to overrule that unanimous opinion of the court of last resort without a more nearly specific warrant." Hand accordingly voted to join Chase and to affirm the dismissal of Gardella's suit.[16]

Within a few weeks, however, Hand had changed his mind. When the Court of Appeals published its decision in February 1949, all three judges wrote opinions. Chase and Frank adhered to their initial views. Chase wanted to follow *Federal Baseball Club*. "It has never been expressly over-ruled, and I do not think it has been overruled by necessary implication," he argued. "Our duty as a subordinate court is to follow the Federal Base Ball Club case." Frank began his opinion by disparaging *Federal Baseball Club* as "an impotent zombi," by which he meant that it lacked any current legal ef-fect. He nevertheless spent the bulk of his opinion drawing the distinction between Gardella's case and *Federal Baseball Club* that had failed to impress Judge Chase—that because of radio and television, baseball had become an interstate enterprise. With broadcasting, Frank concluded, "the games themselves . . . are, so to speak, played interstate as well as intra-state." In finding a way to apply the antitrust laws to baseball, Frank seems to have been heavily influenced by his belief that players were treated unfairly. "We have here a monopoly which, in its effect on ball-players like the plaintiff, possesses characteristics shockingly repugnant to moral principles," Frank declared. "For the 'reserve clause' . . . results in something resembling pe-onage of the baseball player." The only issue before the court was whether the antitrust laws *applied* to baseball, not what the result would be if they were applied, but Frank, who was more outspoken than most judges, was evidently eager to say something about the justice of Gardella's cause. Base-ball contracts, he announced, "are so opposed to the public policy of the United States that, if possible, they should be deemed within the prohibi-tions of the Sherman Act."[17]

Chase thought baseball was not interstate commerce, Frank thought it was, and by the time the judges published their opinions, Hand thought that the issue was a factual question, not a legal one, and thus a matter Gardella should have the chance to prove at trial. Radio and television had indeed changed the character of baseball, Hand had come to believe. When a game in one state was broadcast to another, "the situation appears to me the same as that which would exist at a 'ball-park' where a state line ran between the diamond and the grandstand." But Gardella's claim was not that he had been injured by the broadcasting of baseball games. He was claiming to have been unlawfully excluded from the game. The relevant question, in Hand's view, was thus whether the interstate aspects of baseball "form a large enough part of the business to impress upon it an interstate character" when baseball was considered as a whole. This was the issue that Gardella would have to prove at trial. It was a vague sort of inquiry, Hand conceded, but "I do not know how to put it in more definite terms."[18] The vote was thus two to one to reverse the dismissal of Gardella's complaint and send his case back for a trial.

For the first time since 1922, a court had pierced the armor protecting baseball from antitrust suits. "Danny Gardella may not have been a star," remarked one journalist, "but he may go down in history as the Dred Scott of baseball."[19] (Unlike Gardella, Dred Scott lost his famous case, but the writer must have been thinking of Dred Scott as a symbol for the movement to abolish slavery rather than a successful litigant.) Baseball's lawyers could not have been too surprised, but the decision struck terror in the hearts of club owners, who worried that the reserve clause would not stand up against antitrust attack. "Owners of baseball clubs are acting these days in a manner remindful of southern plantation owners just before Lincoln freed the slaves," observed the veteran sportswriter Henry McLemore. "They are wailing to all who will listen that if Outfielder Danny Gardella wins his $300,000 damage suit against organized baseball and thus puts an end to the reserve clause in baseball contracts, all will be chaos." At the Brooklyn Dodgers' board of directors meeting, Walter O'Malley, the team's lawyer and part owner, warned that Gardella's case "has serious implications" for the business of baseball. Baseball officials recognized that the game faced its worst crisis since the Black Sox scandal of 1919. Commissioner Happy Chandler prepared for battle by retaining the eminent Washington antitrust lawyer John Lord O'Brian, the former head of the Justice Department's antitrust division.[20]

The first decision Chandler and O'Brian had to make was whether to seek review in the Supreme Court. They decided not to. "I do not think the lawyers thought we could win the Gardella case," Chandler later recalled. "That would have been an ideal case if you could win it, you understand. But if you cannot win, then you do not go to court." The way the Supreme Court's commerce clause jurisprudence had been evolving, there was a very good chance that the Court would agree with the Court of Appeals that baseball was a form of interstate commerce, or at least that the players should be given a chance to prove at trial that it was. Appealing *Gardella* to the Supreme Court might only convert a local precedent into a national one and hasten the demise of the reserve clause. *Federal Baseball Club* was still on the books, and there was no reason to give the Court a chance to overrule it. "The Holmes opinion in the Baltimore case is in favor of baseball," Chandler explained. "The fellow who gets the favorable decision in the Supreme Court does not want to go back to court. That is as natural as a goose going barefooted. If you have a favorable decision you do not want to go to court. You let somebody else take it back to court."[21]

Meanwhile, the other players banned from baseball for jumping to the Mexican League began filing antitrust suits of their own. Max Lanier and Fred Martin, both former pitchers for the Cardinals, sued baseball in early March, a month after the Court of Appeals' decision in *Gardella*. Sal Maglie, formerly of the Giants but now working as a gas station attendant in a small town near Buffalo, filed suit two weeks later. Several others threatened to do the same. "I have seen several of the boys and I am telling you, Mr. Rickey, that they have about reached the end of the rope," Mickey Owen reported to the Dodgers' general manager, Branch Rickey. "There aren't any of these boys, and there are about 10 of them, who really wants to sue. They would rather not have anything to do with suits." But without any opportunity to play baseball, the players had no alternative. "Take Martin," Owen continued. "He bought a big home and it is not paid off. He bought it when he thought he was going to have a big future. He has recently had a baby born without a roof in its mouth and they have had a lot of operations and more to come at great expense." Few of the banned players, if any, were qualified for jobs that would pay them anything close to what they had made in baseball. "Some shyster has been calling them wanting them to bring suit," Owen explained. That was what they planned to do, because "they have everything to gain and nothing to lose."[22]

Looking ahead to a string of antitrust trials, Happy Chandler gave in. He announced in June 1949 that he was lifting the suspensions of all the players who had jumped to the Mexican League. "Get your bag packed, boy," he told Mickey Owen, "and get to your club right away." Chandler tried to put a positive spin on recent events by insisting that baseball's legal position had been vindicated when the Court of Appeals had denied a preliminary injunction to Lanier and Martin, but lawyers could recognize that this was bluster. The denial of a preliminary injunction merely returned the Lanier and Martin cases to the trial court, where baseball was in the same perilous position as before.[23] All the banned players but one accepted reinstatement and dropped their lawsuits.

Danny Gardella was the one player who refused reinstatement and chose to litigate instead. By 1949, Gardella was working as a hospital attendant in Mount Vernon, in the suburbs just north of New York. A marginal major leaguer even in his prime, Gardella had been out of the majors for four years. He was 29 years old. Had he been reinstated, he had little chance of making a major league roster. His suit for damages promised to be more lucrative than a baseball career. Both sides began preparing for the trial, which was scheduled for November.[24]

In October, in the midst of the World Series, Gardella and baseball reached a settlement. In exchange for dropping his suit, Gardella received $60,000, a fifth of what he had requested in damages. From the perspective of organized baseball, it was worth at least that much to remove the last outstanding antitrust suit. "I'm so happy about it," Chandler exulted, "I'd go out and get drunk, if I were a drinking man."[25] From Gardella's point of view, $60,000 was probably more than he could realistically have hoped to recover in a lawsuit. Even if baseball was an illegal monopoly, he had not suffered much in damages. He had made much more money in Mexico than he could have in the United States. With the end of the war and the return of many players from military service, even if Gardella had been permitted to play baseball from 1947 through 1949, he would probably have played in the minor leagues. Even if he won the suit, there was not much chance that a court would award him more than $60,000, and of course there was a significant likelihood that he would lose.

The antitrust crisis of 1949 was over. Danny Gardella signed with the St. Louis Cardinals for 1950, but he came to bat only once before the Cardinals sent him down to the minors. He played some for the Cardinals' AA team in Houston and was then released outright. He spent the rest of 1950 playing for an unaffiliated class D team in Bangor, Pennsylvania, where his older brother was the manager. After playing part of 1951 for a team in Quebec, Gardella's baseball career was over. He took a job as a construction laborer. Fifteen years later, when the money had run out, he regretted the settlement. "They gave me $60,000, but my lawyer got 31 of it," he said. "I was interested in carrying through with the suit, but you sell for money because it's real. One has to eat. A principle is invisible no matter how precious it is to you. I feel I sold a principle down the river. I feel the way many of us do when we sell out." With time, however, Gardella came to view his experience in a more positive light, particularly when free agency arrived and he could think of his suit as an early step in that direction. "I feel I let the whole world know that the reserve clause was unfair," he recalled, at the age of 74. "It had the odor of peonage, even slavery."[26]

By the end of the 1949 season, baseball had settled all the antitrust suits arising from the banning of the players who jumped to the Mexican League. The Court of Appeals decision in *Gardella* was still out there, however, as an invitation to additional suits. Baseball would be back in court again very soon.

GLORIFIED WIND JAMMING SESSIONS

The Second Circuit's decision in *Gardella* drew immediate responses from members of Congress sympathetic to organized baseball. Syd Herlong, who had been president of the Florida State League before entering Congress, declared that the decision "could well sound the death knell for the sport." Herlong and the Arkansas congressman Wilbur Mills promptly sponsored bills to exempt baseball and other organized professional sports from the antitrust laws.[27]

Baseball officials and their lawyers recognized, however, that attempting to secure an antitrust exemption from Congress was a risky project. The status quo was mostly favorable to baseball. *Federal Baseball Club* was still on the books, so in principle, at least, baseball was still immune from antitrust suits outside of New York, Connecticut, and Vermont, the states within the Second Circuit. If baseball tried but failed to persuade Congress to legislate an exemption, courts in other circuits might view the failure as evidence that Congress intended baseball to be governed by the antitrust laws, which might make those courts more likely to distinguish or disregard *Federal Baseball Club*. Worse, placing the issue before Congress threatened to open a can of worms, in the form of a highly visible public debate over baseball's antitrust status, a debate that could easily lead to the introduction of bills expressly placing baseball under the antitrust laws.

In late 1949, John Lord O'Brian (figure 4.2), baseball's antitrust counsel, prepared a lengthy memorandum for Happy Chandler in which he weighed the pros and cons of seeking an antitrust exemption from Congress. On one hand, O'Brian observed, Congress had already enacted many similar exemptions for other industries. The Webb-Pomerene Act of 1918, for example, exempted certain export trade associations from the antitrust laws, and the Clayton Act of 1914 had done the same for labor unions. There was nothing unusual about an antitrust exemption. On the other hand, O'Brian continued, the Justice Department was already conducting an investigation into possible antitrust violations in connection with the radio and television broadcast of baseball games, and the department was quite unlikely to agree to any legislative change that would bring this investigation to a halt. Without the support of the Truman administration, O'Brian advised, "it will be so hopeless as to be unwise to make the attempt" to get a bill through Congress.

Figure 4.2: John Lord O'Brian, the former head of the Justice Department's Antitrust Division, represented baseball throughout the antitrust crisis of the late 1940s and early 1950s. O'Brian advised that baseball should neither appeal the *Gardella* decision nor seek a statutory exemption from Congress. Baseball emerged with its exemption intact. LC-B2-5147-14, Prints and Photographs Division, Library of Congress.

Chandler accordingly decided to make no efforts in support of the bills introduced by Herlong and Mills.[28] Baseball would lie low. Congress would take no action for the next couple of years.

Meanwhile, antitrust threats began piling up. Al Widmar, a pitcher for the St. Louis Browns, held out for a higher salary before the 1950 season. "If I don't get at least $10,000 this year," he told the press, "I'll sue baseball in the courts the way Danny Gardella did." Widmar and the Browns reached an agreement before the season began, but club owners could not have failed to realize that any player disappointed with his salary could wield the same bargaining chip. In April 1951, organized baseball found itself defending two antitrust suits. One was filed by Jack Corbett, the owner of the minor league El Paso Texans, who alleged that Happy Chandler had violated the Sherman Act by voiding contracts the Texans had signed with players who were already under contract with teams in the Mexican League. (After the bidding war with the Mexican League fizzled out in 1947, organized baseball and the Mexican League had agreed to respect each other's reserve clause.) The other suit was filed by the pitcher Jim Prendergast, who had just been traded from a minor league club in Syracuse, New York, to one in Beaumont, Texas, where he did not wish to play. Prendergast's suit claimed that baseball's system of labor relations, which compelled him to play in Beaumont or nowhere at all, violated the Sherman Act.[29]

These suits sparked the interest of Congress once again. Emanuel Celler had represented a district in Brooklyn since 1923. By 1951, he was the chairman of the House Judiciary Committee. Celler was an ardent baseball fan and an experienced politician alert to the advantages of being seen as a savior of the game. "Baseball is one of the finest things in American life, but it is in danger," Celler declared. "We should not permit matters to drift any longer." Celler happened to be engaged in a series of hearings into antitrust matters, because he was chairing the Judiciary Committee's subcommittee on the study of monopoly power. Thus far the subcommittee had investigated alleged monopolies in steel, aluminum, and newsprint, but Celler announced that in the summer of 1951 the subcommittee would turn its attention to a very different sort of industry. It would hold hearings on whether the antitrust laws should apply to baseball.[30] Four members of Congress quickly introduced bills to exempt professional sports from the antitrust laws—Herlong and Mills again, as well as Representative Melvin Price of Illinois and Senator Edwin Johnson of Colorado, who was also the president of the Western League, a class A minor league. The antitrust issue was back before Congress, despite baseball's efforts to keep it out.

From the beginning, it was clear that the primary purpose of the hearings was to protect baseball from antitrust litigation. By the time the hearings began, four more antitrust suits had been filed against baseball, bringing the total number of pending cases to six. Celler wrote to Happy Chandler: "The members of the subcommittee are seriously concerned with the possibility that private litigation involving the reserve clause may have disastrous consequences on a great American institution." Celler's public statements were just the same. "There is an obvious necessity to clarify the status of baseball in its relationship to these anti-trust laws," he told the press. "Such clarification is necessary so that the national game [may] be properly protected and its integrity maintained." When the hearings began, the other members of the subcommittee practically competed to proclaim their support for baseball. "The purpose of these hearings," stated Peter Rodino of New Jersey, "has been primarily and solely to assist baseball . . . so that all of us might continue to give our great love and attention to the great pastime."[31]

It was simply good politics to profess a love for baseball. The members of the subcommittee, especially Celler, also had close personal connections with Happy Chandler (figure 4.3), who had left the Senate only a few years before. In Chandler's correspondence with Celler, he addressed him as "My dear Mannie." When Chandler helped Ty Cobb prepare his testimony, he assured Cobb that "Mannie Celler, who is conducting this investigation[,] is my warm good friend." Chandler had possessed no obvious qualifications to be commissioner when he had been appointed to the position in 1945 except for his contacts in Washington, and he put them to good use. As usual, the Washington Senators pitched in by giving Celler free box seats to a game.[32]

In private, some members of the subcommittee thought the hearings were a waste of time, and that Congress had more pressing matters to attend to. The Korean War was at its height, President Truman had just fired General Douglas MacArthur, and congressional committees were investigating allegations that powerful positions in American life were held by communists. When the subcommittee met in executive session, Kenneth Keating of New York complained that he "could not warm up to these hearings with the state of the world as it is." William McCulloch of Ohio felt the same way. Celler had already announced that the hearings would take place, however, and

Figure 4.3: Albert B. "Happy" Chandler left the Senate to be commissioner of baseball from 1945 to 1951. His warm relations with members of Congress helped ensure that baseball retained its antitrust exemption. BL-4330.88, National Baseball Hall of Fame.

McCulloch thought it would look worse to cancel them than to go ahead and hold them. One of the subcommittee's staff members, a young antitrust lawyer from Chicago named John Paul Stevens, advised that "should one of the treble damage suits be successful, the game would suffer."[33] The hearings went on as scheduled.

The subcommittee heard 33 witnesses over 16 days of what one sportswriter aptly called "one of those glorified wind jamming sessions." Some of the witnesses were baseball executives, like Happy Chandler, whose term as commissioner came to end while the hearings were underway, and his successor, Ford Frick. Some were players, like Pee Wee Reese, the Dodgers' shortstop, and Ned Garver, the Browns' pitcher. Writers, coaches, politicians, even the great Ty Cobb—all testified at length about the baseball business. The most common theme was the peril that baseball would be in if

the antitrust laws forced it to abandon the reserve clause. "As to the elimination of the reserve clause, the answer is very plain," Frick declared. "That was
tried in the early days of baseball. The result was chaos." Reese testified that
even the players, the ostensible victims of the reserve clause, were unanimously in favor of keeping it. Another prominent theme came out in testimony and letters from many residents of the western half of the United
States, who urged Congress to do something about baseball's failure to keep
up with the growth of western cities. By 1950, Los Angeles and San Francisco were the fifth- and eleventh-largest metropolitan areas in the country,
but the westernmost major league clubs were still in St. Louis. California
had to settle for minor league teams. "Why should an enormous city like Los
Angeles be shackled to little cities like Sacramento, San Diego, and Portland?" asked Vincent Flaherty of the *Los Angeles Examiner*. "If that isn't monopoly, how else might you interpret it?"[34] But these themes were swamped
by 16 days and 1,600 pages of meandering questions and answers, most with
little apparent purpose.

When the hearings came to an end in October 1951, only one thing was
clear—they had served as excellent publicity for Emanuel Celler (figure 4.4).
"Your hearings will get a fine press all over the land," wrote one admirer.
"Every city, town and village covers the sports." Monopolistic practices in the
steel industry might have been more important, but the baseball hearings
brought Celler much more attention. "Naturally, baseball fans the nation
over are tremendously interested in the hearings," gushed a columnist for the
Long Beach Press-Telegram. "You certainly are a wizard," wrote one friend
from New York. "You have captivated the imagination of all of Baseball loving
America with your present inquiry."[35] Celler might have gone on to serve
nearly 50 years in Congress even without the baseball hearings, but they
could not have hurt.

The purpose of the hearings had been to decide whether to recommend
the enactment of legislation exempting baseball from the antitrust laws, so
when the testimony was over, the subcommittee had to reach a decision.
John Paul Stevens laid out five possible options: the subcommittee could
(1) report favorably on the pending bills to exempt professional sports from
the antitrust laws; (2) do nothing; (3) draft a new bill exempting only the
reserve clause, the part of baseball most at risk, while leaving the rest of the
game open to being governed by the antitrust laws; (4) attempt to write a
code of laws to govern baseball; or (5) report unfavorably on the pending

Figure 4.4: New York representative Emanuel Celler poses with a baseball. As the long-serving chairman of the House Judiciary Committee, Celler held highly visible hearings on baseball's antitrust status, but Congress passed no legislation. LC-USZ62-127299, Prints and Photographs Division, Library of Congress.

bills and leave the antitrust issue to the courts. None of the options was entirely satisfying. The subcommittee members all wanted to allow baseball to keep the reserve clause. "The practice has been so imbedded," Celler observed, "that there will be a tremendous outcry throughout the nation of undue interference if we changed the reserve clause." But none of the members wanted to exempt baseball in its entirety. As Celler put it, because of "concessions, radio and television rights," the game "is tinged with big business." Then again, no one favored drafting new legislation, whether a detailed baseball code or an antitrust exemption just for the reserve clause. And everyone recognized that after so much high-profile testimony, it would look silly for the members of the subcommittee not to issue a report of any kind. They would have to do *something*. Organized baseball, represented throughout the hearings by the distinguished Washington lawyer Paul Porter, urged the subcommittee not to report favorably on any new legislation, for fear that any change in the law would harm baseball's legal position in the pending antitrust cases. For Congress to enact a new exemption would imply that none had existed before, which would be contrary to the view of the law that baseball was pressing in all of the pending cases. In the absence of any support within the subcommittee for any particular course of action, the members unanimously chose Stevens' option five. They would leave the antitrust issue to the courts.[36]

The Celler subcommittee's final product was a book-length report on the history and economics of the baseball business published in May 1952, a year after Celler announced his investigation. The report explained that "organized baseball has for years occupied a monopoly position in the business of selling professional baseball exhibitions to the public," but that "baseball is a unique industry," because "of necessity, the several clubs in each league must act as partners as well as competitors." The report stated that "the overwhelming preponderance of the evidence" offered at the hearings "established baseball's need for some sort of reserve clause." A complete immunity from the antitrust laws would be too broad, however, because it would exempt from antitrust scrutiny aspects of the business that had nothing to do with hiring players, such as the sale of radio and television rights, the management of stadia, and the purchase and sale of advertising. Nor was there any need to legislate a limited exemption just for the reserve clause. "Organized baseball, represented by eminent counsel, has assured the subcommittee that the legality of the reserve clause will be tested by the rule of reason," the rule that governed antitrust cases, in the lawsuits that were already pending. "It would therefore seem premature to enact general legislation for baseball at this time," the report concluded. "Legislation is not necessary until the reasonableness of the reserve rules has been tested by the courts."[37] With that, the Subcommittee on the Study of Monopoly Power ended its investigation of baseball.

Organized baseball publicly hailed the report as a vindication of its business practices. In private, baseball officials recognized that they had survived another close call. Commissioner Ford Frick established a committee of club owners to consider reorganizing the economic structure of the game. "Frick and the owners feel that the Committee was fair and did not hurt their litigation position," Judiciary Committee staff counsel Ernest Goldstein reported to Celler. "Frick's attitude is that they now have an opportunity for constructive changes which must be drafted lest in a future investigation they be found wanting."[38] There were any number of things baseball could do to forestall further congressional antitrust inquiries while still retaining the reserve clause. Teams could be placed in the West. Major league clubs could relinquish some measure of control over the minor leagues. The rules regarding broadcasting could be changed.

Meanwhile, however, there were still those pending antitrust suits. There had been six when the subcommittee had begun its investigation; now, a year later, there were eight. Before baseball could clean its house, these suits would have to be resolved.

Congress had no intention

One of the antitrust suits had been filed by George Toolson, a pitcher in the Yankees' organization. The Yankees were at their peak—they were in the midst of winning five consecutive World Series—and Toolson had little chance of being promoted to the majors so long as his career was controlled by the Yankees. In 1949, he pitched for the Newark Bears, a AAA affiliate of the Yankees. When the Bears folded after the 1949 season, the Yankees assigned Toolson to the Binghamton Triplets, a class A team. Toolson refused to report to Binghamton. He sat out the 1950 season and then filed suit in Los Angeles in the spring of 1951, alleging that baseball was violating the Sherman Act by prohibiting him from playing for a team other than Binghamton.[39]

District Judge Benjamin Harrison dismissed Toolson's complaint, because he considered himself bound to follow *Federal Baseball Club*. "It is not my function to disregard such a decision because it is old," Harrison explained. He was well aware that the prevailing professional conception of interstate commerce had changed completely since 1922, but in his view lower courts had no power to anticipate the overruling of Supreme Court precedent. "We are supposed to be living in a land of laws," he argued. "Stability in law requires respect for the decisions of controlling courts." Writing in the fall of 1951, Harrison also took note of the recently concluded Celler hearings and the possibility that Congress might soon enact legislation that would resolve the antitrust question one way or the other. A court, in his view, ought to stay out of the way. "I believe it is my clear duty to endeavor to be a judge and should not assume the function of a pseudo legislator," he concluded. That meant following *Federal Baseball Club* and determining that baseball was still not interstate commerce. Toolson's lawyer, Howard C. Parke of Santa Barbara, was not surprised. He also expected to lose on appeal to the U.S. Court of Appeals for the Ninth Circuit, he told reporters, but he hoped that the Ninth Circuit would write an opinion that conflicted with the Second Circuit's decision in *Gardella*, because that could be enough to persuade the Supreme Court to hear the case.[40]

Walter Kowalski filed a similar suit just a month after Toolson filed his. Kowalski was a third baseman and outfielder who played for several of the Dodgers' lower level minor league affiliates between 1947 and 1950. His complaint alleged that the Dodgers were violating the antitrust laws by keeping him from playing at higher levels or for other teams in retaliation for his efforts to secure a higher salary. The complaint was dismissed by a district judge in Cincinnati in early 1952, for the same reason Toolson's complaint had been dismissed—under *Federal Baseball Club*, the antitrust laws did not apply to baseball.[41]

The *Toolson* and *Kowalski* cases were both affirmed by courts of appeals in the winter of 1952–1953. The Ninth Circuit disappointed Howard Parke by writing no opinion in *Toolson*, but the court did explain that it reached its decision "for the reasons stated" in the district judge's opinion. In *Kowalski*, the Sixth Circuit held that "the controlling authority is the decision of the United States Supreme Court in *Federal Baseball Club*." The judges would not disregard *Federal Baseball Club*, they explained, "on the speculation that the Supreme Court may change its decision in this regard in the future." The same day, for the same reason, the Sixth Circuit also affirmed the dismissal of the antitrust suit filed by Jack Corbett, the disgruntled owner of the minor league El Paso Texans.[42] With these decisions, Parke and the other lawyers had the lower court conflict they had been hoping for. In the Second Circuit, under *Gardella*, antitrust plaintiffs would be given the opportunity to prove at trial that baseball was interstate commerce. In the Sixth and Ninth Circuits, under *Kowalski* and *Toolson*, plaintiffs would have no such opportunity, because baseball, by definition, was not interstate commerce.

This sort of conflict is the usual reason the Supreme Court agrees to hear a case, so the lawyers for Toolson and Kowalski naturally emphasized it in their petitions for certiorari, the documents in which parties seek Supreme Court review. Toolson's petition reached the Supreme Court in March 1953, two weeks ahead of Kowalski's and Corbett's. Kowalski was now represented by Frederic Johnson, who had been Danny Gardella's lawyer a few years before. Johnson most likely worked in cooperation with Toolson's Santa Barbara lawyers, because the certiorari petitions filed on behalf of Toolson and Kowalski used nearly identical language.[43]

Baseball's lawyers responded the only way they could—they contended that there was in fact no conflict with *Gardella*—but even they must have realized that this was not a persuasive argument. Justice Robert Jackson's law clerk, a recent law school graduate named William Rehnquist, saw right through it. "One can't point to a square conflict in reasoning" between *Gardella* and the other cases, he told Jackson, "but there certainly is a conflict in result." Rehnquist advised Jackson that "on the merits, there can be no doubt of a change between 1890 baseball, 1922 baseball, and 1953 baseball." Not only had the Court expanded its definition of interstate commerce, "but baseball itself has changed, probably much more than the insurance business," which the Court had newly labeled interstate commerce only a decade before. Rehnquist himself had what he admitted was a "strong personal animus in these cases." He explained to Jackson that "this Court should keep its hands off. I feel instinctively that baseball, like other sports, is *sui generis*, and not suitably regulated either by a bunch of lawyers in the Justice Department or by a bunch of shyster lawyers stirring up triple damages suits. But I feel that it might be difficult to couch this result in judicial language." With regret, he recommended that Jackson vote to hear the cases. (Rehnquist was not the only young lawyer working on the case who would go on to bigger and better things. Bowie Kuhn, barely out of law school, helped his firm represent baseball in *Toolson*.[44] Two decades later he would be commissioner of baseball.)

The Court agreed to hear all three cases together—*Toolson, Kowalski,* and *Corbett*. Oral argument was scheduled for October 1953, the week after the World Series. All concerned knew which was more important. "The entire future of professional sports rests on the outcome of the cases," the *New York Times* declared.[45]

Knowledgeable insiders assumed that the Court would finally overrule *Federal Baseball Club* and put an end to baseball's antitrust immunity. "Baseball officials shyly agree, off the record, that baseball can't maintain its claims of being exempt from interstate commerce," reported the veteran Washington sport columnist Shirley Povich. "No baseball man would dare say a word for publication," agreed his New York counterpart, Arthur Daley. "They'd just as soon get it over with once and for all. The realization has gripped them all that they no longer are able to cling to Oliver Wendell Holmes' ruling of 1922." Lawyers contemplated how the reserve clause and other baseball practices would fare when tested by antitrust law. Emanuel Celler predicted that the Court would find that baseball had become interstate commerce. "The years have brought changes," he declared. "More than $100,000,000 in annual revenue makes organized baseball a business." The club owners may have felt a twinge of regret that they had not renewed Happy Chandler's contract as commissioner. Chandler was friendly with some of the Supreme Court justices from his days in the Senate, including Sherman Minton, who had been a senator at the same time, and Tom Clark, who had been in the Justice Department during the period.[46] Ford Frick, the new commissioner, had no similar contacts. He had been a sportswriter, not a politician.

Baseball's lawyers had assured Celler's congressional subcommittee that the club owners were prepared to make fundamental changes in the economic structure of the game. Since the end of the hearings they had begun planning in this direction, and they had even discussed holding meetings with members of Congress to explore possibilities. Once the Supreme Court agreed to hear the antitrust cases, however, baseball slammed the door shut. "Preliminary meetings of the sort suggested," Ford Frick admonished, "would only be an indication of weakness on the part of Baseball."[47] Any visible plans for reorganizing the game would give the impression that baseball was admitting some flaw in its current organization.

Baseball's lawyers had promised Celler's congressional subcommittee that there was no need to enact antitrust legislation, because the courts would soon consider whether the reserve clause was consistent with the rule of reason under the Sherman Act. In the courts, however, baseball's lawyers claimed precisely the opposite: that courts could never consider whether the reserve clause complied with the Sherman Act, because the antitrust laws simply did not apply to baseball. Nothing of significance had changed since *Federal Baseball Club*, they argued in the Supreme Court. The clubs were taking in more revenue than before, and games were broadcast on radio and television, but none of that changed the fundamentally local character of baseball, they contended. The games were still played in one place, before a local audience. "It is the communications companies," baseball's lawyers insisted, "and not the baseball clubs who, in broadcasting, telecasting or telegraphing descriptions of local games, are engaged in interstate commerce." Otherwise, they pointed out, "any local event that attracted the attention of the press or radio or television would become interstate." Radio and television were subject to the antitrust laws; baseball itself was not.[48]

Toward the end of their briefs, baseball's lawyers turned to a different kind of argument. The Supreme Court was traditionally more circumspect about overruling prior cases in which it had interpreted statutes than it was about overruling prior cases in which it had interpreted the Constitution. When the Court interpreted a statute, Congress could always disagree, in effect, by amending the statute to give it a meaning different from the one the Court put on it. Congress's failure to amend any given statute, once interpreted by the Court, could be understood as acquiescence in the Court's decision. With the Constitution, by contrast, Congress had no comparable power. The Court was the final authority on the meaning of the Constitution. Once the Court interpreted a provision of the Constitution, its meaning could not change (without going through the cumbersome process of a constitutional amendment) unless the Court itself made the change. This distinction had long counseled in favor of a special reluctance to overrule statutory interpretation cases.

This point was emphasized in an amicus brief written by the Harvard law professor Thomas Reed Powell. Powell was in his seventies, approaching the end of a distinguished career, when he was hired by the Boston Red Sox to participate in the *Toolson* case. The Red Sox may have sought Powell's counsel because of his reputation as a constitutional scholar, but they likely also knew that Powell was close friends with some of the justices, who could be expected to pay particular attention to what he had to say. Powell concluded his brief with a discussion of the recent Celler hearings, a conspicuous episode in which Congress had considered applying the antitrust laws to baseball—which would have effectively overruled *Federal Baseball Club*—but had declined to do so. "Congress, fully aware of the decision in the earlier baseball case for all these years, has itself failed to modify the situation," Powell observed. There was thus no warrant for the Court to do it.[49]

In making this argument, Powell must have known that matters were not so simple. In one sense, *Federal Baseball Club* had been a case of statutory interpretation; the Court had ruled that the Sherman Act did not apply to baseball. In another sense, however, the Court in *Federal Baseball Club* was interpreting the Constitution rather than any statute. By determining that baseball was not interstate commerce, the Court was not just deciding that baseball was immune from federal antitrust laws. It was deciding that baseball was immune from *all* federal laws that purported to rest on Congress's power to regulate interstate commerce. The holding of *Federal Baseball Club* was not that Congress possessed an authority to govern baseball that it had declined to exercise in the Sherman Act. The holding was that Congress had no such authority, because the Constitution conferred none. At bottom, Justice Holmes had been interpreting the Constitution, not the Sherman Act.

Meanwhile, lurking not far below the surface was the issue of retroactivity. Court decisions, unlike legislation, normally have retroactive effect, even when they change the law. If the Court overruled *Federal Baseball Club*, and if any of baseball's practices were found to violate the antitrust laws, baseball could be required to pay treble damages to all the players and others who had been harmed for conduct that had been lawful at the time it took place. Legislation, by contrast, is normally prospective: new statutes do not apply to conduct that took place before their enactment. Baseball's lawyers alluded to this issue only indirectly, for the most part, by arguing that club owners had made substantial investments, for decades, in reliance on baseball's immunity from the antitrust laws. Only once did they state explicitly their bigger concern. "A decision here that the *Federal Club* case was no longer applicable to professional baseball would penalize retroactively and quite probably disastrously the whole structure of professional baseball," the lawyers declared, near the end of their brief in *Kowalski*. If baseball were to be subjected to the Sherman Act, it would be far better for baseball if Congress were to do it, because Congress could do it prospectively only. "Congress may, if it chooses, pass legislation which would regulate baseball in the future and without penalty to those who have relied upon the *Federal Club* decision," baseball's lawyers pointed out.[50]

Oral argument was "a sort of legal world series," as one account put it. The argument ranged well beyond the question of interstate commerce to encompass a host of collateral issues. Jack Corbett's lawyer complained about baseball's failure to put major league teams on the West Coast, in a transparent attempt to gain the sympathies of Earl Warren, the new chief justice, who had left the governorship of California only two weeks before. The Yankees' lawyer, for his part, looked past the issue of interstate commerce to the dire consequences he expected would flow from the application of the antitrust laws. "Baseball cannot exist in an entirely free economy," he warned. "To apply to it the full rigors of the Sherman Act would destroy it."[51]

At their conference after oral argument, the nine justices spoke in order of seniority, beginning with Hugo Black, who had been on the Court for 16 years. Black explained that if the Court were starting from scratch, he would find that the antitrust laws governed baseball. The difficulty was in dealing with *Federal Baseball Club*. The Court could try to draw a distinction between present-day baseball and the game of 1922, but "that is not realistic," he told his colleagues. He preferred to rest the decision on the argument made by Thomas Reed Powell on behalf of the Red Sox. Because the case involved "no constitutional question," but rather "mere statutory construction," Black concluded that he was inclined not to make any change in the law. He suggested that the Court publish a short *per curiam* opinion—an opinion of the Court as a whole, without any identification of authorship—reaffirming *Federal Baseball Club*.[52]

Stanley Reed disagreed. "The old case was more than statutory construction," he argued; "it was on the constitution." *Federal Baseball Club*, in Reed's view, was not a case about what the words of the Sherman Act meant; it was about whether baseball was interstate commerce, and thus about whether the constitution even gave Congress the power to regulate it. Reed thought the time had come to recognize that "the sport of baseball is a trade under the Act." Like Jerome Frank in the Court of Appeals, he seems to have been influenced by his dislike of the reserve clause. The justices all knew that they were deciding only whether the antitrust laws applied to baseball, not how they should apply if they did, but Reed nevertheless shared his opinion that "the reserve clause violates the anti-trust laws."

Felix Frankfurter took issue with Reed's characterization of *Federal Baseball Club*. The "old case turned on the statute, not the constitution," Frankfurter insisted. He voted to join Black in reaffirming *Federal Baseball Club*. So did William Douglas and Robert Jackson. In a note to himself, Jackson recorded that if he could decide the issue as an original matter, he would find that baseball was interstate commerce. But, he noted, whether to depart from *Federal Baseball Club* was "up to Congress."[53] Harold Burton provided a second vote to reverse. He agreed with Reed that it was time to recognize that baseball was a form of interstate commerce. Thus far there were four votes to stick with *Federal Baseball Club* and two to overrule it. The last three justices to speak, Tom Clark, Sherman Minton, and Earl Warren, all agreed with the majority. Warren was the only one who spoke at length. He acknowledged that there were "very substantial differences in the game" since 1922, "with radio—with television," and with "the farms," the national networks of minor league teams affiliated with each major league club. "All these change the character of the game," Warren conceded. Still, he did not wish to "reverse the old case." Baseball was poised to retain its antitrust immunity by a vote of seven to two.

Justice Black drafted a one-paragraph *per curiam* opinion for the seven justices in the majority.[54] In *Federal Baseball Club*, he explained, the Court had held that the baseball business was not within the scope of the antitrust laws. "Congress has had the ruling under consideration," he continued, "but has not seen fit to bring such business under these laws by legislation." Black's draft concluded: "We think that if there are evils in this field which now warrant application to it of the antitrust laws it should be by legislation. Without re-examination of the underlying issues, the judgments below are affirmed on the authority of *Federal Baseball Club*." Chief Justice Warren promptly sent a memo to Black, suggesting that his short opinion was incomplete. Under *Federal Baseball Club*, Warren pointed out, baseball was not interstate commerce, so Congress could not subject it to the antitrust laws even if Congress wanted to. Warren urged Black "to make it clear that Congress has the right to regulate baseball if and when it desires to do so." He asked Black to add one more clause to the opinion's last sentence, to clarify that the Court was relying on *Federal Baseball Club*, "so far as that decision determines that Congress had no intention of including the business of baseball within the scope of the federal antitrust laws."[55] Black made the change. The final version of the opinion included Warren's suggested language.

Justice Burton dissented in an opinion joined by Reed. Organized baseball was obviously interstate commerce, he pointed out, in light of its "well-known and widely distributed capital investments used in conducting competitions between teams constantly traveling between states." None of his colleagues would have disagreed. There was no dispute that baseball was interstate commerce; the real question was whether to abandon *Federal Baseball Club* or wait for Congress to do it. "It seems to me essential," Reed urged Burton, "to tie down the fact that there was no purpose in Congress to omit baseball from the Sherman Act, and that [*Federal Baseball Club*] was a decision on intra-state commerce." Burton followed Reed's advice. "In the *Federal Baseball Club* case," Burton argued in his dissenting opinion, "the Court did not state that even if the activities of organized baseball amounted to interstate trade or commerce those activities were exempt from the Sherman Act. The Court acted on its determination that the activities before it did not amount to interstate commerce." The Court claimed to be following *Federal Baseball Club*, Burton was suggesting, but it really was not. To follow *Federal Baseball Club* would be to continue to hold that baseball was off-limits to Congress because it was not interstate commerce. What the Court was actually doing, Burton implied, was subtly modifying the holding of *Federal Baseball Club*. The Court was now saying something new: that baseball *was* interstate commerce, but that ever since 1890, when Congress enacted the Sherman Act, the intent of Congress had been that the Sherman Act should not apply to baseball.[56]

This was a point that was easy to miss, but it was one with important consequences for the future. Under *Federal Baseball Club*, the source of baseball's antitrust immunity had been the commerce clause of the Constitution. Congress could not regulate baseball because it was not a form of interstate commerce. Under *Toolson*, however, the source of baseball's antitrust immunity was Congress. Congress *could* regulate baseball, but thus far Congress had chosen not to. *Federal Baseball Club* had rested on the limits of Congress's power, but *Toolson* rested on the vagaries of Congress's choice. From 1953 on, the argument would no longer be about whether Congress *could* bring baseball under the antitrust laws. The argument would be about whether Congress *should*. It was only after *Toolson* that lawyers could begin speaking accurately about baseball having an "exemption" from the antitrust laws, in the sense of an exemption treated as if it were actually intended by Congress.

As an empirical, historical matter, the view adopted by the Court in *Toolson*—that Congress intended to exempt baseball from the Sherman Act—was almost certainly wrong. Baseball was a negligible industry in 1890. The Congress that enacted the Sherman Act most likely did not think about it at all. On the other hand, to the lawyers and judges who had followed the Celler hearings in the papers just two years before, it was clear that at least a few members of the present-day Congress were firmly of the view that the Sherman Act should not apply to baseball. While it was nonsense to think of the 1890 Congress as intending that baseball should enjoy an antitrust exemption, it was not nonsense at all to think the same of the Congress of the early 1950s.[57] Of course, the justices must have known this all very well. Earl Warren, who was responsible for the language in the *Toolson* opinion shifting the ground of the antitrust exemption from the Constitution to Congress, had become a judge only weeks before, after a career in the executive branch. He was not trying to write a historical account of what was in the minds of the drafters of the Sherman Act. He was engaging in pragmatic governance by sending a message to Congress that it had the power to subject baseball to the antitrust laws. The message would be received loud and clear.

Critics have called the result an Alphonse-and-Gaston routine, in which Congress declined to act because it was waiting for the Supreme Court to decide the antitrust issue, but then the Court declined to act because it was waiting for Congress.[58] In fact, though, the Court *did* act, by shifting the foundation of the antitrust exemption to Congress. Before *Toolson*, it was uncertain whether the antitrust exemption was still in effect, and it was almost as uncertain whether Congress had the power to modify it. *Toolson* removed these uncertainties by answering both questions affirmatively. After *Toolson*, there was no doubt about Congress's authority to subject baseball to whatever antitrust regime it chose.

Were the seven justices in the majority influenced by their personal interest in baseball? Maybe, although, as in *Federal Baseball Club*, they showed no signs of it. The one thing we can say is that the fall of 1953 was perhaps the worst time in the history of baseball to be making an argument that could lead to the demise of the reserve clause. Just a week before oral argument, the Yankees defeated the Dodgers to win their fifth consecutive World Series. They had won twelve of the last eighteen and might have won even more had they not lost stars like Joe DiMaggio, Phil Rizzuto, and Joe Gordon to military service in the war years. The most common argument in favor of the reserve clause was that it prevented the wealthiest clubs from signing all the best players. The Yankees were the wealthiest, because they consistently sold more tickets than any other team—in 1950 they attracted more than eight times as many fans as the St. Louis Browns and nearly seven times as many as the Philadelphia A's. If the Yankees could be so strong even with the reserve clause, baseball fans might have worried, imagine how lopsided baseball would become without it.[59]

A more likely, although equally tacit, motive was the reluctance to subject baseball to the possibility of retroactive liability. This is always a concern when a court is asked to change the law, and it is one of the primary reasons courts generally adhere to precedent. Retroactive liability posed an especially large problem in *Toolson*. If the reserve clause was illegal, there were thousands of professional baseball players in the majors and minors with plausible arguments that they had lost money over their careers due to their inability to sell their services to the highest bidder. All might have been entitled to treble damages under the Sherman Act. Baseball could have faced crushing liability for engaging in conduct that was perfectly legal at the time it took place. Even if the justices thought the reserve clause was unfair, they might well have thought that imposing retroactive liability on baseball was even more unfair. All the more reason, then, to let Congress change the law prospectively, and to let baseball clean its house for the future without having to pay for the past.

Within most of the legal world, *Toolson* was eclipsed by another case on the Court's docket in the fall of 1953, *Brown v. Board of Education*, which was argued just a few weeks later. Some savvy Court-watchers saw in the *Toolson* opinion a sign of how the Court would decide *Brown*. One of the states' arguments in *Brown* was that school segregation was an issue for legislatures, not courts, to resolve. In *Toolson*, the Court said just the same thing about baseball and antitrust. If *Toolson* was a preview of *Brown*, some predicted, "separate but equal" would remain the law.[60] This prediction turned out to be wrong, of course, but with the benefit of hindsight we can see *Toolson* as a precursor of *Brown* in a different sense. Both cases were early examples of the pragmatic, instrumentalist nature of the Warren Court, a willingness to justify decisions on explicit policy grounds.

Baseball officials knew they had dodged another bullet, but they also recognized that their antitrust exemption was more precarious than it had been before, now that the Court had made clear that Congress could whisk it away at any time. Baseball would have to tend to its congressional relations more carefully than ever.

BASEBALL BECOMES UNIQUE

The Supreme Court's decision in *Toolson v. New York Yankees*, which preserved baseball's immunity from the antitrust laws, was welcome news for the owners of teams in other professional sports as well. Baseball had been the first significant professional team sport in the United States. When leagues formed in other sports, they modeled their business structures on baseball. The National Football League, organized in 1920 as the American Professional Football Conference and renamed the NFL in 1922, adopted a standard player contract similar to the one used in baseball, under which the club had a renewal option for the following year at the same salary. "From its inception," explained NFL Commissioner Bert Bell, the league "has tried to copy what baseball has done." The National Hockey League, organized in 1917, had a reserve clause modeled after baseball's, as did the National Basketball Association, which was founded in 1946 and first called the NBA in 1949. Indeed, football, hockey, and basketball players had even less bargaining power than baseball players. A baseball player signing his first professional contract at least had his choice of clubs. Football and basketball allocated new players to clubs in annual drafts. A drafted player could bargain only with the club that had selected him. A hockey player could negotiate only with the club that first notified the league of its interest.[1] (Hockey would eventually institute a draft for new players in 1963, and baseball in 1965.)

The NFL, NHL, and NBA also copied baseball's recognition of clubs' territorial rights by requiring some form of consent on the part of existing clubs before a new club could form or an existing club could move too close to another. All this copying was hardly surprising. Baseball offered a conspicuously successful model for organizing a professional sports league.

Football, hockey, and basketball did not participate in the flurry of baseball antitrust litigation at midcentury, but they were watching closely. "There can be no question that organized hockey is based on the same two fundamentals as baseball—the reserve clause and territorial rights," explained Clarence Campbell, the president of the NHL. "The uncertainty as to the legal validity of these two principles of operation is just as great a menace and just as unsettling to the structure of hockey as it is to baseball." Campbell and his NBA counterpart, Maurice Podoloff, both urged Emanuel Celler's 1951 antitrust subcommittee not to forget hockey and basketball in any legislation intended primarily for the benefit of baseball. "Professional basketball, like professional hockey and baseball, relies for its continued existence on the reserve clause contained in the players' contract and on recognition of territorial rights," Podoloff wrote to Celler. Football, hockey, and basketball were much smaller enterprises than baseball, but whatever baseball needed, the other sports needed too.[2]

Toolson was thus as much a relief to the men who ran other sports as it was to those who ran baseball. Thomas Hart, the NFL's lawyer, was "greatly encouraged" by the Supreme Court's decision, he told the press. "Professional football claims the same immunity from federal anti-trust laws as baseball."[3] The owners of hockey and basketball teams must have been equally heartened by the Court's reluctance to subject baseball to antitrust law. Football, hockey, and basketball had not yet been sued under the Sherman Act the way baseball had, but had *Toolson* gone the other way, such suits would surely have been forthcoming.

If *Toolson* was good news for the other team sports, it was bad news for the Department of Justice, which was in the midst of bringing many antitrust cases of its own. Enforcing the antitrust laws had long been one of the department's main functions. Since 1933, it had employed specialized lawyers in an antitrust division to do nothing but litigate antitrust cases. The Justice Department had not participated in *Toolson*, despite the government's interest in clarifying the scope of the antitrust laws. A few months afterwards, Assistant Attorney General Stanley Barnes, the head of the antitrust division, expressed his unhappiness with the decision. "It was the view of the Antitrust Division, and has been the view for many years, prior to the Supreme Court decision, in Toolson versus New York Yankees, that baseball was subject to the antitrust laws," he told a Senate subcommittee in early 1954. Not long after, a committee appointed by Attorney General Herbert Brownell to review the antitrust laws reached the same conclusion. *Toolson* was "difficult to rationalize," the committee reported. "The *Toolson* case is unsound."[4]

From the government's perspective, the real problem was not so much *Toolson* itself but the way judges in two of the government's own cases were interpreting *Toolson*. One case was a suit against a group of theatrical producers who the government alleged were monopolizing the presentation of plays and musicals throughout much of the country. Shortly after *Toolson*, the trial judge dismissed the government's case. "In principle, I can see no valid distinction between the facts of this case and those which were before the Supreme Court" in *Toolson*, the judge reasoned. The theater business was like the baseball business. Both were traveling spectacles. If baseball was exempt from the antitrust laws, so was the theater. The second case was a government suit against the International Boxing Club, an organization the government charged with monopolizing the presentation of championship boxing matches. A trial judge dismissed this case too, again on the strength of *Toolson*. "I feel the principle in this case is the same as that decided by the Supreme Court in the Baseball case," the judge explained. "The Supreme Court laid down a broad principle which I say takes all professional sports out of the Antitrust Act."[5] The Justice Department could live with a narrow antitrust exemption solely for baseball, but an exemption for all sports, or maybe even for all kinds of entertainment, was broad enough to hinder the government's enforcement efforts.

Government antitrust suits had a fast track to the Supreme Court. Under the Antitrust Expediting Act of 1903, the government could bypass the Courts of Appeals and appeal directly to the Supreme Court, which was required to hear the case. (The Expediting Act was already coming in for criticism by the 1950s, for saddling the Court with too many antitrust cases, and the automatic appeal would eventually be eliminated in 1974).[6] The government promptly appealed the theater and boxing cases to the Supreme Court. Just a few months after reaffirming that baseball was not governed by the antitrust laws, the Court was confronted with two more difficult questions, one of which involved another sport. If baseball was exempt from the Sherman Act, what about boxing?

WHERE WOULD THE SNOWBALL END?

Boxing was the country's oldest commercially significant professional sport. John L. Sullivan, the most famous American athlete of the nineteenth century, earned well over $100,000 per year in the 1880s (more than $2 million when adjusted for inflation), a period when the highest-paid baseball players made little more than $1,000. The rise of competing spectator sports in the first half of the twentieth century scarcely dented boxing's popularity. The 1926 fight between Jack Dempsey and Gene Tunney drew over 120,000 spectators; their rematch the following year filled all 105,000 seats of Chicago's Soldier Field. With the spread of television in the early 1950s, boxing became more popular than ever, as weekly boxing programs were among the most-watched early television shows.[7]

Beginning in 1949, championship boxing matches were largely under the control of a corporation called the International Boxing Club, which was owned by two sports-minded entrepreneurs, James D. Norris and Arthur Wirtz. Norris and Wirtz also owned, among other things, the Chicago Blackhawks hockey team and a substantial share of New York's Madison Square Garden. (The Norris Trophy, given annually to the NHL's top defensive player, and the NHL's former Norris Division, now the Central Division, were both named for Norris's father, James E. Norris, who owned the Detroit Red Wings and part of the New York Rangers.) The IBC held contracts giving Norris and Wirtz the exclusive right to promote bouts in the nation's principal arenas. In the early 1950s, a boxer could not participate in a championship fight that was not controlled by Norris and Wirtz through the IBC. The government filed suit in 1952 against Norris, Wirtz, and the IBC, alleging that this arrangement violated the Sherman Act.[8]

The Supreme Court decided *Toolson* while both sides were preparing for trial. The IBC's lawyers immediately asked Judge Gregory Noonan to dismiss the case on the ground that there was no basis for distinguishing between boxing and baseball. When the government's lawyer tried to argue that *Toolson* exempted only baseball from the antitrust laws, Noonan had little patience. "Do you think the government should take the position that the Supreme Court meant only baseball as against football, college or professional, and basketball?" the judge asked. "Where would the snowball end?" A month later, in a different antitrust suit against the IBC, this one filed by a manager of professional boxers, the federal Court of Appeals in Chicago reached the same conclusion. "We agree that a professional boxing contest is not to be distinguished legally from that of a professional baseball game," the court held. "Obviously each involves a contest of physical skill and endurance taking place in a particular locality. The success of each depends upon the support of the public in the purchase of tickets and the sale of radio and television rights. Each baseball game is unique; no two are exactly alike. Each boxing contest is unlike any other. The profitable promotion of each depends on the same elements." It would make little sense, the judges reasoned, for antitrust law to apply to one but not the other. "Under the mandate of the Supreme Court," the Court of Appeals concluded, "we must hold that it was not the intention of Congress to extend the provisions of the Anti-Trust laws to athletic contests such as those involved in boxing."[9]

In the Supreme Court, the government's task was to draw a line between baseball and boxing, and to persuade the justices that the reasons for inferring an antitrust exemption for one did not apply to the other. The origin of the exemption, the government reminded the Court, was the 1922 *Federal Baseball Club* case, a decision that was only about baseball. There had never been a comparable decision holding that boxing was not a form of interstate commerce. Even if the reasoning of *Federal Baseball Club* applied to boxing, the government continued, boxing had never relied on immunity from the antitrust laws the way baseball had. Baseball had built up an elaborate structure, the "farm system" linking major and minor league clubs, that was premised on an exemption from the Sherman Act. In boxing, by contrast, no comparable organization had been built up. Finally, the government pointed out, in 1951 Congress had held extensive hearings as to whether baseball should be exempt from the antitrust laws, and the clear view of the members of Congress who participated in those hearings was that it should. Boxing had never received any similar consideration in Congress. These reasons, the government argued, were enough to infer that Congress intended the Sherman Act to apply to boxing, even though the Court had inferred a contrary intent for baseball.

The practical consequences of an antitrust exemption, the government continued, would be very different in the two sports. Baseball teams needed to cooperate to maintain rough equality among them, because public interest in the sport would suffer if one team became too much better than its competitors. An antitrust exemption allowed baseball to develop the organization necessary to achieve that level of cooperation. An exemption would not facilitate the maintenance of a similar equality in boxing, because boxing was an individual sport, in which talent disparities were inherent in the individuals who entered the ring. Boxers would not become any more equal if boxing were exempt from the antitrust laws. That was why there was no comparable degree of organization in boxing. Boxing did not need an antitrust exemption. If baseball ever lost an antitrust challenge, the sport would need to make far-reaching organizational changes. If the government prevailed in its suit against the IBC, by contrast, there would be no substantial change to the structure of boxing. The IBC would have to dissolve, but otherwise the sport would remain the same. For all these reasons, the government argued, the antitrust exemption the Court had recognized in *Toolson* should not also apply to boxing.[10]

The IBC was represented by Whitney North Seymour, one of the leaders of the midcentury bar. Seymour had just finished serving as president of the New York City Bar Association; a few years later he would become president of the American Bar Association. He was also an experienced Supreme Court advocate. Seymour had argued many cases in the Court on behalf of the federal government as assistant solicitor general in the Hoover administration, and he would argue many more in private practice. Just a few years before, he had represented Paramount Pictures in the studio's appeal in the government's massive antitrust case against the film industry.[11] There was no lawyer better suited for the task of persuading the Court that the antitrust exemption recognized in *Toolson* should apply just as well to boxing.

If there was any relevant difference between boxing and baseball, Seymour argued, it was that baseball involved *more* interstate commerce than boxing. Baseball teams moved constantly from state to state throughout the season to fulfill a schedule of 154 games. Boxers crossed state lines much less often, because they fought only infrequently. Baseball, meanwhile, was a much larger business than boxing. If baseball was exempt from the antitrust laws due to its minimal connection with interstate commerce, boxing should be exempt all the more. Otherwise, Seymour contended, the two sports were the same. They were both displays of strength and skill. They were both broadcast nationally on radio and television. "The analogy between boxing and baseball is such that Congress, not having intended (as this Court stated in the *Toolson* case) to include baseball within the scope of the antitrust laws, cannot logically be said to have had a contrary intent as to boxing," Seymour concluded. "John L. Sullivan was the recognized heavyweight champion when the Sherman Act was adopted. Congress, in 1890, must be deemed to have been quite as aware of the existence of boxing as it was of the existence of baseball. There is no rational basis for imputing to Congress an intent to have the words of the Sherman Act exclude baseball while at the same time intending that the same statutory words should include boxing or any other sport."

Seymour reserved his strongest words for the government's argument that baseball should be treated differently because of its greater reliance on the Court's precedents. "This is a rather startling theory," he chided. Precedent ordinarily did not work that way. Parties were normally allowed to cite precedent in their favor without having to prove that they had actually relied on that precedent. If the government's theory were accepted, Seymour argued, "legal argument would not then be confined to precedents, as is now the case, but would in effect involve an appellate court in a trial of the factual justification for the citation of each precedent. Stability in the law would decline and each case would tend to become a legal transient. The most ancient and respected precedents would be the hardest to support because of the difficulty of excavating proof of reliance in support of practices long followed. By the same token, recent decisions would be valueless because they would not have had time to acquire the patina of reliance which the Government here contends is prerequisite to citation as precedent." This view, he argued, "is alien to the fundamental concept of *stare decisis*," the principle that courts should respect their prior decisions.[12]

The justices were in a bind. In *Toolson*, they had reaffirmed baseball's antitrust exemption by ascribing to Congress an aim that everyone recognized as fictional—the intent to exclude baseball from the Sherman Act. This intent was fictional not because members of Congress actually had the opposite intent, but because they had no intent in the matter at all. When Congress passed the Sherman Act in 1890, members had given no thought to baseball one way or the other. Like all legal fictions, this one served a specific purpose—in this instance, the purpose of making clear that the source of baseball's exemption rested with Congress rather than the Constitution, and thus clarifying that Congress had the authority to subject baseball to the antitrust laws if it wished. But having imputed to Congress a fictional intent to exempt baseball, the Court left itself adrift when it came to other sports.

In trying to figure out whether boxing should also be exempt, the justices could not use any of the traditional materials of legal interpretation. The text of the Sherman Act, the statute's legislative history, the surrounding context—all the tools that would be useful in determining what members of Congress truly intended in a real sense were worthless for the task at hand. *International Boxing Club* would have to be decided, not by deciding what real people actually intended, but by divining whether Congress's fictional intent was to exempt all sports or just baseball.

In making that determination, the justices had nothing to go by other than their understandings of what they had done in *Toolson* and their own views as to sound policy. Was *Toolson* grounded on the unique qualities of baseball or on the general characteristics of sports? Would boxing fans benefit or suffer if the government had the power to break up a monopoly of boxing promoters? The arguments in *International Boxing Club* were couched in terms of what Congress did or did not intend, but these were the questions that really mattered.

Justice Robert Jackson died a month before oral argument. He would not be replaced by John Harlan until a few months later, so the Court had only eight members when it decided *International Boxing Club*. All eight had participated in *Toolson* the previous year. They split six to two in favor of subjecting boxing to the antitrust laws. The majority was further split four to two. Justices Harold Burton and Stanley Reed had dissented in *Toolson*. In their view, baseball should have been governed by the antitrust laws, so they had little trouble concluding that boxing should be covered as well. The other four justices in the majority—Earl Warren, Hugo Black, William Douglas, and Tom Clark—had also been in the majority in *Toolson*. They had to draw a line between baseball and boxing.

Warren's opinion for the majority began by acknowledging that were it not for *Federal Baseball Club* and *Toolson*, it would be clear to all that boxing was a form of interstate commerce and was thus governed by the Sherman Act. The only question was whether the reasoning of *Toolson* applied to boxing as well. "*Toolson* is not authority for exempting other businesses merely because of the circumstance that they are also based on the performance of local exhibitions," Warren declared. "None of the factors underlying the *Toolson* decision are present in the instant case." Baseball had been judicially declared immune from the antitrust laws ever since *Federal Baseball Club* in 1922, but there was no analogous decision immunizing boxing.

In 1951, Congress had held extensive hearings on baseball's relationship to the antitrust law and had determined to leave matters as they were, but there had been no comparable hearings on boxing. In light of these differences, Warren's majority opinion concluded, if boxing promoters wanted an exemption from the Sherman Act, "their remedy, if they are entitled to one, lies in further resort to Congress."[13]

On the very same day, in *United States v. Shubert*, the Court unanimously reversed the trial judge's dismissal of the government's other antitrust suit, the one against the theatrical producers. All eight justices found that the theater business was interstate commerce subject to the Sherman Act. Warren wrote that opinion too, and he took the opportunity to say more about the baseball cases. "In *Federal Baseball*," Warren explained, the Court "was dealing with the business of baseball and nothing else." *Toolson* was also about the baseball business: it was "a narrow application of the rule of *stare decisis*." Baseball's antitrust exemption thus applied neither to the theater nor to boxing.[14]

Only two justices, Felix Frankfurter and Sherman Minton, were of the view that the principles underlying the antitrust exemption recognized in *Toolson* applied just as well to boxing. "It would baffle the subtlest ingenuity to find a single differentiating factor" between the two sports, Frankfurter insisted. Whatever were baseball's attributes that justified immunity from the Sherman Act, boxing, and indeed most "other sporting exhibitions," had those same attributes. The Court was thus treating like cases unalike. "If *stare decisis* be one aspect of the law," Frankfurter concluded, "to disregard it in identic [*sic*] situations is mere caprice." Minton emphasized the absurdity of a decision that, in effect, treated boxing but not baseball as interstate commerce, when in fact both sports required participants to travel from state to state.[15] As a matter of pure logic, it was hard to understand why baseball and boxing should be treated differently.

Of course, there is often more to Supreme Court decisions than pure logic, and *International Boxing Club* is a good example. "It would seem that the boxing decision is basically one of 'policy,'" one lawyer observed shortly after the Court's opinion was published. "It appears the Court felt baseball was a clean and honest sport, capable of carrying on unhampered; whereas boxing, scandal-ridden and degenerate, needed to be subject to close scrutiny." Another lawyer agreed that "it is no more than a policy decision, a decision based on the practical requirements of the two respective business-sports."

Boxing did have a reputation for corruption at the time, in light of the sport's association with organized crime, which resulted in some high-profile incidents of boxers accepting bribes to lose fights. Baseball had experienced similar episodes, most notably during the 1919 World Series, but by the mid-1950s they were safely in the past. Baseball was popularly perceived as much cleaner than boxing, and that perception was almost certainly correct. "What the court did was to permit baseball to get out of bed with its perhaps evil bedfellows," explained Shirley Povich, the veteran *Washington Post* sports columnist. Boxing's "behavior might have brought a crack-down on the whole caboodle of 'em, by act of Congressmen outraged by the thin pretense interstate commerce, and thus monopoly, is not involved. Now baseball is no longer responsible for the sins of others." A similar interpretation of the Court's decision was offered, a bit more subtly, by none other than Felix Frankfurter in his dissenting opinion. "Whatever unsavory elements there be in boxing contests is quite beside the mark," he noted—a thinly veiled charge that his colleagues had taken those elements into account. "It can hardly be that this Court gave a preferred position to baseball [in *Toolson*] because it is the great American sport."[16]

Perhaps the justices' personal views of baseball and boxing played a role in their decision in *International Boxing Club*, but, as with *Federal Baseball Club* and *Toolson*, all we can do is speculate. This is the kind of question as to which, by its very nature, there is unlikely to be any direct evidence one way or the other. Lurking behind the decision, however, was a very different policy question, one that may well have loomed larger in the justices' minds than a simple preference for baseball over boxing. Unless limited in some way, *Toolson*'s exemption for baseball threatened to spread like ivy, because virtually all of the sports and entertainment fields had the same basic structure as baseball. They all consisted of a series of performances, each located in a single state, with interstate travel between. Taken to its logical extreme, *Toolson* would have declared most of sports and entertainment exempt from antitrust law. That would have been a big change. To pick only the most conspicuous example, the Justice Department had been litigating antitrust issues against the leading film studios for decades, an effort that had culminated only a few years before in the Supreme Court's *Paramount Pictures* decision, which affirmed most of a trial court decree reorganizing the movie industry. It would have come as a shock to learn, after all that, that the studios were not governed by the Sherman Act in the first place.

Unless the Court were to dramatically change antitrust law, a line had to be drawn somewhere between baseball and the movies. The problem was that there was no place to draw a principled line. One could hardly argue that sports involved less interstate commerce than the theater, for example, or that baseball involved less interstate commerce than other sports. It would not be plausible to impute to the Congress that enacted the Sherman Act in 1890 an intent to pick and choose among sports or types of entertainment. Any line would be arbitrary.

It is not clear whether the justices anticipated this problem when they decided *Toolson*. It was not mentioned in the dissenting opinion or in the briefs filed on George Toolson's side of the case, so it is possible that the justices overlooked it or did not take it as seriously as they might have. The root of the problem, as the justices must have realized by the time they had to decide *International Boxing Club*, was that baseball's antitrust exemption was the lone remaining vestige of a legal order that was long gone. Under the conception of interstate commerce that prevailed by midcentury, all professional sports, and the entire entertainment industry, should have been forms of interstate commerce governed by the Sherman Act. It would have been logically consistent for the Court to say so, but that would have required overruling *Federal Baseball Club* and *Toolson*. On the opposite extreme, it would have been logically consistent for the Court to exempt all sports and entertainment from the Sherman Act, but that would have required wholesale changes to antitrust law. There were a variety of positions in between that would not have required overruling past cases, but none of them was logically consistent.

Faced with this dilemma in *International Boxing Club*, the Court cut its losses. It drew the line where it would do the least damage to the internal logic of the law. The exemption was for baseball, period. Everything else was subject to the Sherman Act, just as it would have been in the absence of *Federal Baseball Club*. One can understand *International Boxing Club* as an exercise in damage control. The Court chose the least bad of the available options, the one that confined incoherence to the smallest realm of life. The law hung together, with the one exception of baseball. Boxing, like any other nationwide business, was governed by the Sherman Act. Two years later, the IBC was found liable for violating the antitrust law, a judgment that would be affirmed by the Supreme Court in 1959. The boxing monopoly was broken up.[17]

But what would the next problem be? *Toolson* had created the monster of *International Boxing Club*; what new monster would *International Boxing Club* create?

UNREALISTIC, INCONSISTENT, OR ILLOGICAL

"I'm not out to wreck football," Bill Radovich insisted. "I wouldn't want to do anything like that. I put twenty-two years into the game. But I didn't like to have a man tell me I could play for one club and nobody else."[18] Radovich had been a lineman for the Detroit Lions. Although he had not been drafted out of the University of Southern California, Radovich was good enough to play in the Pro Bowl after his rookie season of 1938. He remained with the Lions through 1941, entered the Navy in early 1942, and remained there until the end of the war, when he rejoined the Lions in time for the 1945 season. Several publications named him to their all-NFL teams in 1945.

Before the 1946 season, Radovich asked to be traded to the Los Angeles Rams, so he could be closer to his ailing father. "I had to do it," Radovich later recalled. "My father didn't have any insurance. I couldn't live back there [in Detroit] and keep expenses going here for my family." The Lions' owner, Fred Mandel, refused to trade him. As Radovich remembered it, "the little creep said I'd either play in Detroit or I wouldn't play anywhere." Radovich jumped to a newly formed league, the All America Football Conference, which played its first season in 1946 and had a team in Los Angeles, the Dons, which offered him twice what he had been making with the Lions. Just as baseball had done when faced with competition from new leagues, the NFL blacklisted all the players who jumped to the AAFC, including Radovich. He stayed with the Dons through the 1947 season. In 1948, with his playing career winding down, he was offered a position as player-coach with a minor league team, the San Francisco Clippers. He was on the verge of accepting the offer when it was withdrawn. The Clippers played in the Pacific Coast Professional Football League, which had entered into an agreement with the NFL in which its clubs would effectively serve as farm teams for the NFL clubs. One term of the agreement prohibited clubs in the Pacific Coast League from hiring players like Radovich who were on the NFL's blacklist.[19]

Barred from most of professional football, Radovich found work as a waiter in Los Angeles. One of his customers turned out to be a young San Francisco antitrust lawyer named Joseph Alioto, who was then early in a career that would see him become a prominent attorney and later the mayor of San Francisco. At the time, Alioto had been in private practice for only a few years, after a period working in the Justice Department's antitrust division. Alioto outlined a legal argument on the back of a cocktail napkin, an argument he would turn into an antitrust suit against the NFL, alleging that the blacklist and the NFL's reserve clause violated the Sherman Act.[20]

The time was perfect for an antitrust suit against football. Radovich and Alioto filed the suit in the summer of 1949, just a few months after the Court of Appeals for the Second Circuit had decided, in *Gardella*, that baseball might be a form of interstate commerce subject to the Sherman Act. Baseball's antitrust immunity looked to be on its last legs. The Celler hearings of 1951 and the *Toolson* decision of 1953 were still well in the future. "It is obvious," the NFL's lawyer reflected, "that the complaint herein was born of a hope encouraged by language in one of the opinions in the *Gardella* case that the *Federal Baseball* case was an 'impotent zombi' and would be overruled by the Supreme Court."[21] If baseball was going to be governed by the antitrust laws, no doubt football would be too.

The NFL's lawyer was John Cromwell Bell, Jr., the older brother of league commissioner Bert Bell. Sports antitrust litigation was nothing new to the Bells; their father, John senior, had been counsel to National League president John Tener during the Federal League battles of the 1910s. At the NFL's annual meeting in November 1949, John junior advised the assembled owners that the league "had a 50–50 chance to win the case." He told them that he had retained John Sutro, a well-known San Francisco attorney, to act as local counsel, and that Sutro was even less optimistic; he thought the league was certain to lose. The problem, Bell explained, was that the law was in the midst of changing. "A number of federal judges were making decisions on interstate commerce cases now that six to ten years ago would not be considered in that category," he told the owners. With baseball's status as interstate commerce so uncertain, it was hard to predict whether football would be classified as interstate commerce—so hard, Bell observed, that "in his opinion the case hinges on the thinking of the judge who would hear the case."[22]

The owners had an immediate decision to make, because Radovich's lawyer had offered to settle the case for a payment of $13,000, twice Radovich's annual salary with the Dons, and four times his salary with the Lions. That was a substantial sum, but it was much smaller than the $35,000 in damages Radovich had requested in his complaint, an amount that under the

Sherman Act would be tripled to $105,000 if the court found it justified. Bell advised that if the NFL went to trial and lost, the damage award would likely be smaller, but that the league's total cost could amount to $50,000, taking into account the attorneys' fees and the cost of travel to take depositions from witnesses scattered across the country. Bert Bell had spoken with Happy Chandler, the commissioner of baseball, and Chandler had urged him to settle the case, just as baseball had recently settled the *Gardella* case, in order to avoid a court decision declaring that sports were governed by the antitrust laws. On the other hand, John Cromwell Bell noted, if the league settled with Radovich, there was a good chance that other blacklisted players would file identical lawsuits, and the bill would grow much higher. "The National Football League should defend this suit," Bert Bell declared to the owners. "If the Supreme Court of the United States finally decides that the National Football League should come under interstate commerce, . . . we better find it out as soon as possible." The owners voted unanimously to turn down Radovich's settlement offer. They would test football's antitrust status in court.[23]

"The *Gardella* case is identical to the case at bar," Alioto argued on Radovich's behalf. "The slavish 'reserve' clause was the subject of the *Gardella* case, just as it is the subject of this case." Danny Gardella and Bill Radovich had both jumped to upstart competing leagues, and both had been blacklisted in retaliation. "The black-listing in both cases," Alioto contended, "was the direct result of a combination and conspiracy among the defendants to monopolize the baseball and football business."[24] Radovich's case, however, took a very long time to proceed through the courts. Both sides recognized that football's antitrust status depended in part on baseball's, so they agreed to wait until *Toolson* was over before continuing to litigate.

Meanwhile, the All America Football Conference folded after the 1949 season. Three AAFC teams—Cleveland, San Francisco, and Baltimore—joined the NFL (although the Baltimore team would disband a year later). AAFC players were allowed to rejoin NFL teams. It was too late for Bill Radovich, who played his final season, in 1949, with the Edmonton Eskimos of the Canadian Football League. The league turned down another settlement offer from Radovich and Alioto in 1952. It was clear by then that by paying off Danny Gardella, baseball had only invited copycat lawsuits. The NFL would "defend this case," Bert Bell told the owners at their annual meeting, "so that we would not get into the same difficulties as baseball did in the Gardella case."[25]

The Supreme Court finally decided *Toolson*, and reaffirmed baseball's antitrust exemption, in late 1953. Now the tables were turned. Before *Toolson*, when baseball seemed on the verge of being subjected to the Sherman Act, Joseph Alioto had repeatedly argued that football was just like baseball. After *Toolson*, Alioto had to emphasize the differences between the two sports. It was the NFL's lawyer, Marshall Leahy, who contended that baseball and football were alike. "All of the factual issues which could be raised in the Radovich case were thoroughly considered by the courts in the various baseball cases," Leahy argued. He must have enjoyed quoting Alioto's own words, from a few years earlier, on the similarities between the two sports. "Counsel for both parties," Leahy concluded, "have always considered that the baseball and football cases presented identical problems." Indeed, the Supreme Court's decision in *Toolson* so discouraged Alioto that he told Leahy he wanted to give up. It was only at Radovich's own insistence that Alioto continued litigating. Alioto, Leahy needled, had "a client who fancies himself to be a more capable attorney than his learned counsel." Judge George B. Harris dismissed Radovich's complaint on the ground that football was entitled to the same exemption as baseball.[26]

Radovich appealed (represented by a new lawyer, Maxwell Keith), and this time the changing law worked to his advantage. In his opening brief, Keith tried gamely to argue that *Toolson* exempted only baseball. "The Supreme Court never once mentioned the word 'sport,'" he noted, "but intentionally used the words 'business of baseball' throughout the reported decision." A month later, the Supreme Court decided *International Boxing Club*, and Keith's argument suddenly grew much more plausible. In his reply brief, filed a few months after, Keith had a more confident tone. "The plain fact of the matter," he asserted, was that "the Supreme Court failed to go where appellees ask this court to go. It held specifically that 'sports' were within the antitrust laws."[27]

Now the question had become more complicated. The NFL could rely on *Toolson* to argue that football was exempt, Radovich on *International Boxing Club* to argue that football was not exempt. "Which of the two tides catches professional football?" asked Court of Appeals Judge Richard Chambers. There was no easy answer. "We confess that the strength of the pull of both cases is about equal," Chambers admitted. The court was "caught between the commands of the two cases."[28]

The only way to solve this problem, the Court of Appeals concluded, was to determine whether the business of football was "more like the business of boxing or like the business of baseball." Framed this way, the choice was obvious. "Football is a team sport," Chambers reasoned. "Its operation has just about the same aspects as baseball." Boxing, by contrast, "is an individual sport. In professional football, very good arguments do exist for the indulgence of restraints on individual players." If players could switch teams whenever their contracts expired, the richest teams would dominate the poorest, and fan interest in the game would suffer, to the detriment of all teams. "In boxing," Chambers continued, "arguments for restraints on the individual's right to contract seem rather hollow." Boxers would not become more evenly matched if one organization monopolized the sport. "Further," he concluded, "it appears reasonable to us to assume that if Congressional indulgence extended to and saved baseball from regulation, then the indulgence extended to other team sports." The reasons underlying baseball's exemption from the Sherman Act applied just as well to all professional team sports, including football. The NFL, the court held, was exempt from the antitrust laws.[29]

The Supreme Court had no obligation to hear the case, and indeed, after two contentious sports antitrust cases in the past three years, the justices might well have preferred to leave the issue to the lower courts for a while. In *Radovich*, however, the federal government entered the case as a friend of the court to support Radovich's request for review. "The petition presents a question of public importance which this Court should resolve," Solicitor General Simon Sobeloff asserted, "namely, whether all businesses involving team contests are beyond the purview of the Sherman Act."[30] The government had no particular interest in whether Radovich himself won or lost, but according to the logic of the Court of Appeals, all team sports would be exempt from the antitrust laws. The Justice Department had no pending investigations concerning the basic business structure of any team sports, but no one knew what the future would bring. The government had been active for several years in monitoring the antitrust implications of sports *broadcasting*, as we will see in the next chapter, and while the Court of Appeals' decision in *Radovich* would have been unlikely to hinder these efforts, the Justice Department was being careful to preserve its authority. The Supreme Court pays close attention to the government's views as to which cases merit review. The chances of having a case heard go up dramatically if the Justice

Department says it should be heard. The Court exhibited such deference in *Radovich*. It agreed to revisit the scope of the antitrust exemption yet again.

By now there was little new to be said on either side of the question. Radovich's lawyers pointed out that the line the Court had drawn in *International Boxing Club* and *Shubert* had been between baseball and everything else, not between team sports and individual sports. In every significant respect, they argued, football was just like boxing. No court (until this very case) had ever held football immune from the antitrust laws. Congress had never granted any such immunity. "Like the boxing business," the government added, "a holding that the business of football is exempt from the statute would be, not to continue an exemption previously judicially determined, but to create a new exemption." The NFL responded by emphasizing the similarities between baseball and football. Both were team sports with a reserve clause necessary for equalizing the strength of the teams. "The only distinguishing feature" between the two sports, the NFL argued, "is that one sport is called 'baseball' and the other 'football.'" It would be absurd to impute to Congress an intention to treat the two differently. "It is inconceivable," the league alleged, "that the same reserve clause sanctioned in baseball should warrant condemnation when adopted by football."[31]

Radovich reached a Supreme Court with two new members since the Court had decided *International Boxing Club* two years before. John Marshall Harlan had replaced Robert Jackson, and William Brennan, the newest justice, had taken his seat just a few months before oral argument, following the retirement of Sherman Minton. Harlan and Brennan were the only members of the Court approaching the issue afresh. Neither could see any reason to treat football differently from baseball. They could "find no basis for attributing to Congress a purpose to put baseball in a class by itself," they declared, in a dissenting opinion written by Harlan. "If the situation resulting from the baseball decisions is to be changed, I think it far better to leave it to be dealt with by Congress," Harlan concluded, "than for this Court to becloud the situation further, either by making untenable distinctions between baseball and other professional sports, or by discriminatory fiat in favor of baseball." Felix Frankfurter agreed. He had dissented in *International Boxing Club*, so for him football presented an easier case than boxing: if boxing was covered by the antitrust exemption, football should obviously be covered too.[32]

Shortly after the oral argument in *Radovich*, Justice Tom Clark confided to Harlan that he too thought that football should be covered by the same antitrust exemption baseball had secured in *Toolson*. "Tom said he would canvass other members of the Court," Harlan told Brennan and Frankfurter, "to see whether he could obtain a 'Court' for that disposition."[33] But Clark could not find a fifth vote to exempt football from the antitrust laws, and when he could not, he sided with the majority—indeed he wrote the majority opinion. In *International Boxing Club*, "the Court was careful to restrict *Toolson's* coverage to baseball," his opinion began. Clark seemed a little tired of the issue and a little peeved that the Court had to say it again. "Since *Toolson* and *Federal Baseball* are still cited as controlling authority in antitrust actions involving other fields of business," he continued, "we now specifically limit the rule there established to the facts there involved, i.e., the business of organized professional baseball." It is unusual for the Supreme Court, or indeed any court, to admit that one of its decisions makes little sense, but Clark acknowledged that there was no principled basis for treating baseball differently from other sports. Baseball was simply the beneficiary of an old case from an earlier era that had never been overruled. "If this ruling is unrealistic, inconsistent, or illogical," Clark declared, "it is sufficient to answer . . . that were we considering the question of baseball for the first time upon a clean slate we would have no doubts" that the sport was governed by the antitrust laws. "But *Federal Baseball* held the business of baseball outside the scope of the [Sherman] Act." The result might amount to discrimination in favor of baseball, but "the orderly way to eliminate error or discrimination, if any there be, is by legislation and not by court decision." Football was subject to the antitrust laws, even though baseball was not.[34]

The decision "vindicates my feeling that a player shouldn't be treated like a piece of furniture," Bill Radovich declared. "For a professional athlete," Maxwell Keith exulted, "this is emancipation." The men who ran football were, not surprisingly, less happy. The decision was "a great disappointment," admitted NFL commissioner Bert Bell. "I always thought that under the Constitution of the United States all people were regarded as being equal," he lamented. "Evidently, under the Supreme Court decision, baseball, a team sport, is different from football, a team sport." Edwin Anderson, president of the Detroit Lions, called the decision "inconceivable."[35] Professional football faced an uncertain future. The reserve clause, the player draft, the system of territorial rights—no one knew how these fundamental features of the game would fare under the scrutiny of the Sherman Act.

Radovich was roundly mocked in the sporting press. "How can pro football be a monopoly in restraint of trade if pro baseball, which conducts the same kind of store under the virtually the same conditions, isn't?" asked Joe Williams of the *New York World Telegram*. "Stripped of its legal gibberish," charged the Philadelphia columnist Hugh Brown, the decision was "the Supreme Absurdity." "After reading the decision," another columnist chided, "we don't know whether to pass it or bat it."[36] Even the more serious newspapers had their fun. An editorial in the *Wall Street Journal* imagined this discussion:

Q: Daddy, what is a sport?
A: A sport is a game played indoors or outdoors, sometimes in teams, sometimes man to man.
Q: Like prize-fighting, Daddy?
A: Well, no.
Q: Like professional football, Daddy?
A: Well, no.
Q: Well, what is a sport, Daddy?
A: Professional baseball.
Q: Is that the only one, Daddy?
A: Yes.
Q: That's funny, Daddy. Baseball is a sport, but football and prize-fighting aren't. How is that?
A: The Supreme Court says so.

On reading the Court's opinion, the *New York Times* chimed in, "an old vaudeville act comes to mind." The decision reflected what the *Times* saw as "a tendency on the part of the court to proceed on the assumption that the law is not what the Congress or previous opinions of the Supreme Court itself have held it to be, but what it now thinks it should be."[37]

Lawyers were just as critical. *Radovich* "borders on the absurd," scoffed Philip Kurland of the University of Chicago, one of the leading constitutional scholars of the era. The doctrine of *stare decisis* "ought not to be applied in a manner which can be justified only in terms of judicial fiat." The *Harvard Law Review*'s annual summary of Supreme Court decisions concluded that "a better course might have been to overrule *Toolson*." The decision was mocked even within the Supreme Court. Justice Harold Burton had dissented back in

Toolson: he thought the antitrust laws should apply to all sports. If only his colleagues had agreed with him about baseball, he must have been thinking, the Court would not have tied itself up in knots over football. Roger Cramton, who would go on to a career as a law professor at Cornell, was one of Burton's law clerks. Had Congress enacted a statute treating baseball and football differently for antitrust purposes, Cramton told Burton, the Court might well find the statute unconstitutional, as an arbitrary distinction with no rational basis. "But the Court," he needled, "apparently does not feel itself bound by the same considerations of fair play and reasonableness which it applies to the state and federal legislatures!"[38] There was no escaping the incongruity the Court had created in *Toolson* and *Radovich*.

Critics sometimes accused the Court of classifying football as a business but baseball as a sport. The imaginary father-son dialogue that appeared on the editorial page of the *Wall Street Journal* was one example. Another such critic was the Brooklyn congressman Emanuel Celler, who was still the chair of the House Judiciary Committee. "They can't make fish of one and fowl of the other," Celler complained. "If football is a business, then baseball is a business. It has more of the earmarks of business than football has."[39] This sort of criticism has persisted up to the present. It is inaccurate: in none of the cases did the Court mention any distinction between a sport and a business, much less place baseball in one category and football or any other sport in the other. In *Federal Baseball Club*, back in 1920, the Court of Appeals had called baseball a sport rather than a business, but the Supreme Court never had. In all three cases from the 1950s—*Toolson*, *International Boxing Club*, and *Radovich*—the justices were careful to explain that if the precedent of *Federal Baseball Club* did not exist, there would be no doubt that all professional sports, including baseball, were forms of interstate commerce governed by the antitrust laws. Baseball's unique status was not a product of romanticism among the justices about the national pastime. It was a result of the justices' aversion to overruling the Court's prior cases, even when, like *Federal Baseball Club*, those cases were vestiges of a very different climate of constitutional thought. Nevertheless, for decades critics would continue to repeat the mistaken notion that baseball was exempt from the Sherman Act because the Supreme Court viewed it as a sport, in contrast to other sports, which the Court viewed as businesses.

Some of the sharpest critics of *Radovich* were members of Congress. "It is difficult to be rational about a decision which in one fell swoop put football in and left baseball out," grumbled John Byrnes, whose congressional district included Green Bay, Wisconsin, home of the NFL's Packers. "It is sufficient to say that a highly inequitable and discriminatory situation has been created which threatens the very life of professional football." Oren Harris of Arkansas counted no NFL teams among his constituents, but he was no happier. "I do not want to be construed as having an attitude of any disrespect for the highest Court in the land," Harris declared. "But to me this is a most ridiculous decision."[40] Emanuel Celler declared that his committee would immediately consider legislation to set matters straight. So did Estes Kefauver, the chair of the Senate Subcommittee on Antitrust and Monopoly. Bert Bell, the NFL commissioner, began a furious lobbying campaign to secure an antitrust exemption for football. Baseball officials, meanwhile, began to worry that if Congress determined to treat all sports equally, the outcome might be legislation stripping baseball of its own exemption. "For 35 years, the men who run organized baseball have huddled under a legal umbrella raised for them by Justice Oliver Wendell Holmes," noted *Sports Illustrated*. "The umbrella is now leaking badly."[41] The stage was set for another round of congressional hearings, this time encompassing all sports, not just baseball.

As for Bill Radovich himself, the Supreme Court decision in his favor only reversed the dismissal of his complaint and returned his case back to the trial court for litigation. His playing career had ended a decade earlier. He had tried to break into the movies, without much success except for some bit parts. By the time the Supreme Court reinstated his suit, Radovich was selling cars in the San Fernando Valley. In the spring of 1958, the two sides reached a settlement. Radovich abandoned his suit in exchange for a payment of $42,500, probably much more than he lost by virtue of the NFL's blacklist. He remained in Los Angeles until his death in 2002, a dedicated supporter of the football team at USC, where he had started in the 1930s. He would be remembered not for his accomplishments on the field but for filing the lawsuit that cemented baseball's unique legal status.[42] No other sport would enjoy baseball's exemption from the antitrust laws.

A POLITICAL FOOTBALL

The *Radovich* case touched off a decade of activity in Congress. The notion that baseball should be the only sport exempt from the antitrust laws was so unpopular and so strongly criticized in the press that two bills were introduced in the House of Representatives, the day after *Radovich* was decided, to equalize the treatment of the four major professional sports, baseball, football, basketball, and hockey. By the time the House's Antitrust Subcommittee began holding hearings four months later, in June 1957, members had introduced five more bills. Hearings on the seven bills lasted for 15 days. The House heard from 51 witnesses, whose testimony sprawled over nearly 2,500 pages of printed transcript. But nothing happened. When the hearings were over, the subcommittee took no action on any of the bills.[1]

The issue came back to Congress the following year, when the House Judiciary Committee favorably reported a bill to subject the four major sports to the antitrust laws in most respects. An amended version of the bill was approved by the House as a whole. It was now the Senate's turn to hold extensive hearings, which took up most of July 1958 and involved 37 witnesses, including many of the same people who had testified in the House the previous summer. At the end of the hearings, the Senate Antitrust Subcommittee voted to take no action on the bill. Once again, a flurry of legislative activity had yielded no legislation.[2]

Every year was just the same. In 1959, the House and Senate both held hearings on sports antitrust bills, six in the House and three in the Senate. None of these bills made it out of committee. In 1960, a sports antitrust bill survived the Senate antitrust committee, after another round of hearings, and made it to the Senate floor. The full Senate voted to return the bill to the committee. More bills were introduced in 1961, 1964, and 1965, and there were yet more hearings in 1964 and 1965. None of the bills was enacted.[3]

By the mid-1960s, almost a decade had passed since baseball became the only sport exempt from the antitrust laws. Congress's failure to correct the anomaly was a source of repeated complaint on the part of congressmen and sports officials alike. "A solution is overdue," lamented Senator Philip Hart of Michigan, who saw the issue year after year as a member of the Senate Antitrust Subcommittee. When baseball commissioner Ford Frick appeared at the 1964 hearings, he noted that he was testifying about antitrust matters for the thirteenth time. Warren Giles, the president of the National League, testified a couple of weeks after Frick. "The first time I appeared in connection with the sports bill was a long time ago," Giles told the committee. Back then, he explained, "I didn't need glasses, but I need them now." Committee reports routinely recited the number of times Congress had tried, without success, to equalize the antitrust treatment of the major sports. "Approximately 60 bills have been introduced dealing with the status of professional team sports under the antitrust laws," acknowledged a 1965 report recommending the enactment of a bill to treat all four sports equally.[4] That bill became the sixty-first.

The remarkable thing about Congress's failure to enact sports antitrust legislation is that scarcely anyone favored the status quo. In nearly a decade of hearings, not a single witness testified that baseball *should* be treated differently from the other sports for antitrust purposes. Barely any members of Congress thought so either. Virtually everyone agreed that the anomaly created by *Radovich* made little sense as a policy matter. There was near unanimity among all concerned that the antitrust laws should apply to baseball as much or as little as they applied to other sports. Yet nothing happened. When all this legislative activity sputtered out after a decade, baseball's odd antitrust exemption had not changed a bit.

A SENSIBLE SPORTS BILL

One reason for the absence of legislation was the difficulty of reaching agreement on the details. There was no serious dispute about the big picture: baseball did not deserve special treatment. The New York senator Kenneth Keating (figure 6.1), who was one of the most active congressional proponents of sports legislation until he lost his 1964 reelection bid to Robert Kennedy, spoke for virtually everyone when he declared that the four major sports "are essentially alike and, therefore, logically should be treated alike in our laws." Even baseball favored extending its antitrust exemption to the other sports, on the theory that an exemption only for baseball would be less likely to withstand future attacks in Congress or the Supreme Court than an exemption for all four sports. "Baseball firmly believes that the antitrust laws are not appropriate for the regulation of any organized team sports," explained Commissioner Ford Frick. "Football, basketball and hockey, as well as baseball, should have exemption for their sports practices."[5] Baseball

Figure 6.1: Kenneth Keating, who represented New York in both houses of Congress, was one of the most active proponents of legislation to equalize the antitrust treatment of the four major professional sports until he lost his 1964 reelection bid to Robert Kennedy. LC-USZ62-110565, Prints and Photographs Division, Library of Congress.

had nothing to lose from an exemption covering the other sports. It would lose a great deal if its own exemption were to disappear.

There was agreement on the goal, but not on the best way of reaching it. Two months after *Radovich*, when the *Congressional Quarterly* polled members of Congress as to their preferred solution, 147 members returned the questionnaire: 43 wanted the antitrust laws to cover all sports, 29 wanted all sports to be exempt from the antitrust laws, 12 wanted to exempt only baseball and football (the two most commercially successful sports), one wanted to exempt only baseball, and 62 were undecided. Representative Torbert Macdonald of Massachusetts, who had been captain of the Harvard football team in his younger days, conducted a similar poll of the nation's sportswriters a couple of months later. The results were just as divided. Of the 275 sportswriters who responded, 95 thought all sports should be exempt from the antitrust laws, 70 thought all sports should be covered by the antitrust laws, 57 said that only baseball and football should be exempt, 33 said only baseball deserved an exemption, and 20 were undecided.[6]

This diversity of opinion was reflected in the bills that were introduced in Congress, some of which proposed covering all sports, some exempting all sports, and some exempting all sports only in certain respects. Of the seven bills introduced in the House in 1957, for example, two provided that baseball should be governed by the antitrust laws, one extended baseball's exemption to the other three major sports, and the remaining four exempted the major sports from the antitrust laws for some purposes but not others. One of these bills, for example, provided that the antitrust laws would cover sports, except with respect to playing rules, the organization of leagues, territorial agreements, and the employment of players, the areas in which club owners believed they most needed protection from antitrust suits. All seven bills would have equalized the treatment of the major sports, but they would have done so in very different ways.

The antitrust laws should apply to all sports, many argued, because professional sports were big businesses. "The answer to the anomaly resulting from the Supreme Court decision isn't for Congress to pass legislation holding that football, baseball and the others are just games played for fun, while other activities depending on spectators for profits are businesses," the *Philadelphia Inquirer* editorialized. "If Congress wants to end the confusion—and strike a healthy note of realism—it should start by recognizing the profit-making motive in professional sports, and treat them as it does other enterprises." Baseball "is the only cartel that is legally permitted to operate in this great, free-enterprise-conscious Nation of ours," insisted *Town and Country* magazine. "The men who run baseball are, by and large, able business executives, not philanthropists." Baseball's reserve system depended on its antitrust exemption, agreed the *New Republic*, so to broaden the exemption would only be "to extend this modern form of chattel slavery to other major professional sports."[7] On this view, the anomaly that needed correcting was the failure to include baseball within the antitrust laws, because baseball was a business like any other. Widening the exemption to include other sports would only compound the mistake.

But was it true that sports were businesses like any other? Many argued that sports teams had legitimate needs to cooperate on matters like playing rules, scheduling, and the equalization of team strength, issues that were not present in any other industry. "If the antitrust laws are applied to these sports," Kenneth Keating worried, "many such rules, regulations and practices so vital to their existence will be destroyed. The end result will be chaos in the sporting world, and the biggest loser of all will be the general public." The lesson many drew, as Keating argued in *Sports Illustrated*, was that "Congress should not apply to sports the same laws it applies to U.S. Steel or General Motors."[8] When one viewed the question from this perspective, the true anomaly was not baseball's antitrust exemption but the lack of a parallel exemption for football, basketball, and hockey.

Once the issue was before Congress, there was a third option as well. If there were some aspects of the sports business amenable to antitrust coverage, but others that deserved exemption from the antitrust laws, perhaps the solution was to draft a statute more finely tuned than the Sherman Act, one that applied antitrust law only where it was needed. For example, teams needed to cooperate to establish playing rules. It would have seemed absurd to subject to antitrust analysis an agreement among football teams that the ball needed to be advanced ten yards to achieve a first down, or an agreement among baseball teams that the game should last nine innings. These were parts of the sports business with little parallel in other industries. On the other hand, sports teams bought and leased real estate, employed clerical staff, sold food, purchased advertising, and performed many other tasks just like ordinary businesses did. It was hard to fathom why a baseball team should be exempt from the antitrust laws when it entered into contracts with hot dog vendors or billboard companies.

But if a finely tuned statute could answer these questions easily, there were others that were much harder, particularly the questions involving the employment of players. What about baseball's reserve clause? Or the football draft? Was an antitrust exemption necessary to insulate these traditions from antitrust attack? Or were these precisely the kind of exploitative practices the antitrust laws were intended to prohibit? On such points there was little agreement.

Baseball, of course, was eager to preserve the complete exemption it had enjoyed ever since 1922. Commissioner Ford Frick took every opportunity to testify in favor of the status quo. "The question naturally arises as to what great public urgency now demands that baseball should be completely subjected to the antitrust laws," Frick argued in 1957. Were antitrust law brought to bear, "I do not see better baseball, or lower admission prices, or better ball parks, or anything better for the fan. In short, I see baseball set back 50 years." "The application of the antitrust laws," he contended the following year, "would be inappropriate and disastrous." From baseball's point of view, the ideal outcome was a statute specifying that baseball was not covered by the antitrust laws, because such a statute would prevent the Supreme Court from overruling *Toolson* and deciding that baseball, because it was so obviously a form of interstate commerce, was subject to the Sherman Act. As Frick put it, baseball needed statutory protection "against a future reversal by the Supreme Court."[9] Statutes could be repealed too, of course, but an antitrust exemption declared by statute *and* court decision would be stronger than one secured by court decision alone.

The outcome baseball feared the most was the complete demise of the antitrust exemption, because baseball officials feared that the reserve system would be found to violate the Sherman Act. "I cannot conceive of baseball surviving without a reserve clause," the longtime executive Branch Rickey worried in 1957. "Without it there would be chaos." American League president William Harridge warned the House Antitrust Subcommittee that abolishing the exemption would mean the end of professional baseball. "I am sure the reserve clause in the major leagues is responsible for stabilizing the game," he testified. "I think it would be very doubtful that the major leagues could operate without a reserve clause."[10] Baseball had something to gain from congressional action, but because it was starting from such a favorable position, it had a lot more to lose.

Baseball accordingly cranked up its formidable lobbying machine, to a degree that had not been necessary since the antitrust crisis of the 1910s. With minor league clubs in virtually every congressional district, clubs typically owned and operated by local residents, baseball could exploit connections with nearly every member of Congress. Bobby Hipps, for example, had been the president of the class B Tri-State League until it folded in 1955. Hipps lived in Asheville, North Carolina, the home of the Tri-State League's Asheville Tourists. He was personally acquainted with three members of Congress: George Shuford, who represented Asheville; Hugh Alexander, who represented the district just to the east; and Robert Ashmore, whose South Carolina district was just to the south. When organized baseball wrote to the owners and presidents of all the minor leagues and all minor league clubs, asking for help in urging Congress not to repeal baseball's antitrust exemption, Hipps volunteered for action. So did Art Kowalski, general manager of the class A Topeka Hawks, who prevailed on his friend George Docking, the governor of Kansas, to write letters to each member of the state's congressional delegation. "In this period of world unrest and uncertainty we all need stabilizing recreational outlets such as baseball," Docking urged. "To do anything to threaten the fundamental structure of the sport at this time could be a marked disservice to all our people." When unfavorable legislation seemed on the verge of being enacted, baseball pushed this network of contacts as hard as it could. "THE TIME IS NOW for us to go all out on contacting our friends in the House of Representatives," exhorted George Trautman, the head of the minor leagues, in a letter circulated to all the minor league clubs. "Please do this AT ONCE."[11]

The men who ran major league clubs did their part as well. "To keep the Justice Department from being overworked," cracked Bill Veeck, "baseball has enlivened the halls of Congress with its own lawyers (you may read lobbyists if you're a cynic)." Securing the game's antitrust exemption "will require hard work on the part of every one of you," Ford Frick lectured the owners of all the major league clubs. "You cannot pass positive Federal legislation by sitting idly by and leaving the job to one or two people." They did not sit idly by. For instance, Joseph Cairnes, the president of the Milwaukee Braves, argued in a letter to Wisconsin representative Alvin O'Konski that to remove baseball's antitrust exemption "would take away from baseball certain rights which have been essential to the conduct of the game over the years. . . . Professional baseball has, I am sure, many friends in the Congress," Cairnes suggested, "and I feel quite confident that they will protect our interests." In this case, at least, Cairnes was right. "I have faith and confidence enough in you people," O'Konski responded, "that I will vote on this matter in accordance with the wishes your group expresses." Organized baseball printed up pamphlets, suitable for distributing to members of Congress and the press. As Frick put it, to ensure favorable antitrust treatment, baseball would "marshal all our forces for an all out effort at the next session of Congress."[12]

The National Football League also pushed hard for legislation. Football lacked the political advantage of baseball's widely dispersed minor league structure. The 12 clubs of the NFL were located in 11 and then 12 cities (the Cardinals shared Chicago with the Bears until they moved to St. Louis in 1960), but football did not enjoy the benefit of minor league franchises in congressional districts all over the country. The key to "favorable legislation in Washington," Commissioner Bert Bell told the owners, was thus "the support of Congressmen and Senators from states where there are no professional football teams." Bell repeatedly traveled to Washington from his office in the suburbs of Philadelphia to discuss antitrust issues with members of Congress. The NFL hired a lobbyist to keep up with all the pending bills. "Our man in Washington has done a great job," Bell reported to the owners in 1959. "He knows everything that is going on in Washington. We are in good shape." The league published a 43-page brochure, "The Story of Professional Football in Summary," which it sent to every member of Congress. The brochure emphasized that the Supreme Court's decision in *Radovich* "jeopardizes the continued existence of professional football."[13] Although football lacked baseball's tradition and grassroots political muscle, the sport was beginning to rival baseball in commercial success. Football, like baseball, could make itself heard in Congress.

The NFL was primarily interested in securing an antitrust exemption to protect its reserve clause and its player draft, both of which were left exposed to attack after *Radovich*. If either "should now be held by the courts to be an unreasonable restraint of trade," Bell warned the Antitrust Subcommittee, "organized professional football, the highly competitive and colorful sport that we know today, would come to an end." Football needed an exemption just as much as baseball did, Bell testified. "The National Football League from its inception has tried to copy what baseball has done," Bell told members of Congress. If baseball deserved an exemption, so did football. The draft was essential, argued George Halas, the owner and coach of the

Chicago Bears. "It protects the public by insuring evenly balanced competition," "it protects college football by preventing professional football teams from signing college players prior to graduation," and "it protects the players by encouraging them to complete their college studies." The draft and the reserve clause "are designed to promote competition, not to stifle competition," agreed Bell. "This is, I think, the essential difference between professional team sports and ordinary businesses. Application of the antitrust laws to the sports aspects of professional team sports would, it seems to us, have exactly the opposite effect from that which it has on ordinary businesses."[14]

Basketball and hockey were smaller enterprises than baseball and football, but both employed the reserve clause, and basketball had a football-style player draft, so both did what they could to help put pressure on Congress for an antitrust exemption that applied equally to all sports. "Professional basketball could not continue without substantially the same draft system we now have," insisted Maurice Podoloff, the president of the National Basketball Association. Abolishing the draft "would result in a mad scramble for players, which would only result in creating an intolerable situation." Clarence Campbell, the president of the National Hockey League, predicted that without the reserve clause hockey would suffer the same fate.[15] The four major sports were united in urging Congress to enact legislation that would exempt them from the antitrust laws, either completely or at least in the areas that concerned them most, involving the organization of leagues and the employment of players.

Antitrust suits were not just a theoretical possibility. In the late 1950s, all four of the major sports were preparing to defend lawsuits inspired by the Supreme Court's decision in *Radovich*. In late 1957, the National Football League Players Association announced plans for a $4.2 million suit against the NFL, in which it would allege that the NFL was violating the Sherman Act. The suit was a bargaining chip in the Players Association's effort to force the NFL to recognize it as the players' representative in labor negotiations and in the association's attempt to secure higher salaries for the players. The tactic worked. Within a few weeks, the NFL agreed to recognize the association as the players' formal representative, to pay players a minimum annual salary of $5,000, to pay additional amounts for exhibition games, and to provide medical care and continued salaries for players injured in the course of their duties. A year later, when NFL players determined to seek a pension, the association returned to the same tactic; it threatened another antitrust suit. The National Hockey League Players Association filed an antitrust suit against the NHL in the fall of 1957. The following year, the star basketball player Jack Molinas, who had been suspended from the NBA for betting on games, brought an antitrust suit against the league, claiming $3 million in damages. The Portland Beavers, a minor league baseball team, sued the major leagues under the Sherman Act in 1959, in the hope that *Radovich* presaged the end of baseball's antitrust exemption.[16] All these lawsuits added to the sense of urgency underlying the efforts of the four major sports to persuade Congress to exempt them from the antitrust laws.

These efforts encountered opposition, however, from sources both inside and outside the world of sports. The Justice Department was wary of any legislation that would limit the scope of the antitrust laws. Victor Hansen, who ran the Antitrust Division, explained that "the Department's view" was that an "antitrust exemption should be extended only upon a very strong and clear showing that team sports cannot survive under the present status of antitrust's application. Exemptions from antitrust should not be lightly proffered." While some baseball players with established careers, like Robin Roberts of the Phillies and Stan Musial of the Cardinals, testified to the necessity of the reserve clause, other players took the opposing view. The pitcher Jim Prendergast had spent his entire career in the minor leagues, except for a brief stint toward the end with the Boston Braves. Early in his career, in the late 1930s, he had been in the Yankees' minor league organization, stuck behind a top-notch pitching staff on one of the greatest teams of all time and not allowed to reach the majors with any other team. His career ended in 1951, he testified, when he was suspended from baseball for refusing to sign the contract that had been offered him. The reserve clause "is a weapon used by the owners," Prendergast told the House Antitrust Subcommittee. "They can reach out, no matter where you play, and use the reserve clause to keep you from making your living." Jackie Robinson, who had retired in 1956 after nearly a decade as the most well known player in the game, attacked the reserve clause on similar grounds in the Senate. A substitute on "say, a Boston Red Sox team, the fellow who sits on the bench," Robinson argued, was "perhaps better than the No. 1 man that is playing second base or third base for the Washington Senators or some other team, and yet he has no opportunity to show his talents because he has to sit and be a substitute." As a result, "he is not able the following year to be paid or compensated for his real ability because he has not had an opportunity to express it."[17] Within baseball, opinion was divided as to the proper reach of the antitrust laws.

The same division was evident within football. Some established players, like Chuck Bednarik of the Eagles and Norm Van Brocklin of the Rams, testified in favor of the reserve clause and the draft. But others, like William Howton of the Packers (who was president of the NFL Players Association) and Kyle Rote of the Giants, urged Congress not to grant football an exemption from the antitrust laws, for fear that club owners would use the exemption to conspire to blacklist players who tried to negotiate higher salaries. Two of the leading college football coaches, Bud Wilkinson of the University of Oklahoma and Bowden Wyatt of the University of Tennessee, argued that the draft was unfair to players, because it deprived them of the ability to sell their services to the highest bidder. "I have never understood the logic in a boy becoming the property of someone without any choice in this matter, and also without any compensation," Wilkinson testified. "He has a skill that apparently is merchandisable, and someone now says, 'This skill belongs to me.'"[18] Despite their best efforts, the major sports were unable to present a unified front to Congress.

Almost everyone agreed that the four major sports should be treated equally, but there was considerable controversy over exactly how. Disagreement flared up year after year, in response to the particular language of each year's bill. In 1958, for example, Representative Emanuel Celler introduced a bill stating that the antitrust laws would apply to the four major sports, except for agreements or activities "reasonably necessary" to the equalization of teams, the right to operate within specified geographic areas, the preservation of public confidence in the honesty of games, and the regulation of broadcasting. (Celler had favored a statute exempting the major sports from antitrust law when the Dodgers were in Brooklyn, but once they moved to Los Angeles he became an ardent opponent of an antitrust exemption.) The bill drew immediate opposition from baseball on the ground that there was no way to predict what a court would consider "reasonably necessary." The bill "will provoke endless litigation," worried Robert Carpenter, the owner of the Phillies. "This is not an exemption," Ford Frick complained in a letter to members of Congress. "It is merely a requirement that sports rules and agreements must be defended in court whenever challenged." Baseball printed and circulated a pamphlet spelling out its concerns. "The words 'reasonably necessary' look fair and reasonable, but they are deceptive," the pamphlet explained. "Under the Celler bill, baseball in a trial would be required to establish that its rules, agreements and activities were reasonably necessary within the undefined meaning of the bill. This greatly encourages plaintiffs to attack baseball, because the Celler bill says baseball as a whole is subject to the antitrust laws and so gives the plaintiff a running start."[19]

These complaints attracted sympathy from many members of Congress. When the House Judiciary Committee reported the bill favorably, 15 committee members joined in a pair of dissenting statements. "The present bill would force organized professional team sports to run a gantlet of legal proceedings to save themselves from complete ruin," the dissenters argued. "This bill is an open invitation to every disgruntled player to litigate the fine points of the game in courts throughout the land." On the floor of the House, a group of representatives including Kenneth Keating introduced a substitute bill that removed the "reasonably necessary" language, and after extended debate, the House approved the substitute rather than the original bill. The following day Keating received some grateful mail from Walter O'Malley, owner of the Los Angeles Dodgers, who at that moment was perhaps the most reviled person in Keating's home state of New York because of the Dodgers' move from Brooklyn just a few months earlier. "I hope it will not jinx you to get a letter from the feller with the horns," O'Malley joked. "Seriously, I am personally delighted that your long fight for a sensible sports bill ended so well yesterday."[20] The episode illustrated how agreement on the broad outlines of sports antitrust policy could splinter over the details. There would be even more disagreement down the road, when the bill approved by the House could not survive a Senate subcommittee.

A different controversy over statutory language erupted at the next session of Congress, when Senator Estes Kefauver introduced a bill that would have exempted the four major sports from the antitrust laws in the same general areas as the 1958 Celler bill, but added that the exemption would cover a player draft only if players gave their written consent to be subject to the draft. This time it was football and basketball that raised the alarm. Commissioner Bert Bell foresaw the end of the NFL because the best college players would inevitably bypass the draft and be bought up by the wealthiest teams, who would dominate the others. "If passed in its present form," declared NBA president Maurice Podoloff, the bill "will, in our opinion, ultimately destroy professional basketball."[21] Kefauver's bill died in committee. Once again, disputes over exactly how to apply antitrust law to professional sports prevented Congress from changing the status quo.

One of the reasons for Congress's failure to correct the anomaly of baseball's antitrust exemption was that there was simply no agreement about the best way to do it. Bills were introduced year after year, proposing a variety of methods of equalizing the antitrust treatment of the major sports, but there was never enough support for any one of them. That wasn't the only obstacle, however. Throughout the late 1950s and early 1960s, professional sports faced a series of other controversies, and these issues kept intruding into the debate. A second reason for the lack of any legislation was that the antitrust debate was never just about antitrust.

ALL THE LAWYERS IN AMERICA

The most important of these other issues was broadcasting. In 1921, when a Pittsburgh radio station aired the first broadcast of a major league baseball game, club owners were faced with a difficult new question. If baseball was on the radio, would club revenues rise or fall? "At that time baseball had no idea of what the impact of radio might be," Ford Frick recalled. "There were a lot of clubs that thought it would be harmful; some thought it would be helpful." Some teams, including the Cubs and the White Sox, began selling broadcast rights to radio stations in the 1920s. Others, like the Yankees, Giants, and Dodgers, prohibited the radio broadcast of their games for fear that fans would not come out to the ballpark if they could listen at home for free. "The new radio craze is already crimping attendance at anything where the feast is for the ear rather than the eye," worried the *Sporting News*. "What will become of baseball?"[22] By the late 1930s, as it became clear that radio could fuel fans' interest in the game and that there could be significant income in the sale of broadcast rights, these doubts evaporated, and all clubs put their games on the radio.

The general acceptance of broadcasting, however, only created new dilemmas. "As broadcasting became more prevalent," Frick remembered, "and as they began to carry broadcasts of one game into the town of another club, while that club was playing, it became a severe problem." In 1936, to prevent teams from competing for the same fans, Commissioner Kenesaw Mountain Landis barred teams from broadcasting into the territory of other teams. That still left minor league clubs unprotected from the effects of major league broadcasts. Given the choice between listening to a major league game on the radio and attending a local minor league game in person, fans in minor league cities could be expected to opt for the former often enough to cause substantial damage to minor league attendance. In 1946, to preserve the health of the minor leagues, the major league clubs adopted Major League Rule 1(d), which prohibited a major league club from broadcasting a game into the territory of any other club, major or minor, without the consent of that club.[23] The major leagues needed the minor leagues to develop their players. Rule 1(d) embodied a judgment on the part of the major league clubs that the value of keeping the minor leagues alive exceeded the gains to be had from radio broadcasting into minor league towns.

The effect of Rule 1(d) was to take major league baseball off the radio in large sections of the country. It quickly attracted the attention of the Justice Department, whose lawyers viewed the rule as a classic conspiracy to restrain trade, in which a cartel of producers (the major league clubs) had agreed among themselves to limit the supply of their product (the broadcasting of games). At a 1949 conference with representatives of the Antitrust Division, baseball's lawyers offered a compromise. They proposed a revised rule, under which a broadcast would require the consent of the local team only if the local team was either playing a home game at the time or broadcasting an away game into its home territory. The parties settled on a restriction narrower than baseball would have liked. Beginning in 1949, major league clubs could broadcast into minor league territories without the consent of minor league clubs, except during minor league home games. At the time, baseball's antitrust worries were at their peak. Just a few months earlier, the *Gardella* decision had poked a large hole in baseball's antitrust immunity. The other players who had jumped to the Mexican League had all filed antitrust suits of their own. The last thing the club owners needed was yet another lawsuit, this one from an opponent much more formidable than any of the others. Two years later, when the Justice Department reopened its investigation into baseball broadcasting, the owners had no stomach for another fight. They agreed to repeal Rule 1(d). The major league teams began broadcasting their games into minor league cities, even while the minor league teams were playing.[24]

Minor league attendance plummeted, just as baseball officials had feared. With the ability to hear major league games on the radio, and increasingly even to watch them on television, fans stopped going to minor league ballparks. In 1949, there had been 59 minor leagues. By 1953 there were only 39, "and many of these 39 are weak and wobbly, and may fold before the present season is ended," lamented Senator Edwin Johnson of Colorado, who was also president of the class A Western League. In 1949 there had been 17 minor league clubs in Ohio, but by 1953 there were only two.[25] People who had once gone to see the Lima Phillies or the Marion Red Sox of the class D Ohio-Indiana League could stay home and listen to the major league Cleveland Indians instead. The clubs in Lima and Marion folded after the 1951 season.

Baseball locked horns with the Justice Department again in 1953, when club owners decided to sell nationwide television rights for a "Game of the Week." The arrangement would have required the owners to deal collectively with one of the television networks. Baseball's lawyers, afraid to litigate against the government, sought assurances from the Justice Department that this sort of collective action would not amount to an antitrust violation, but Stanley Barnes, the head of the Antitrust Division, advised that the department would not approve the proposal. The "Game of the Week" was abandoned for the time being.[26]

The broadcasting of football games was raising similar issues at the same time. In 1951, the National Collegiate Athletic Association announced that it would ban the live televising of college football. College sports programs earned revenue primarily from ticket sales to football games. Gate receipts tended to drop when games were shown on television. The colleges did earn some revenue from television, but not nearly enough to make up the shortfall. The Justice Department began an antitrust investigation of the proposed ban, for the same reason that it disapproved of restrictions on radio and television coverage of baseball.[27]

The National Football League was grappling with the same question. In January 1951, the league adopted a broadcasting rule modeled on baseball's, under which teams were barred from permitting their games to be broadcast, either on radio or television, into the home territory of another team, on the same day that the other team was either playing at home or broadcasting an away game into its home territory. Because virtually all NFL games were played on Sundays, the rule had the effect of ensuring that the local team's game would be the only one available on radio or television. When the Justice Department threatened to sue, the NFL refused to back down the way baseball had. "All the lawyers in America have worked on this," complained George Marshall, owner of the Washington Redskins, at the owners' annual meeting. "The deal baseball made with them would be terrible for us to make with them." The government accordingly filed an anti-trust suit against the NFL in the fall of 1951, midway through the football season, in which it alleged that football's broadcasting rule violated the Sher-man Act. The Justice Department planned to file similar suits against the NCAA and any other sports organizations that restricted the broadcasting of games, announced Assistant Attorney General H. Graham Morrison. "If any sport sells a ticket, it is offering a commodity on the market," he declared. "The American people are entitled to have free of monopoly the right to see or hear what they want."[28]

After two years of litigation, Judge Allan Grim of the federal district court in Philadelphia agreed in part with the government. The NFL's broadcasting rule "is a clear case of allocating marketing territories among competitors, which is a practice generally held illegal under the anti-trust laws," Grim rea-soned. He acknowledged that sports teams could not compete in a business sense as fully as enterprises in other industries, because if the stronger teams drove the weaker teams out of business, the entire league would fail, as no team could operate without a league. Football thus needed special rules "to help the weaker clubs in their competition with the stronger ones and to keep the League in fairly even balance." The ban on televising games into cities whose teams were playing at home was one such rule, Grim held. Without it, fans in cities with weaker teams would stay home and watch the stronger teams on television, thus depriving the weaker teams of ticket sales and weak-ening them even further. Because this aspect of the NFL's broadcasting rule promoted competition, Grim concluded, it did not violate the Sherman Act. But the ban on televising outside games when the home team was playing an away game was different, in Grim's view. This part of the rule did not protect the ticket revenue of weaker teams. It merely ensured that local spectators would not switch their allegiance to stronger teams in other cities after seeing them on television. Such a change in allegiance might deprive the home club of ticket sales or television revenue in the long run, Grim acknowledged, but he determined that these losses were too speculative to support the restric-tion on broadcasting. The NFL could give local teams a monopoly when they were playing at home, but not when they were playing away from home.[29]

At the end of the opinion, Judge Grim addressed one of the defenses raised by the NFL—that in light of *Federal Baseball Club*, the Sherman Act did not apply to football, because football was not a form of interstate commerce. Whether football enjoyed baseball's status under the antitrust laws was still an open question in the early 1950s. Not until 1957 would the Supreme Court make clear, in the *Radovich* case, that baseball was the only sport exempt from the Sherman Act. But Judge Grim had little doubt that *Federal Baseball Club* applied only to the internal organization of sports leagues, not to the sale of radio and television rights. Whether or not football or baseball was a form of interstate commerce, *broadcasting* clearly was.[30]

The NFL's attorneys advised the owners not to appeal, and the owners unanimously voted to rewrite the broadcasting rule to comply with Judge Grim's opinion. There was little chance of persuading an appellate court that the broadcasting of football games was not interstate commerce. There was a substantial risk that an appeal would only make matters worse, because an appellate court might well have decided in the government's favor for home games as well. Commissioner Bert Bell made the best of the situation. "Football won the most important part of its case," he told the press. The court "understood the vital need of professional football today, namely, the protection of our home gate."[31] It was clear, however, that in dealing with the new world of television, sports leagues would have to maneuver carefully around the obstacles posed by antitrust law.

For the next decade, whenever the question of how to end baseball's anomalous antitrust status reached Congress, the question of broadcasting was not far behind. This made legislation even more difficult to obtain, because there was just as much disagreement over the antitrust implications of broadcasting as there was over baseball's antitrust exemption.

On one side of the debate were football and baseball, which urged Congress to exempt sports broadcasting from the antitrust laws. "The wholesale televising of major league games will eventually destroy the love of baseball," argued Frank Shaughnessy, the chairman of the National Association of Professional Baseball Leagues, the umbrella organization for baseball's minor leagues. Television was killing the minor leagues, and "without the minor leagues," Ford Frick testified, the "major leagues cannot exist."[32]

On the other side were the Justice Department and the broadcasters, who reminded Congress at every opportunity that an antitrust exemption for sports broadcasting would harm the millions of fans who watched games on television. The kind of bill baseball favored, warned Assistant Attorney General Robert Bicks, "could conceivably result in a virtually complete blackout of sports broadcasts and telecasts." Robert Swezey, the executive vice president of a New Orleans television station affiliated with the NBC network, reported that the station's weekend telecasts of major league baseball games attracted approximately 325,000 viewers, more than any other daytime programming the station offered. New Orleans had a minor league club, the Pelicans, that typically drew only a few hundred fans to its games. If baseball were allowed to black out major league telecasts to protect the Pelicans' gate receipts, Swezey explained, a great many fans would suffer for the benefit of only a few. "I have no desire to bore the Committee with philosophical banalities," he concluded, "but in passing, at least I think we must recognize the similarity of this situation to many others which have developed as a normal consequence of social and economic progress and the inexorable change in popular tastes, customs, and habits. The fate of the minor leagues is actually not dissimilar in many respects to that of the Chautauqua and vaudeville circuits, which also had their day."[33] If the minor leagues could survive only with legislation allowing major league teams to collude to restrict telecasts, maybe they didn't deserve to survive.

Broadcasting was not the only issue that kept nosing its way onto the agenda whenever Congress considered legislation to rectify the anomaly of baseball's antitrust exemption. Another was the migration of major league baseball teams. For half a century after 1903, when the Baltimore Orioles moved to New York, not a single American or National League team had changed cities, despite substantial population shifts and the development of air travel. In 1953, the Braves left Boston for Milwaukee and the dam had burst: five more teams moved to new cities in the next eight years. Most of them, like the Braves, abandoned metropolitan areas they shared with another team in favor of cities in which they would be the only one. In 1954, the St. Louis Browns became the Baltimore Orioles. The Philadelphia A's moved to Kansas City in 1955. In 1958, the Brooklyn Dodgers moved to Los Angeles, and the New York Giants moved to San Francisco. In 1961, the Washington Senators became the Minnesota Twins. (The Braves would move again to Atlanta in 1966, and the A's would continue on to Oakland in 1968.) All of these moves were important events in the lives of baseball fans and elected officials in the affected metropolitan areas. Whenever baseball's antitrust status was before Congress, there was inevitably a great deal of interest in the relationship between antitrust law and the ability of baseball teams to move to new cities.

This was most true in New York, where the departures of the Dodgers and Giants were widely perceived as major injuries to the city. The 1957 hearings took place amid rumors of the impending moves, and New York's congressional delegation was interested in little else. "Let's go right into it," Emanuel Celler began, when National League president Warren Giles appeared before the antitrust subcommittee. "Let's put the fat right in the fire. What do you know about the contemplated or intended removal of the Giants and the Dodgers to the west coast?" Celler claimed that his interest in the topic was related to the question of baseball's antitrust exemption, but Kenneth Keating was more honest. "I don't have as lofty ideals as that," he admitted. "I want to see the Dodgers stay in Brooklyn. I would like to see the Giants stay in New York." Long stretches of the hearings were devoted to grilling Walter O'Malley, the owner of the Dodgers, and Horace Stoneham, the owner of the Giants, about their plans. "Baseball has been dealt a severe blow by the baseball magnates," Celler declared to the press. "Their conduct demonstrates the need to make the antitrust laws applicable to baseball."[34] This was nonsense as a legal matter. Applying the antitrust laws to baseball would only make the leagues *less* able to prevent teams from changing cities. Without an antitrust exemption, competitors in an industry cannot agree to prohibit their rivals from moving. But for a New York politician seeking to take a visible public stand against his city's loss of major league teams, the antitrust question provided an ideal platform.

The Senators began threatening to leave Washington for Minneapolis in 1958, a development that was deeply disturbing to many members of Congress. "The House of Representatives numbers among its members many hard-core dyed-in-the-wool, old-fashioned baseball fans," admitted Francis Walter of Pennsylvania, who had served in the House for the past 25 years. In the Senate, agreed John Carroll of Colorado, "being for baseball is like being for mother love and against sin." New York's congressional delegation had been angry about the Dodgers and Giants, but the whole Congress was angry about the Senators. It was not long before Senators' owner Clark Griffith was called to testify. Karl Mundt, who had represented South Dakota in Congress since 1939 and had thus lived in Washington nearly as long as he had lived in South Dakota, introduced a bill to exempt baseball from the antitrust laws only so long as a major league team remained in Washington. "Washington is everybody's second hometown, and all Americans take an interest in the Washington baseball club," Mundt argued. "Having baseball as a national sport, without a baseball club in Washington, would be like trying to have a rodeo without any horses."[35]

The question of where teams would be located became even more important in 1959, when a group of promoters led by the New York lawyer William Shea announced plans for a new major league, the Continental League, which would have teams in growing cities like Dallas, Houston, Atlanta, and Denver as well as New York. The announcement made it even harder for Congress to reach agreement on the terms of an antitrust exemption, because members of Congress from prospective Continental League cities now had an incentive to weaken baseball's reserve clause, to free up the players who would stock the rosters of the new league's teams. Members of Congress from cities with American and National League teams now had an even more powerful incentive than before to strengthen the reserve clause, to prevent their teams from losing players to the Continental League. Any antitrust reform would favor one group or the other. One of the bills introduced in 1960 granted an antitrust exemption to football, basketball, and hockey, but allowed baseball a similar exemption only if major league teams agreed that each one could control only 40 players at a time. This provision would have made thousands of minor league players available to the Continental League.[36] Once again, it proved impossible to disentangle one specific question—whether antitrust law should treat baseball differently from other sports—from broader and more politically salient issues.

The NFL also faced a challenge from a new league, the American Football League, which hired antitrust lawyers well before its teams played any games. The AFL was organized in late 1959 to begin play in the fall of 1960 with teams in several cities lacking NFL clubs, including Dallas and Minneapolis. The NFL responded by announcing that it would expand by adding two new teams, which would be located in Dallas and Minneapolis. The AFL owners interpreted this move as an attempt to suppress competition from the new league. "They're out to continue their monopoly of professional football," complained AFL commissioner Joe Foss. "There are antitrust laws that take care of such situations." Foss fired off a letter to the owners of NFL teams, warning them that "to follow your present 'scorched earth' policy is heresy to the cities involved, the American sporting public and especially to the Senate's Anti-Trust Committee." Robert Dedman, the AFL's lawyer, recommended a three-step approach: "(1) Seek to have the Justice Department take action; (2) Seek to have the Kefauver Committee [the Senate Antitrust

Subcommittee] take action; and (3) As a final step, have the AFL and member clubs take action." As the *Sporting News* put it, "this promises to be a fat year for the lawyers."[37]

The AFL followed Dedman's advice to the letter. Foss first met with lawyers in the Justice Department's antitrust division in an effort to persuade the government to bring an antitrust suit against the NFL. The AFL owners lobbied their senators to take some action, either to urge the Justice Department to file suit or to have the Senate conduct an antitrust investigation of its own. Ultimately, the AFL filed its own antitrust suit against the NFL, a suit that would endure for two years, until the AFL lost in 1962, on the ground that it had not proven that the NFL intended to destroy the AFL when it expanded to Dallas and Minneapolis.[38] During the two years the suit was pending, any new antitrust legislation would favor either NFL cities, by offering sports leagues more protection, or AFL cities, by offering less. Like the Continental League, the AFL made it more difficult to reach agreement on the details of any plan to address the differential treatment of baseball and other sports.

If the anomaly of baseball's antitrust exemption could have been considered on its own, perhaps it would have been possible to reach some legislative compromise that would have treated baseball like other sports. But the antitrust exemption was never considered on its own. It was always linked with more complicated questions, particularly broadcasting, team relocation, and the rise of new leagues. As a result, the baseball anomaly persisted, year after year, despite the consensus that it should be eliminated.

The end of an era

Some of these other issues were eventually resolved. Until 1961, each professional football team sold television rights on its own, but in 1961 the NFL negotiated a league-wide contract with the CBS television network. The Justice Department returned to Judge Grim in Philadelphia, who held that the CBS contract was inconsistent with his 1953 opinion. The NFL immediately turned to Congress, joined by the other three major sports, which saw Grim's decision as a threat to their own television contracts. Despite opposition from the Justice Department and the National Association of Broadcasters, within two months Congress enacted the Sports Broadcasting Act of 1961, which exempted from the antitrust laws agreements like the one between the NFL and CBS, in which professional sports teams pooled their television rights and sold them as a single package. The act provided that the exemption would not apply to any agreement in which the broadcaster was prohibited from televising any games in any area, except within the home territory of a league member on a day when the team was playing at home. At the request of the National Collegiate Athletic Association, another provision of the act specified that the antitrust exemption would not apply if the NFL allowed the telecast of games on Friday nights or Saturdays from stations located within 75 miles of the site of a college football game taking place that day. Once football had sufficient financial incentive to separate broadcasting from the other antitrust issues it faced, legislation followed quickly. Revenue sharing from a league-wide television contract would be an important step in the NFL's rise to surpass baseball as the nation's most popular televised sport.[39]

The issue of competition from new leagues was also put mostly to rest, at least for a while. The Senators moved to Minneapolis in 1961, but baseball promptly placed a new American League team in Washington, also called the Senators, in large part to placate the members of Congress who had been threatening to withdraw baseball's antitrust immunity. When the National League agreed to add two new teams in 1962, one in New York and the other in Houston, the Continental League disbanded. The AFL, by contrast, flourished. It was so successful that the NFL and the AFL reached agreement in 1966 on a merger of the two leagues. The merger was at risk of being attacked on antitrust grounds, so the leagues applied to Congress for a statute immunizing them from such attack. The result, obtained in just a few weeks, was a law providing that the Sherman Act "shall not apply to a joint agreement by which the member clubs of two or more football leagues . . . combine their operations."[40]

By the mid-1960s, a decade had passed since the Supreme Court declared that baseball was the only sport exempt from the antitrust laws. Football, the most commercially successful of the other sports and thus the one with the most to gain from an antitrust exemption, had spent years lobbying unsuccessfully for one. But football had also discovered that for most purposes it did not need one. On the two occasions when the NFL had some pressing reason to seek antitrust immunity—to sell league-wide television rights in 1961 and to merge with the AFL in 1966—the league had no trouble securing that immunity from Congress, in narrow statutes tailored specifically to the issue at hand. The NFL had every reason to expect that should some other need for antitrust immunity arise, another statute would be just as easy to get. Back in 1957, when the Supreme Court had allowed Bill Radovich to bring an antitrust suit against the NFL, the league's owners had worried about future challenges to the player draft and the reserve clause. A decade later, no such challenges had materialized. None was on the horizon. An antitrust exemption had seemed crucial to the NFL's success in 1957, but by 1966 it no longer looked so important.

Baseball had also lobbied for a statutory exemption, but baseball's incentive in that direction was always smaller than football's because baseball already enjoyed the exemption conferred by the Supreme Court. In 1957, after *Radovich*, there was some danger that Congress would take the exemption away, either in whole or in part, by enacting new antitrust law to cover all sports. By 1966, that danger had largely dissipated. Baseball, like football, had little motive to seek legislation. The issue dropped off the agenda of Congress.

For a decade, every year had seen the introduction of several bills to modify baseball's antitrust exemption, and sports hearings had been an annual staple of the House and Senate Antitrust Subcommittees. Nothing had been accomplished. Baseball was still the only sport exempt from the antitrust laws. Virtually everyone agreed that this made no sense. Few members of Congress, if any, believed that baseball deserved better treatment than the other sports because it was the national pastime. Yet the anomaly was as firmly a part of the law as ever.

THREE MONTHS OF STATE
ANTITRUST LAW

The debates surrounding baseball's antitrust exemption, from the 1920s through the 1960s, had been about whether the sport would be governed by *federal* antitrust law. States had antitrust law too, but it had been dormant for a very long time. In Illinois, for example, the state legislature had passed an antitrust statute in 1891, a year after the enactment of the federal Sherman Act, but between 1905 and 1960 the state did not file a single enforcement action under the law. Ohio enacted a similar statute in 1898, but its record of enforcement was nearly as sparse. In 1956, when a committee of the New York Bar Association surveyed antitrust activity in 35 states, it discovered that during the previous two decades there had not been *any* suits filed under state antitrust law in 30 of them.[1] State antitrust law existed on paper, but in practice it was nearly defunct.

If there was one business that could be fertile ground for state antitrust law, however, it was baseball, because baseball was immune from federal antitrust law. Back in 1922, when the Supreme Court decided *Federal Baseball Club*, the Court had held that the regulation of baseball was for the states, not for the federal government. Later challengers to the baseball monopoly had not taken up the Court's implicit invitation to rely on state law, because they had focused instead on overturning *Federal Baseball Club*. State antitrust law was still lingering on the books, waiting for some litigant with the motive and the legal skills to use it.

That litigant finally arrived in 1965. It was the government of Wisconsin, which invoked Wisconsin antitrust law in a last-ditch effort to prevent the Milwaukee Braves from moving to Atlanta.[2] Wisconsin's suit forced baseball to confront a challenge it had not faced for half a century, since the pre–*Federal Baseball Club* antitrust cases of the 1910s. There was a brief period in 1966, largely forgotten now, during which the future of baseball was genuinely in doubt, because of the threat posed by state antitrust law.

THE HOMES OF THE BRAVES

The makeup of the National and American Leagues was remarkably stable in the first half of the twentieth century. After 1903, when the Baltimore Orioles moved to New York to become the Highlanders (later the Yankees), there would be no more franchise moves for the next 50 years. By the early 1950s, much of the population had moved west, but the 16 major league baseball teams were still where they had been a half century before. Los Angeles, the fourth largest city in the country, had no major league team, while Boston and St. Louis, cities with less than half of Los Angeles's population, had two teams each. In an era before commercial air travel was a routine part of life, teams traveled between cities on trains. Los Angeles and San Francisco (the eleventh-largest city, with a population slightly less than Boston's) were too far to reach by overnight train. But there were other growing cities within a train trip of existing major league teams that lacked teams of their own. The biggest was Milwaukee.

Meanwhile, there were five major league cities with two or more teams, and Boston was the smallest of the five. The Braves, the city's National League club, were consistently among the worst of the league's eight teams, both in revenue and performance on the field. Between 1901 and 1952, the Braves finished in the top half of the league in per-game attendance only six times, and in the top half of the standings only 13 times. The team reached the World Series only twice, in 1914 and 1948. By 1952, when the Braves finished in seventh place and drew fewer than 3,700 fans per game, owner Lou Perini had seen enough. In 1953, he moved the Braves to Milwaukee.

The move rejuvenated the club. In Boston, the Braves had been last in the league in attendance, but in brand-new Milwaukee County Stadium they led the league in attendance every year between 1953 and 1958. In Boston, they had enjoyed very little success on the field, but in Milwaukee they finished in second place three of their first four years, and then they won the National League pennant in 1957 and 1958. In 1957, led by a young Hank Aaron, the league's most valuable player, the Braves beat the Yankees to win their first World Series since 1914. By moving to Milwaukee, a perennial loser had transformed itself into one of the most successful and popular teams in baseball. Many Milwaukee residents felt that the city had been transformed as well. "The National spotlight has been focused on our city because of the phenomenal success of the Milwaukee Braves," exulted the city's parks commissioner.[3] Milwaukee was in the big leagues.

The Braves' change of fortune in Milwaukee opened the eyes of the other club owners to the profits that could be made from leaving a city with more than one team for a city with none. Within a few years the St. Louis Browns moved to Baltimore, the Philadelphia A's to Kansas City, the New York Giants to San Francisco, and the Brooklyn Dodgers to Los Angeles. Before 1953, there had been five cities with multiple teams, but by 1958 Chicago was the only one left.

The Braves' newfound success did not last long, however. In 1957 the team drew 2.2 million fans to Milwaukee County Stadium, but attendance declined every year thereafter, until it bottomed out in 1962 at 767,000. After finishing first in 1957 and 1958, the Braves gradually settled into mediocrity on the field, finishing no better than fourth after 1961. When the Braves had first arrived in Milwaukee in the spring of 1953, 15,000 people had been waiting at the train station to see them. Thousands of fans had driven to the stadium even before the season started, just to sit in the seats and stare at the field. "Now, nine years later," remarked *Sports Illustrated*, "the long, wild party is over." As the magazine's headline put it, there was "No More Joy in Beertown."[4]

Part of the decline in attendance was simply that the novelty of a major league team had worn off, but the real problem was more fundamental. Television was becoming an ever more important part of baseball. The sale of broadcast rights was a growing source of revenue, and television played an indispensable role in encouraging attendance by cementing the allegiance of local fans by allowing them to follow the team on the road. Milwaukee was smaller than most other major league cities, and its television market was disproportionately smaller, because Milwaukee was hemmed in from all directions. To the south, less than a hundred miles away, was Chicago, a city with two long-established teams that also broadcast their games on television. To the east was Lake Michigan and then the state of Michigan, where residents were already watching telecasts of the Detroit Tigers. The natural television market for a Milwaukee baseball team lay to the north and the west, in Wisconsin, Minnesota, and Iowa. But much of that market was whisked away in 1961, when the American League's Washington Senators moved to Minneapolis, only 300 miles to the northwest. By 1964, Milwaukee had the third-smallest television market among the 20 major league teams. Only in Houston, where a new National League team began play in 1962, and in Kansas City did television broadcasts reach fewer homes. But the Houston Colt .45s (later the Astros) and the Kansas City A's were the only teams for hundreds of miles around. Their television markets had room to grow. Milwaukee had no such prospects.[5]

After the 1962 season, Lou Perini sold the Braves to a group of investors from Chicago led by an insurance executive named William Bartholomay. Bartholomay assured fans that he had no intention of moving the Braves to another city. "This has been and will be a Milwaukee-Wisconsin franchise," he declared in the press release announcing the purchase. "It already has a great baseball tradition and we are tremendously pleased to become part of it." But the Braves continued to lose money. By early 1964, the team's new owners had already hired a consulting firm to survey other cities. Midway through the 1964 season, the Braves announced that they would move to Atlanta the following year. As the club's owners explained to the National League, "the economic situation in Milwaukee is untenable."[6] The city of Atlanta had a population even smaller than Milwaukee's, but it was one of the fastest growing cities in the country, and it sat at the center of an immense untapped television market encompassing the entire southeastern United States.

The news of the Braves' impending move was a serious blow in Milwaukee. "Many thoughtful businessmen and citizens in this community are sick and tired of having our town treated like a backwoods frontier outpost," complained one local magazine. Milwaukee mobilized as best it could. Local business leaders tried to persuade the National League not to allow the Braves to move, but the league was unsympathetic. "The television and radio rights for Braves' games would have to produce more revenue," insisted league president Warren Giles, "if a better 'picture' of a Milwaukee operation is to be created." The leaders of the Milwaukee business community offered to buy the Braves from the Bartholomay group to keep them from moving, but Bartholomay wouldn't sell. (One of these local boosters was a young man in the car-leasing business named Bud Selig, who would later bring major league baseball back to Milwaukee as the principal owner of the Brewers, and who would eventually become commissioner of baseball.) When their offer to purchase the Braves was declined, they tried to buy the Kansas City A's and move them to Milwaukee, but Charlie Finley, the A's owner, wouldn't sell either.[7] Wisconsin's congressional delegation, led by Senator William Proxmire and Milwaukee Representative Henry Reuss, repeatedly threatened to introduce legislation revoking baseball's antitrust exemption if the Braves were allowed to move.[8] But none of these efforts paid off.

The county of Milwaukee was able to buy a little time at the end of the 1964 season by suing the Braves for breach of contract, on the ground that the team's lease for Milwaukee County Stadium did not expire until the end of 1965. The county persuaded a Milwaukee trial judge to issue a temporary restraining order, barring the Braves from applying to the National League for formal permission to move until the county's suit had been decided. "The very minute they vote to approve this transfer, we'll slap an injunction on everybody," declared county attorney George Rice. "We'll chase all these fellows down . . . and we'll slap them all in jail, players and all." The league capitulated. Club owners voted that the Braves should play in Milwaukee for the 1965 season, and then move to Atlanta in 1966.[9]

Given a year's reprieve, local officials began to consider whether the law might offer a way to force the Braves to remain in Milwaukee permanently. Eugene Grosschmidt, chairman of the Milwaukee County Board of Supervisors, threatened an antitrust suit if the National League allowed the Braves to leave. The county was prepared to file "antitrust litigation in an attempt to seek an overruling of the U.S. Supreme Court Case of 1922, with which you are all familiar," Grosschmidt cautioned the owners of National League clubs. "While you might have been advised by your respective attorneys that the likelihood of this happening is minimal," he warned, the law had changed considerably since the Braves had moved to Milwaukee in 1953. "The U.S. Supreme Court has overruled the 'separate but equal' doctrine on racial matters; it has broached the thicket and assumed full jurisdiction over reapportionment; and it has expanded the doctrine of due process to unheralded lengths. These are just a few indicators that the 1922 Decision may not survive if a chain of events transpires, requiring a direct assault upon it."[10]

Behind the scenes, Milwaukee's lawyers were far less optimistic. "We do not believe that the county would prevail in such an antitrust action," explained John MacIver. "It has been held with virtual uniformity that professional baseball is not subject to regulation under the antitrust laws." Just twelve years before, in *Toolson*, arguments against baseball's antitrust exemption had been rejected by the Supreme Court, "and we have no reason to believe they would be accepted today." Even if the county was able to convince the Court to overrule *Toolson*, MacIver advised, a court would be unlikely to order the Braves to stay in Milwaukee, because "a court would find damages an adequate remedy." Rudolph Schoenecker, another Milwaukee lawyer, agreed. An antitrust suit was almost certain to fail, he predicted, but even if the county won, the suit wouldn't keep the Braves in Milwaukee. The city's best hope was to persuade the National League to expand and place a new team in Milwaukee, but "any anti-trust proceeding would only serve to antagonize the very people who can give us a franchise in the first place. And since the outcome of such litigation is so doubtful, there would seem to be no advantage in pursuing that course." When a member of the County Board of Supervisors introduced a resolution authorizing the county to bring an antitrust suit against the Braves, "the reception was awfully cold," Schoenecker reported. The county decided, for the time being, not to sue baseball but rather to attempt to lure some other major league team to move to Milwaukee.[11]

When the county stepped aside, the leaders of the Milwaukee business community looked farther afield. They turned for advice to the Washington, D.C., lawyer Louis Oberdorfer, who had just returned to private practice after four years as assistant attorney general. (He would later serve many years as a federal judge.) Oberdorfer suggested a different legal theory: rather than trying to persuade the Supreme Court to overrule *Federal Baseball Club* and *Toolson*, a suit could be brought against the National League under *state* antitrust law, an area of law that neither *Federal Baseball Club* nor *Toolson* had explicitly addressed. Bronson La Follette, Wisconsin's newly elected attorney general, agreed that the state would be the plaintiff in such a suit. Within weeks, the state of Wisconsin filed suit against the National League and its ten clubs, alleging that the Braves' move from Milwaukee to Atlanta would violate state antitrust law.[12]

Wisconsin's suit was not the first against baseball to be based on state anti-trust law, but it was the first in a very long time. In 1914, Hal Chase had used state antitrust law in his successful defense against the White Sox's suit to pre-vent him from jumping to the Federal League. Chase persuaded a New York trial judge that organized baseball was a monopoly that violated the law of New York. The following year, when the Federal League filed its antitrust suit against organized baseball, it relied on state antitrust law as well as the federal Sherman Act. When the parties reached a settlement after Judge Kenesaw Mountain Landis delayed his decision for an entire year, Landis explained that he would have ruled in favor of the Federal League, but he never said whether he would have based his ruling on state law or federal law. The Balti-more Terrapins' suit against baseball, the one that reached the Supreme Court in 1922, included a state law claim as well as a claim under the Sherman Act, but the Terrapins gave up the state law claim when they lost in the Court of Appeals, so they could get to the Supreme Court more quickly. The Terrapins' suit appears to have been the last one to invoke state antitrust law before Wis-consin revived the tactic. Danny Gardella's 1948 suit against baseball was based entirely on federal law, as were the suits filed in the early 1950s by George Toolson, Walter Kowalski, and Jack Corbett. Relying solely on federal antitrust law made perfect sense at the time, because the conventional wis-dom was that the Supreme Court would overrule *Federal Baseball Club* and hold that baseball was interstate commerce. As a result, no one had tried to use state antitrust law as a weapon against baseball in nearly half a century.

At the National League's midsummer meeting in July, league president Warren Giles reminded the assembled owners that as part of the deal allow-ing the Braves to move to Atlanta, both the Braves and the city of Atlanta had promised to indemnify the league and its clubs for any liabilities arising from the move. The Braves and Atlanta, not the league, would be the ones to pay if the suit was successful. The owners accordingly voted not to revoke the permission they had already granted for the Braves to move to Atlanta for the 1966 season.[13] The stage was set for a battle in court.

The lawsuit was a stroke of genius in one sense. In *Federal Baseball Club*, the Supreme Court had held that baseball was not governed by the federal Sherman Act because it was not interstate commerce. The implication, which would have been clear to all lawyers at the time, was that baseball was properly regulated by the states rather than the federal government. In basing its suit on state law, Wisconsin had a strong argument that it was doing exactly what the Supreme Court had told litigants to do. In *Toolson*, the Court had held that baseball was exempt from the Sherman Act because such was the intent of Congress. But *Toolson* had said nothing about any intent of Congress with respect to state law. Again, by basing a suit on the law of Wisconsin, the state could say that it was bringing precisely the kind of suit the Court had left available.

But if the strategic decision to rely on state antitrust law was a clever one, the suit itself bordered on the absurd. Antitrust law prohibits competitors in an industry from reaching anti-competitive agreements that harm customers—for example, agreements to divide up markets by restricting where firms can locate. Had baseball been completely free of such agreements, any club could have moved to any city at any time, without needing the permission of the other clubs, just as in any other industry. If antitrust law were applied as strictly as possible, it would have been even *easier* for the Braves to leave Milwaukee. It would have been plausible to argue that antitrust law prohibited the league from preventing a club from changing cities, but it was counterintuitive, at the least, to argue that antitrust law *required* a league to prevent a club from changing cities. The state was standing antitrust law on its head. The state contended "that the playing of professional baseball violates state antitrust laws," the Braves' lawyer joked. "So what do they want to do? They want to keep us in Milwaukee where we will continue to violate their antitrust laws."[14] As a logical matter, the suit was hard to understand.

Of course, Wisconsin didn't sue the Braves to clarify the antitrust laws. The suit was the last weapon available in the battle to keep the Braves from moving to Atlanta. More important than logic, from the state's perspective, was that the suit would be filed in Milwaukee, where it would be heard by a Milwaukee judge. The baseball entrepreneur Bill Veeck got right to the point. "I wonder," he mused, "if there is a judge sitting on a Milwaukee bench who would want to go down in local history as the man who let the Braves depart."[15]

Baseball is in trouble

Wisconsin's antitrust suit against the Braves and the National League landed in the courtroom of Judge Elmer W. Roller. It was "hardly a friendly venue," recalled Bowie Kuhn, the New York lawyer who represented the National League (and who would become commissioner of baseball a few years later). "It soon became apparent to defense counsel that Judge Roller had no sympathy for anything we had to say." Behind the judge's back, baseball's lawyers referred to him as "Steam Roller." Before Roller could take any action in the case, the city of Atlanta filed a suit of its own against the Braves, in Atlanta. In December 1965, an Atlanta judge ordered the Braves to play in Atlanta in 1966 on the ground that if they played anywhere else the Braves would breach their contract to use Atlanta's newly built stadium. Judge Roller responded in January with a preliminary injunction of his own, ordering the Braves to play in Milwaukee for the 1966 season. The Braves were now subject to contradictory orders from two hometown judges. "You have two states involved and the Braves seem to be under orders in both states," lamented baseball commissioner William Eckert (figure 7.1). "I don't have an answer for this one." National League owners

Figure 7.1: Baseball Commissioner William Eckert expresses his happiness with the decision of the Wisconsin Supreme Court that baseball did not violate state antitrust law by allowing the Braves to move from Milwaukee to Atlanta. At upper left is a picture of Atlanta Stadium, the Braves' new home. BL-689.2009.9, National Baseball Hall of Fame.

worried that the conflicting court orders would prevent the Braves from playing anywhere at all in 1966, an outcome that would have been financially disastrous for the league.[16]

The trial before Judge Roller began in late February and lasted into early April. It produced 7,000 pages of testimony and nearly 600 exhibits. When it was over, Roller worked frantically to produce his 175-page opinion before opening day of the 1966 baseball season. He missed his self-imposed deadline by one day. Roller announced his decision on April 13, the day after the Braves made their Atlanta debut, a 13-inning 1–0 loss to the Pittsburgh Pirates.

Roller held that the National League and its ten clubs had violated the antitrust law of Wisconsin. The defendants "have combined and conspired among themselves to monopolize the business of Major League professional baseball within the State of Wisconsin," he concluded. This monopoly power "requires the defendants to exercise reasonable control" over the business of baseball, and "to follow reasonable procedures in the issuance of memberships in the National League." He determined that the league's decision to allow the Braves to move to Atlanta, coupled with the league's refusal to grant Milwaukee a replacement team, "was an unreasonable exercise of the monopolistic control of the business of Major League professional baseball," in violation of Wisconsin law. The judge awarded the state damages of $5,000 from each club, but more important, he ordered the National League to place a new team in Milwaukee beginning with the 1967 season. Until the league agreed to do so, he ordered the Braves to play their home games in Milwaukee.[17]

Judge Roller stayed the enforcement of his order pending the defendants' appeal to the Wisconsin Supreme Court, so the Braves remained in Atlanta for the time being. But the decision was a serious threat to baseball. For the first time since the Hal Chase case of 1914, the organization of the game had been held up to the standards of antitrust law, and had been judged illegal. "Baseball is in trouble," intoned the columnist Arthur Daley. Everyone expected the case to be appealed, maybe all the way to the U.S. Supreme Court. If the higher courts upheld Judge Roller's application of state antitrust law to baseball, the entire structure of the game might have to be torn down and rebuilt. Fans of opposing teams had their fun. When the Braves traveled to New York to play the Mets a few days later, one spectator hung a sign above the Braves' dugout reading "Beat Atl'waukee, or is it Milwanta?"[18] Inside the game, however, Roller's decision was no joke.

The lawyers and economists who won the case for Wisconsin celebrated their victory. "You have laid the groundwork for what is likely to be a reversal of previous Supreme Court decisions," the economist Robert Nathan predicted to the lawyer Willard Stafford. "I should think the League would promise the franchise rather than risk the strong prospect of a reversal of earlier court decisions on the monopoly aspects of baseball." Stafford replied that the league and its clubs "have never done anything reasonable yet, so possibly the United States Supreme court will have occasion to weigh your testimony this winter."[19] But they both knew that the victory was not yet complete. First they would have to defend it in the Wisconsin Supreme Court.

The Wisconsin Supreme Court set the case on an expedited schedule. Briefs were filed in May, oral argument took place in June, and the court would issue its opinion in July, as the Atlanta Braves dropped into a tie for eighth place in the ten-team National League, fourteen games behind Pittsburgh. Only a bit more than three months would elapse between Judge Roller's decision and that of the Wisconsin Supreme Court.

The Braves' primary argument before the Wisconsin Supreme Court was that under *Toolson* and *Radovich*, the Supreme Court's sports antitrust cases of the 1950s, baseball was exempt from *all* antitrust law, not just federal antitrust law. Back in the 1920s, under *Federal Baseball Club*, the Court had found that baseball was off-limits to federal regulation because it was not interstate commerce. In the 1950s cases, by contrast, the Court rested baseball's antitrust exemption on a decision by Congress not to subject baseball to antitrust law. That decision, the Braves argued, was evidence of a congressional determination that principles of antitrust law, whether state or federal, were simply unsuited for baseball. The Braves noted that Congress had considered sports antitrust bills every year since *Radovich* but had enacted none of them, a pattern that showed, the Braves contended, that Congress had no desire to change the status quo. Finally, the Braves' brief argued, the application of state antitrust law would make no sense as a policy matter. If a Wisconsin court could require baseball to place a team in Wisconsin, what would prevent courts in other states from doing the same thing? If different states imposed different obligations on the game, the result would be chaos. There had to be a single, uniform, national antitrust policy with respect to baseball. And that policy had already been chosen by Congress: it was to leave baseball immune from the antitrust laws.[20]

The state responded by attacking the first step of this chain of reasoning. Congress had never shown any intention to preempt state law, Wisconsin argued. Where a federal statute and a state statute came into conflict, the federal statute prevailed, but here there was no federal legislation at all with respect to baseball. It was well established that the Sherman Act itself did not preempt state antitrust law, the state pointed out, so it was simply inconceivable that the *inapplicability* of the Sherman Act could preempt state antitrust law. In *Toolson* and *Radovich*, the Supreme Court had said nothing one way or the other about state law. The only thing the Court had ever said about state law and baseball had been back in *Federal Baseball Club*, when the Court had explained that baseball games "are purely state affairs" and were thus properly regulated by the states. In the absence of any explicit statement from either Congress or the Supreme Court that state regulation was preempted, the state concluded, the Wisconsin Supreme Court should follow the normal presumption that the state was free to regulate.[21]

The case presented the Wisconsin Supreme Court with a difficult legal question, but the justices were doubtless aware that they faced a difficult political question as well. They all had to run for reelection, with the exception of Justice Thomas Fairchild, who was nominated to the federal court of appeals by President Lyndon Johnson while the case was pending. Fairchild remained on the state supreme court while awaiting Senate confirmation, but he knew his future was safe. The other six justices had to reckon with the possible cost to their careers of allowing the Braves to leave Wisconsin. For five of the six, this concern was alleviated by the fortuity that they had been elected to the court within the past few years, to serve ten-year terms. They would not have to face the voters for several years after their decision. But this was no protection to the longest serving member of the court, Chief Justice George Currie, whose last election had been way back in 1957. He would have to run for reelection while the Braves' case was fresh in the voters' minds.

Given the political context, it is something of a surprise that four of the seven justices voted to allow the Braves to leave Milwaukee, and that one of them was Chief Justice Currie. (It is less of a surprise that Justice Fairchild was chosen to write the majority opinion.) The Braves' lawyers could not have been heartened by the first few paragraphs of the opinion, because the court's majority agreed with the state that baseball had violated the state's antitrust law. State law followed the federal Sherman Act in prohibiting agreements "in restraint of trade or commerce." Baseball, the majority observed, was built upon just such an agreement, because the American and National Leagues "have complete power to control participation in major league baseball, and to control the number of teams and the location of their home games." The majority determined that the clubs were using this power unlawfully, by in effect conspiring not to engage in business in Wisconsin. The "defendants have, by agreement among themselves to transfer the Braves, terminated very substantial business activity in Wisconsin, and are totally and effectively preventing its resumption at the present time," the majority declared. "On their face, these facts support a conclusion that there is a combination or conspiracy in restraint of trade or commerce."[22]

But the four justices in the majority concluded that the state's antitrust law did not apply to baseball. They did not agree as to exactly why: Justice Fairchild's opinion provided two reasons, and explained that neither of them was supported by all four justices, but Fairchild did not specify how many favored each one. The first reason was that Congress, by refusing to legislate in the wake of *Toolson* and *Radovich*, had shown its intent to immunize baseball from all antitrust scrutiny, whether state or federal. The "silence of Congress in this context demonstrates congressional recognition that league structure and the related agreements and rules are integral parts of baseball as it exists, and that the application of the familiar type of antitrust legislation is inappropriate," Fairchild held. "We deem it unrealistic to interpret these decisions of the supreme court of the United States plus the silence of Congress as creating a mere vacuum in national policy, leaving the states free to regulate the membership of the baseball leagues." By not acting, Congress had implicitly preempted state antitrust law.[23]

The majority's second reason for finding state law inapplicable was that "since baseball operates widely in interstate commerce, the regulation, if there is to be any, must be prescribed by Congress." The extent to which states could regulate interstate commerce was a very old question of constitutional law, one that was governed by a large and ever-growing number of Supreme Court opinions. At bottom, the question was largely about the dangers that might result from inconsistent state laws in any given area. Some of the justices in the majority were worried that "if Wisconsin can reach her problem by application of her antitrust statute, other states would have equal standing to apply other types of regulatory rules and procedures," rules that would presumably favor their home states at the expense of others. This sort of inconsistent state regulation of baseball had not arisen yet, Fairchild conceded, but it was likely enough to arise in the future that "we should not read into the silence of Congress permission for the individual states to regulate these matters."[24]

The three dissenters rejected both rationales. The mere silence of Congress, they argued, "in no way constitutes an expression of intent that Congress exclusively occupy the field or that there shall be no control whatsoever." The more natural inference from Congress's inaction was that the states remained free to regulate baseball. The majority's second reason posed "a more difficult problem," the dissenters acknowledged, but in their view the Supreme Court had allowed states much more latitude to regulate interstate commerce than the majority recognized. State regulation was permissible, even if it had incidental effects on interstate commerce, so long as the state regulated evenhandedly, without preferring local interests. "What the trial court has directed is not the curtailment or burdening of interstate commerce," the dissenters insisted, "but its emancipation from the monopolistic practices of baseball. . . . It can hardly be argued that it is in the national interest to preserve a monopoly that may with impunity flout the laws of the state of Wisconsin and injure its citizens and economy." Any burden that might be incidentally imposed on interstate commerce was outweighed, in their view, by the salutary effect of controlling this monopoly with state law.[25]

Wisconsin had lost its case. Baseball was now free from Judge Roller's order requiring it to put a team in Milwaukee for the 1967 season. Perhaps it was a coincidence, but once the cloud of litigation was lifted, the Atlanta Braves began playing a lot better. The day after the Wisconsin Supreme Court decision was announced, the team was in ninth place. From that day forward, they were the best team in the National League, with a record good enough to lift them into fifth by the season's end. For Chief Justice George Currie, on the other hand, the future was not so bright. Judicial elections are usually not seriously contested, but Currie faced an opponent who missed no opportunity to blame him for allowing the Braves to leave Milwaukee. Currie lost in a landslide. It was the first time in state history that a sitting chief justice had been defeated in an election.[26]

The state's only remaining hope was to persuade the U.S. Supreme Court to hear the case. The state's lawyers knew this would not be an easy task, because the Court accepts only a small percentage of the cases presented to it. They spent considerable time trying to convince the federal government to file an amicus brief in support of their petition to the Court. Arlen Christensen, Wisconsin's deputy attorney general, flew to Washington to meet with Donald Turner, the lawyer in charge of the federal Justice Department's antitrust division. Christensen argued to Turner that the federal government had a strong interest in ensuring that the states were able to enforce their own antitrust laws, only to have Turner respond that the Justice Department's lawyers thought that the Wisconsin Supreme Court had decided the case correctly. The only amicus support Wisconsin could obtain was from Illinois attorney general William Clark, who had no particular interest in regulating baseball, but who was charged with enforcing Illinois's new antitrust act and was worried that his own state's courts would emulate the Wisconsin Supreme Court and find that congressional silence was enough to preempt state antitrust law.[27]

Wisconsin's petition emphasized the paradox created by the decision of the state supreme court. In *Federal Baseball Club*, the U.S. Supreme Court had held that baseball had too little involvement in interstate commerce to be governed by federal antitrust law. But now, the state supreme court had held that baseball had too *much* involvement in interstate commerce to be governed by state antitrust law. "Baseball thus becomes the only non-regulated industry in the United States," the petition pointed out; the game was "completely free to disregard both federal and state antitrust laws." Wisconsin urged the Court to correct this anomaly.[28]

The Supreme Court declined to hear the case, in a manner that raised an interesting question of Supreme Court procedure. There are nine justices, and the Court's normal internal rule is that it takes four of them to vote to hear a case. Three of the justices voted to grant Wisconsin's petition: Hugo Black, William Douglas, and William Brennan. But only eight of the justices voted. Abe Fortas, the newest justice, recused himself from the case. Fortas had joined the Court only a year before. He had previously been a prominent Washington lawyer. He did not explain why he recused himself, but the state's attorneys (some of whom were prominent Washington lawyers as well) assumed it was because his former law firm had represented the commissioner of baseball in other matters, and perhaps even in this very case. Whatever the reason for it, Fortas's recusal provided the state's lawyers with one final argument. If it took four out of nine justices to hear a case, they contended in the state's petition for rehearing, then when only eight justices are available, three should be enough to hear a case.[29] But the Court rejected this argument as well. After a year and a half of litigation, the case was over. Milwaukee had lost the Braves for good.

Baseball had escaped one more antitrust challenge, but just barely. For three months in the spring and summer of 1966, baseball was governed by state antitrust law. And if just one member of the Wisconsin Supreme Court had voted differently, baseball would have lost the case on appeal as well.

What would have happened then? The National League would have been subject to a court order to place a team in Milwaukee for the 1967 season. Other cities desiring major league teams would have been emboldened to file antitrust suits of their own, claiming that the existing clubs were monopolists who were unlawfully conspiring to refuse to do business with them. Players wishing to change teams—whether established stars seeking higher salaries or minor leaguers hoping to advance in a different organization—would have been motivated to sue baseball as well. Baseball would have found itself fending off state law antitrust suits from all directions, just as it had to do with federal antitrust suits in the wake of *Gardella v. Chandler* in the late 1940s and early 1950s.

Had baseball lost in the Wisconsin Supreme Court, on the other hand, the prospect of all this litigation would most likely have prompted the U.S. Supreme Court to hear the case. In the U.S. Supreme Court, baseball would almost certainly have won. If Wisconsin could apply its own antitrust law to require the National League to place a team within the state, the other 49 states would have been able to do just the same. One could easily imagine elected officials from Alaska to Florida filing copycat suits in order to bring major league baseball to their states. What would happen when the Maine Supreme Court ordered the National League to put a team in Portland, or the Hawaii Supreme Court required the American League to put one in Honolulu? The constitutional law regarding the extent to which states could regulate interstate commerce would have been flexible enough for the U.S. Supreme Court to quash all this silliness before it got started. Any doubt on this score would be removed six years later, when the question reached the Supreme Court as a side-issue in the Curt Flood case, and none of the justices favored the application of state antitrust law.

The story has an epilogue that also involves state antitrust law. Baseball added four new teams in 1969, but because of the Braves' lack of commercial success in Milwaukee, as well as the acrimony created by the litigation, baseball bypassed Milwaukee in favor of three cities with smaller populations—San

Diego, Seattle, and Kansas City. (The fourth, Montreal, was larger than Milwaukee.) Fortunately for Milwaukee, however, the American League's new Seattle Pilots were so undercapitalized that they could not last more than a single season in Seattle. Bud Selig, who had been one of the leaders of Milwaukee's effort to keep the Braves, secured baseball's approval to purchase the Pilots and move them to Milwaukee, where they became the Brewers. Only five years after the Braves left, Milwaukee had a team again.

Now Seattle had lost a team. Before the 1970 season began, Seattle, King County, and the state of Washington filed a lawsuit against the American League. One of the suit's two claims was identical to Wisconsin's suit against the Braves: Seattle contended that the American League had violated Washington state antitrust law by allowing the Pilots to move to Milwaukee. (The other claim was a novel one: Seattle alleged that in various public statements, American League officials had promised that a team would play in Seattle for many years to come, that these promises had created a contract between the city and the American League, and that the American League had breached this contract by permitting the Pilots to leave.) After six years of on-again, off-again settlement negotiations, the case went to trial in Everett, Washington, just outside Seattle, in 1976. Seattle's lawyers presented evidence to a jury of Washington residents for four weeks, and that was enough to persuade baseball to give in. The two sides reached a settlement, under which the American League would place a new team in Seattle for the 1977 season. That team, the Mariners, has played in Seattle ever since.[30]

THE CURT FLOOD CASE

The Supreme Court's most recent and best known treatment of baseball's antitrust exemption was the 1972 case *Flood v. Kuhn*. Unlike the previous antitrust challenges to baseball, this one was brought by a star player, the Cardinals' center fielder Curt Flood, who was still near the peak of his career. For that reason the case received much more attention from the press and from baseball fans than the earlier antitrust challenges, which had been brought by obscure players and by a moribund team in a defunct league. The outcome, however, was just the same. The Court acknowledged that baseball's antitrust exemption was a historical vestige that made little sense, but once again the Court reaffirmed that the exemption was so fundamental a part of baseball that it should be overturned only by Congress, not by the courts.[1]

Flood v. Kuhn was roundly criticized when it was decided, and it has continued to be mocked ever since. At the time, the veteran sports columnist Red Smith called the Court's decision a "cop-out" and "a disappointment" that demonstrated that "this Court appears to set greater store by property rights than by human rights." The benefit of hindsight has scarcely changed the prevailing view: the decision has been called "an object lesson in conservative principles run amok," and "an almost comical adherence to the strict rule against overruling statutory precedents."[2] As critiques like these suggest, the case ended up being about much more than a technical point of antitrust law. Race, labor relations, and the generation gap of the 1960s—all were wrapped up in *Flood v. Kuhn*.

A PIECE OF PROPERTY TO BE BOUGHT AND SOLD

Curt Flood (figure 8.1) is best remembered today for his lawsuit, but before the suit he was one of the premier outfielders of the 1960s. He was a Gold Glove winner—one of the three best defensive outfielders in the National League— every year between 1963 and 1969. In four of those seven years he led the National League in putouts by an outfielder. Flood hit for much less power than the leading National League outfielders of the era, players like Hank Aaron, Willie Mays, and Roberto Clemente, but he finished in the top ten in batting average five times during that span, and he played in three all-star games.

Figure 8.1: Curt Flood, one of the premier outfielders of the 1960s, filed an antitrust suit against baseball after he was traded from the Cardinals to the Phillies. He lost in the Supreme Court, but free agency would come to baseball a few years later. BL-5193.70, National Baseball Hall of Fame.

At the end of the 1969 season, when Flood was 31 years old, a veteran of 12 years with the St. Louis Cardinals, he was traded to the Philadelphia Phillies. Being traded to a team in another city had been an occupational hazard for baseball players for nearly a century, of course, because of the reserve clause, which allowed clubs to control the course of their employees' careers indefinitely. There were six other players involved in the Cardinals-Phillies trade, including the Cardinals' catcher Tim McCarver and the Phillies' star first baseman Dick Allen. All six moved to a new city and duly reported to their new teams, like countless players who had been traded in the past. Flood did not.

Instead, Flood did something no star player in the history of the game had done since John Montgomery Ward led the player revolt of 1889–1890. He challenged the economic organization of professional baseball. With the backing of the Major League Baseball Players Association, along with the assistance of Marvin Miller, the Association's executive director, and Richard Moss, the association's general counsel, Flood retained as his lawyer former Supreme Court Justice Arthur Goldberg, who had left the Court only four years before. Goldberg, Miller, and Moss had all worked together at the United Steelworkers union in the 1950s, Goldberg as general counsel, Moss as Goldberg's assistant, and Miller as an economist and negotiator. Goldberg agreed to represent Flood without charge. "The case is of tremendous interest to me," he told Miller, "and I would regard it as *pro bono* work, a public service to upset a series of unconscionable rulings that should have been overturned by courts a long time ago." ("Arthur Goldberg for expenses!" Miller exclaimed in his memoir. "That was like Sandy Koufax pitching for pass-the-hat").[3]

Assisted by this high-powered group of advisors, Flood drafted a letter to baseball commissioner Bowie Kuhn. "Dear Mr. Kuhn," the letter began,

After twelve years in the Major Leagues, I do not feel that I am a piece of property to be bought and sold irrespective of my wishes. I believe that any system which produces that result violates my basic rights as a citizen and is inconsistent with the laws of the United States and of the several States.

It is my desire to play baseball in 1970, and I am capable of playing. I have received a contract offer from the Philadelphia Club, but I believe I have the right to consider offers from other clubs before making any decisions. I, therefore, request that you make known to all the Major League Clubs my feelings in this matter, and advise them of my availability for the 1970 season.

Kuhn responded with a letter that, while stating the law accurately, was a bit tone-deaf to Flood's grievance and to the players' increasing dissatisfaction with the one-sided labor relationship that had traditionally governed the game. Even the letter's salutation—"Dear Curt," in contrast with Flood's "Dear Mr. Kuhn"—drove home the point that the club owners dictated the conditions of the players' employment. "I certainly agree with you that you, as a human being, are not a piece of property to be bought and sold," Kuhn began. "That is fundamental to our society and I think obvious. However, I cannot see its applicability to the situation at hand." Kuhn reminded Flood that he had signed a contract that allowed him to be traded, and that his contracts had included such a clause ever since he began playing. "Under the circumstances," Kuhn concluded, "I do not see what action I can take."[4] Two weeks later, Arthur Goldberg and his colleagues filed an antitrust suit against baseball on Flood's behalf.

Flood knew the lawsuit would mean the end of his baseball career, and that he would be sacrificing a considerable amount of money. His $90,000 salary in 1969 made him one of the highest paid players in the game. On the Cardinals only Bob Gibson earned more, and Gibson was one of the greatest pitchers of all time. Flood turned 32 in January 1970. His skills had already begun to decline, but his lawsuit meant that he would give up at least a few more years of baseball. "I knew in advance that the litigation might take years," Flood explained while the suit was still pending. Even if he won, he realized, he "could not expect my athletic skills to survive prolonged disuse."[5] Only a player who had already grown disenchanted with baseball and who had already contemplated retirement would have made the sacrifice.

The reserve clause had been analogized to slavery for nearly a century, but because Flood was the first African-American player to challenge it, Flood's suit took on racial connotations that had not been part of the earlier antitrust suits. Flood himself did much to encourage those connotations: he famously referred to himself as "a well-paid slave" in an interview with Howard Cosell that aired on ABC's *Wide World of Sports*. But his suit would have acquired cultural resonance as a black-white conflict even without Flood's help, simply because of the surrounding environment. By 1970, high-profile black athletes in all sports were speaking out against the racial makeup of the industry, in which team owners and other powerful officials were typically white, while the performers in their employ were increasingly black. At the 1968 Summer Olympics in Mexico City, Tommie Smith and John Carlos, the gold and bronze medal winners in the 200 meters, raised their fists in the "black power" salute during the medal ceremony. Muhammad Ali, stripped of his heavyweight title for refusing to fight in Vietnam, told *Esquire* magazine that boxers "are just like two slaves in that ring. The masters get two of us big old black slaves and let us fight it out while they bet: 'My slave can whup your slave.'"[6] The primary legal ground for Flood's suit, antitrust law, had nothing to do with race, but the cultural meaning of the suit was much broader than its strict legal basis.

While race relations in the world of sport were in the midst of controversy, so too were labor relations, and that change would also have a profound effect on the substance and the perception of Flood's suit. Baseball players had sporadically tried to organize since the late nineteenth century, with little practical effect, but that changed in 1966, when the Major League Baseball Players Association, under the leadership of new executive director Marvin Miller, began acting as a real labor union.[7] In 1968, the Players Association negotiated its first collective bargaining agreement. By 1970 the Association had obtained the right to impartial arbitration of grievances. The invigorated Players Association was essential to Flood's suit in an immediate practical sense, in that it provided the funding and the legal expertise that allowed the suit to proceed, but it was also important in a less direct way. A decade earlier, without the labor consciousness among players that the association both embodied and promoted, a player like Flood might never have had the confidence to challenge the reserve clause.

The association's executive board, composed of one player representing each team, voted unanimously to support Flood's suit, but the suit was more controversial among the players than the vote suggested. The Boston Red Sox's star outfielder Carl Yastrzemski fired off a letter to Miller complaining about the vote and threatened in the press to resign from the Players Association. The pitcher Jim Bunning, one of the most active members of the Players Association, initially voted as the Phillies' representative to support Flood's suit, but soon reconsidered when he contemplated what might happen if Flood won. "I believe our support should be withdrawn," he urged Miller. "I believe complete abolishment of the reserve system would be harmful to the game of baseball."[8] Despite such dissent, however, the Players Association would continue to back Flood's suit until the end.

The lawsuit filed in January 1970 included three legal theories supporting the claim that the reserve clause was illegal. The first was that the reserve clause violated the federal Sherman Antitrust Act. Arthur Goldberg and his colleagues must have expected that they would lose on this argument in the District Court and the Court of Appeals. The Supreme Court had twice held baseball exempt from the Sherman Act, in *Federal Baseball Club* and again in *Toolson*. But an issue cannot reach the Supreme Court without being litigated up the ladder of lower courts, so the only way to persuade the Supreme Court to reconsider its prior opinions was to accept losses at the two levels below. The second legal theory was that the reserve clause violated the antitrust laws of the states in which baseball teams were located. This was the argument that had lost by a vote of four to three in the Wisconsin Supreme Court. It had never been tried out in a federal court, so Flood's lawyers might have hoped for a more receptive audience. They had to expect, however, that if they won on this claim in a lower court, baseball would appeal, so the issue would get to the Supreme Court win or lose. The third theory was one that drew on the wider cultural perceptions of the lawsuit. Goldberg and his colleagues argued that the reserve clause was a form of slavery inconsistent with the Constitution's Thirteenth Amendment and with the federal statutes forbidding involuntary servitude. Although the reserve clause had been colloquially compared with slavery almost since the clause's inception, this was the first time the claim had been made in court.[9]

The complaint also included a fourth theory that had nothing to do with the reserve clause—an argument that the St. Louis Cardinals, a team owned by the Anheuser-Busch beer company, were violating the antitrust laws by selling only Anheuser-Busch products at their games, and that the New York Yankees, owned by the CBS television network, were violating the antitrust laws because CBS was refraining from bidding for the rights to broadcast games. The complaint alleged that Flood suffered from both practices: if the Cardinals sold other kinds of beer they would earn more money, which could be spent on player salaries, and if CBS bid for the rights to broadcast games, the cost of those rights would increase, and players like Flood would share in the revenues. As it turned out, both allegations were simply wrong. The Cardinals sold other brands of beer at their games, and CBS had in fact bid for broadcast rights. This fourth theory was accordingly dismissed at an early stage of litigation, leaving only the three arguments at the core of the case—that the reserve clause was unlawful under federal antitrust law, state antitrust law, and the Thirteenth Amendment.[10]

~ The case was assigned to Judge Irving Ben Cooper, who had been a federal judge since 1962 and a judge in the New York state courts for many years before that. He was best known for losing his temper in court and screaming at lawyers and witnesses, a habit that led the American Bar Association and the New York County Lawyers Association to oppose his nomination to the federal bench. "He seemed to have a persecution complex," recalled one of his fellow judges. A lawyer who practiced before him testified that she had "seen Judge Cooper screaming in a tantrum on the bench like a baby in a high chair." Cooper promptly scheduled Flood's case for trial. This was a puzzling decision, because the purpose of a trial is to resolve factual disputes between the two sides, but there were no factual disputes in Flood's case. Both sides agreed about the facts. Their disagreement was over the law that should govern those facts. The most charitable interpretation of Cooper's decision to hold a trial is that he was allowing the two sides to present facts that might help the Supreme Court decide whether or not to overrule its prior cases on the antitrust exemption. A less charitable but perhaps more plausible explanation is that a trial—especially a lengthy trial at which many of the witnesses would be famous sports figures—would focus public attention on Judge Irving Ben Cooper.[11]

The lawyers were well aware that the testimony they put on at trial would be relevant, if at all, only for the Supreme Court, so they tailored their strategies accordingly.[12] After Flood told his story and Marvin Miller explained how the reserve clause worked, the remaining witnesses on Flood's side were all intended to demonstrate that baseball could continue as a profitable business even if the reserve clause were modified. The witnesses included the retired players Jackie Robinson and Hank Greenberg, the economist Robert Nathan, the men in charge of the other three major professional sports leagues (Pete Rozelle, commissioner of the National Football League, J. Walter Kennedy, commissioner of the National Basketball Association, and Clarence Campbell, president of the National Hockey League), and Alan Eagleson, the executive director of the National Hockey League Players Association. Arthur Goldberg and his colleagues were laying the groundwork for an appeal to the Supreme Court, where one of their arguments would be that baseball would suffer no harm if the Court overruled its prior cases and held that baseball was governed by the federal antitrust laws.

When it was baseball's turn to present evidence, its lawyers also laid the groundwork for a Supreme Court argument, by putting on witnesses who testified that they had recently made considerable investments in the game in reliance on baseball's antitrust exemption. Francis Dale, the leader of a consortium that had recently purchased the Cincinnati Reds, explained that he would not have put his money into the Reds had he anticipated that a court might remove the exemption. John McHale, who owned 10 percent of the Montreal Expos, said the same about his own investment and added that he would not recommend purchasing a baseball team if baseball were to lose its exemption. Bob Reynolds, part owner of the California Angels, agreed. This was testimony that had no bearing on any issue Judge Cooper would have to decide. It was the cornerstone of an eventual argument before the Supreme Court that it would be unjust to revoke baseball's antitrust exemption, in light of the enormous investments that had been made in reliance on the exemption's continued existence.

Cooper issued his opinion in August 1970, toward the end of Flood's first season out of baseball. The outcome was no surprise. If Cooper had been tempted to place baseball under the federal antitrust laws, that temptation was removed in July, when the Court of Appeals for the Second Circuit (which sat above Cooper in the hierarchy of federal courts) held itself bound by the Supreme Court's prior decisions. The occasion was an antitrust suit filed by two American League umpires, who alleged that their firing was a violation of the Sherman Antitrust Act. "We freely acknowledge our belief that *Federal Baseball* was not one of Mr. Justice Holmes' happiest days," Judge Henry Friendly explained. Friendly also acknowledged "that the rationale of *Toolson* is extremely dubious and that, to use the Supreme Court's own adjectives, the distinction between baseball and other professional sports is 'unrealistic,' 'inconsistent' and 'illogical.'" Nevertheless, Friendly concluded, "we continue to believe that the Supreme Court should retain the exclusive privilege of overruling its own decisions. . . . While we should not fall out of our chairs with surprise at the news that *Federal Baseball* and *Toolson* had been overruled, we are not at all certain the Court is ready to give them a happy despatch."[13] In Flood's case, Cooper quoted Judge Friendly's opinion at length and simply explained that "baseball remains exempt from the antitrust laws unless and until the Supreme Court or Congress holds to the contrary."[14]

The state antitrust claim allowed Cooper more discretion, because there was no Supreme Court precedent to dictate a result. Here Cooper agreed with both of the rationales employed by the majority of the Wisconsin

Supreme Court in the Milwaukee Braves' case a few years earlier. If Congress intended baseball to be exempt from federal antitrust law on the ground that the sport had relied on such an exemption for many years, Cooper suggested, it would be unlikely that Congress would have intended the game to be governed by state antitrust law instead. Even if that were wrong, Cooper added, the need for uniform law throughout the United States would counsel against allowing each state to apply its own antitrust law as it saw fit.

Cooper also rejected the argument that the reserve clause was a form of slavery inconsistent with the Thirteenth Amendment and the federal statutes barring involuntary servitude. No one was forcing Flood to play baseball, Cooper reasoned. He had every right to retire or to take up some other kind of work. He might make less money, but that would be his own choice, and it was the lack of choice that was the essential element of slavery. Flood had lost the first round. Few could have been surprised.

While the case was appealed, Flood returned to baseball, but without success. The Washington Senators traded three marginal players to the Phillies for Flood, and signed him for one year for $110,000, a very high salary for the era. Flood desperately needed the money. After a year out of baseball, however, his skills and his physical condition had deteriorated too much. After managing only seven singles in thirteen games, he retired for good.

While Flood floundered on the field, the Court of Appeals affirmed Judge Cooper's decision in all respects. Baseball's exemption from federal antitrust law may have been illogical, Judge Sterry Waterman wrote, but only the Supreme Court or Congress could revoke it. State antitrust law could not govern baseball either, because of the dangers of inconsistent state commands. "We readily acknowledge that plaintiff [Flood] is caught in a most frustrating predicament which defendants [baseball] have zealously seized upon with great perspicacity," Waterman noted. "On the one hand, the doctrine of stare decisis binds the plaintiff because of an initial holding that baseball is not 'interstate commerce' within the Sherman Act, and, on the other hand, after there have been significant changes in the definition of 'interstate commerce,' he is now told that baseball is so uniquely interstate commerce that state regulation cannot apply." But that dilemma was the fault of the Supreme Court, Waterman concluded, and the Supreme Court was the only court with the power to correct it. The reserve clause was not slavery, the Court of Appeals concluded, because Flood had the option not to play. Judge Leonard Moore supplemented the court's short opinion with a lengthy concurrence in which he traced the history of baseball and the antitrust exemption, in order to argue that the exemption should remain in place. Baseball had acquired "such a national standing that only Congress should have the power to tamper with it," Moore declared. "If baseball is to be damaged by statutory regulation, let the congressman face his constituents the next November and also face the consequences of his baseball voting record."[15]

The stage was finally set for the Supreme Court to reconsider baseball's antitrust exemption, but Arthur Goldberg and his colleagues first had to persuade the Court to hear the case. That task was even more difficult than usual in the fall of 1971, because Justices Hugo Black and John Harlan, both gravely ill, retired in September. Both would die before the end of the year. Their successors, Lewis Powell and William Rehnquist, would not be confirmed until January, so the Court had to work with only seven justices. It takes the vote of four justices for the Court to hear a case, which meant that Flood needed four of seven rather than the usual four of nine. He got four, but just barely. When the initial vote was taken, only two justices—William Douglas and William Brennan—wanted to hear the case.[16] Douglas circulated a draft of a dissenting opinion from the decision not to hear the case, in which he emphasized how much the law had changed since *Federal Baseball Club*. Congress had not spoken, he acknowledged, but, he insisted, "I do not see how the unbroken silence of Congress can prevent us from correcting our own mistakes."[17] Douglas's draft dissent was enough to persuade Warren Burger and Byron White to change their minds and become the third and fourth votes to hear the case. Baseball's antitrust exemption would come before the Court one more time.

Retrospective operation

No one outside the Court knew which justices had voted to hear the case and which had not, and the Court's personnel had turned over almost completely in the nineteen years since *Toolson*, so the outcome was impossible to predict. William Douglas was the only justice remaining who had participated in *Toolson*, and he had sided with the majority in reaffirming baseball's antitrust exemption, so baseball's lawyers may have erroneously counted him as a vote in their favor. On the other hand, just a few months earlier

Douglas had taken two actions that seemed to point in the opposite direction. In January, Douglas had been the only member of the Court to dissent from the decision not to hear the *Salerno* case, the umpires' antitrust litigation against baseball. In March, Douglas had issued an in-chambers opinion in favor of the 21-year-old basketball star Spencer Haywood. Haywood had signed a contract with the Seattle SuperSonics of the National Basketball Association, in violation of an NBA rule that prohibited teams from signing any player less than four years after his high school class had graduated. When the NBA threatened to disallow the contract, Haywood filed an antitrust suit against the NBA alleging that the rule amounted to an unlawful group boycott under the Sherman Act. The trial court granted a preliminary injunction allowing Haywood to play for the SuperSonics while the litigation proceeded. When that injunction was stayed by the Court of Appeals, Haywood appealed to Justice Douglas for an order lifting the stay and reinstating the injunction. (Individual justices have the authority to decide such matters, and Douglas was the justice with responsibility for the Ninth Circuit, which included his home state of Washington.) Douglas ruled in favor of Haywood and lifted the stay. "The decision in this suit," he wrote, "would be similar to the one on baseball's reserve clause which our decisions exempting baseball from the antitrust laws have foreclosed." He explained his view that "this group boycott issue in professional sports is a significant one."[18] Strictly speaking, Douglas's decision was a narrow procedural ruling preserving the status quo pending litigation. Its only effect was to allow Haywood to play for the SuperSonics in the 1971 playoffs. (As it turned out, the SuperSonics did not qualify for the playoffs. Haywood and the NBA settled their lawsuit shortly after Douglas's decision.) To lawyers reading the tea leaves, however, Douglas's opinion, combined with his interest in hearing the *Salerno* case, must have suggested that Douglas was willing to reconsider the baseball precedents.

William Brennan was the only other Justice who had been in office long enough to have participated in *Radovich*, the 1957 case declining to extend the antitrust exemption to football. Brennan had been one of the dissenters in *Radovich*; he would have treated football and baseball identically. But that knowledge offered little insight into whether Brennan would be willing to overrule the Court's baseball cases. Byron White was the only justice who had been in the sports business: he was a star running back in the NFL for three years before entering the Navy during World War II. White's career provided little guidance as to his views in the *Flood* case, however. He might have been expected to have sympathies for professional athletes, but he might just as well have been thought to have some attachment to the traditions of professional sports, one of which was the reserve clause. Some of the other justices were baseball fans, none more so than Harry Blackmun, who kept a baseball encyclopedia behind his desk and loved to talk about the game.[19] Again, though, this was scant guidance, because one could simultaneously be a fan of players and of the larger world of organized baseball, and those instincts would pull in opposite directions. In trying to handicap the case, the lawyers were in the dark.

Flood's lawyers had to make two basic points in their argument. The easy one was to show that baseball was clearly a form of interstate commerce, a big business like any other, and that the Court's 1922 decision to the contrary in *Federal Baseball Club* was thus no longer correct. The much more difficult point in Flood's argument was to persuade the Court that it would be possible to subject baseball to the antitrust laws, after the game had been exempt for so long, without unfairly harming the club owners. Arthur Goldberg and his colleagues accordingly devoted much of their brief to arguing that the owners had not truly relied on the exemption in making investments in the game. "Upon what have Baseball investors actually 'relied'?" the brief asked. It was hardly reasonable for team owners to believe that a 1922 decision meant they need not worry about engaging in anticompetitive practices half a century later. There was always a chance that either Congress or the Court would apply the antitrust laws to baseball. All that an investor could rely upon, the lawyers contended, was his estimate of baseball's ability to lobby Congress to preserve the exemption. But "wishful thinking about lobbying skill, however well-advised, is simply not 'reliance' in a jurisprudential sense," the brief argued. "It is opportunism."[20]

Removing the exemption, the brief continued, would not harm the owners in any event, because the game could be just as successful without such severe restrictions on a player's freedom to choose his employer. The other professional sports were all subject to the antitrust laws, and they were doing just fine. Indeed, the brief noted, two of the owners of baseball teams were simultaneously investors in professional football teams, in Cincinnati and Los Angeles, despite their awareness that football, unlike baseball, was governed by antitrust law. As Goldberg and his colleagues concluded this section of the brief, "so much for 'reliance.'"[21]

As a final attack on the claim that it would be unfair to revoke the antitrust exemption now, after the owners had made investments in reliance on it, Flood's brief argued that the Court could provide that its decision would have prospective effect only—that is, that the Court had the power to hold that only baseball's future actions, not anything done in the past, would be governed by antitrust law.[22] The lawyers had to tread lightly here, because the argument opened up a fundamental question about the nature of the legal system, one that the Court was unlikely to be eager to address. If a court could announce a change in the law that would take effect only in the future, did that mean that judges were making the law?

The traditional conception of the judge's role was that judges *found* the law. They did not make it. As the eighteenth-century English judge William Blackstone put it, in the classic formulation of this view, a judge was "not delegated to pronounce a new law, but to maintain and expound the old one." Judges sometimes had to overrule past decisions that no longer made sense, but it followed from this idea of the judge's role that in such cases the judge was not *changing* the law, but merely elaborating a better understanding of what the law had always been. The most well known statement of this conclusion was again from Blackstone. "The subsequent judges do not pretend to make a new law, but to vindicate the old one from misrepresentation," Blackstone explained. "For if it be found that the former decision is manifestly absurd or unjust, it is declared, not that such a sentence was *bad law*, but that it was *not law*." The logical implication was that when a court overruled a past decision, the new understanding of the law would apply to everyone, even to people who had taken actions in reliance on the old understanding. Court decisions applied retroactively to conduct that took place before the decisions had been announced. "I know of no authority in this court to say that ... decisions shall make law only for the future," Justice Oliver Wendell Holmes declared in 1910. "Judicial decisions have had retrospective operation for near a thousand years."[23]

Over time, however, this traditional view came under pressure from a couple of directions. Lawyers gradually came to think of judges not as finders of law but as interstitial makers of law, filling in the gaps where legislatures had failed to provide a rule. Meanwhile there were always occasional cases in which courts held that new rules would not apply retroactively, because it seemed unfair or impractical to apply them to conduct that had taken place when the rule was different. By the mid-twentieth century, it was clear that in exceptional cases courts had the power to change the law prospectively. In a 1969 case, for example, the Supreme Court determined that a municipal utility had issued bonds in an unconstitutional manner, because the bond issue had been approved by an electorate restricted to people who paid property tax. Many other utilities had issued bonds in just the same way. To declare all those bonds void, and thus valueless, would have been a hardship to all the people who had purchased them. The Court accordingly declared that "we will apply our decision in this case prospectively." The general rule, the Court explained, was that "where a decision of this Court could produce substantial inequitable results if applied retroactively, there is ample basis in our cases for avoiding the injustice or hardship by a holding of nonretroactivity." The Court did the same with some of its major criminal procedure decisions of the 1960s. To give full retroactive effect to the new requirement of *Miranda* warnings, for instance, would have been to reverse the convictions of thousands of criminals who had been found guilty before *Miranda* warnings were invented. Rather than opening up the prisons, the Court held that *Miranda* would be applied prospectively only.[24]

Curt Flood's lawyers argued that the Court could do the same with baseball's antitrust exemption. If the obstacle to abolishing the exemption was that club owners had made irreversible investments in reliance on it, they suggested, the appropriate response was to abolish the exemption prospectively. The lawyers must have realized, however, that they were skating on thin ice. To change the law prospectively was to drop all pretense that judges were finders rather than makers of law, and that was still a bit uncomfortable for a profession whose formal discourse required judges to speak and write as if they were merely discovering a law that already existed. Worse, the cases applying new rules prospectively normally applied them to the parties in the case. What was "prospective" about prospective overruling was that the new rule would not be applied to *others* who had relied on it. Flood's lawyers were urging something even more out of step with the traditional judicial role—that the Court should change the law and not even apply that change to the past conduct of the parties before it. That looked and felt like legislation, not statutory interpretation. It was not clear whether the Court even had the power to do what Flood's lawyers were asking. The authority given to federal courts by the Constitution has always been interpreted to mean that federal courts cannot decide abstract questions or hypothetical cases. If the Court announced a rule but did not apply that rule to the parties before it, would the Court improperly be deciding an abstract question? There was no obvious answer.[25] The suggestion that the Court could overrule *Federal Baseball Club* and *Toolson* prospectively sounded like a simple one, but there was quicksand just below its surface.

Most of Flood's brief was taken up with the argument that the Court should abolish baseball's exemption from federal antitrust law. The lawyers devoted only a few pages to the other issue in the case, whether baseball was subject to state antitrust law, and they abandoned their third argument, that the reserve clause was a form of slavery. The slavery claim had fared miserably in the lower courts, and its prospects at the Supreme Court were no better. The success of the state antitrust claim depended in large part on the success of the federal claim. If the Court decided to stick with its view that Congress intended baseball to be exempt from federal antitrust law, the Court would also be likely to find that Congress did not intend baseball to be governed by state antitrust law instead. On the other hand, if the Court could be persuaded that baseball should be governed by federal antitrust law, Flood would win the case, and there would be little need to obtain a ruling that state law applied as well. The lawyers nevertheless repeated the arguments they had made in the lower courts. Congress had never expressed any intention to insulate baseball from state law, they pointed out. Nor would state antitrust law be an insupportable burden on interstate commerce, they contended, because there was no evidence that the law of one state would come into conflict with the law of another.[26]

The brief concluded with a rhetorical flourish invoking the abandoned slavery argument. Although Flood's claim "has not been rested in this Court on the national policies against slavery and peonage cited below, these policies do add urgency to his suit," the lawyers declared. "For it is not right for this country to tolerate in any area of its national life, and perhaps particularly in what professes to be its national sport, arrangements which deny human beings the dignity and freedom guaranteed all Americans by Constitution, statute, and our ideals. The time has come to bring the national sport into the national mainstream."[27]

Baseball countered with two primary arguments, one old and one new. The old one was that baseball had relied on the antitrust exemption in building the game. In the years since *Toolson*, the clubs had continued "to invest millions of dollars in player contracts ... to build private stadiums and enter into long term leases on public stadiums ... to acquire new franchises at costs reaching ten million dollars each . . . and to make numerous other commitments, all in reliance upon baseball's antitrust exemption and in particular upon the validity of baseball's reserve system." To whisk away the exemption now, after all this investment, would be to upset the settled expectations of those who financed the game. "The fact is," baseball's brief insisted, "that nothing could be more central to investor concern than baseball's antitrust status." Meanwhile the exemption had no adverse consequences for antitrust policy in any other business, baseball pointed out, because the Court had been careful to limit the exemption to baseball. As Congress had repeatedly considered changing the law in this area, but had never done so, the brief argued, the logical inference was that Congress approved of the status quo. A change in the law now, after all these years, would "directly threaten the very structure of the game. Almost every traditional element" of baseball "would be vulnerable to costly and disruptive litigation." Only Congress could bring about orderly change, the brief concluded, because "there is no technique of prospective overruling" that would not subject baseball to retroactive liability.[28]

The new argument was that baseball's antitrust exemption had another basis, apart from the Court's decisions in *Federal Baseball Club* and *Toolson*. Now that baseball players had formed an effective labor union and were engaging in collective bargaining, baseball argued, federal labor law exempted the reserve clause from antitrust scrutiny because it was a mandatory subject of collective bargaining and because the union had agreed to it in the most recent contract. Having consented to the reserve system in negotiating the contract, baseball's brief contended, the players could not turn around and challenge the system as a violation of antitrust law. The point was amplified by the Yale law professor Ralph Winter in an article published just as the briefs were being filed. An employee who was a member of a labor union could not complain that he was denied the opportunity to negotiate an individual employment contract, Winter pointed out; that was precisely the function of a union, to bargain on behalf of all the employees together. This was an argument with particular resonance for Arthur Goldberg, not just because he had spent most of his career as a union lawyer, but because only a few years before, toward the end of his short tenure as a Supreme Court Justice, he had written the leading opinion making this very point. Baseball's lawyers were able to throw his words right back at him. Goldberg had declared that "collective bargaining activity concerning mandatory subjects of bargaining under the Labor Act is not subject to the antitrust laws." The history of federal labor policy made clear, Goldberg had written, "that Congress intended to foreclose judges and juries from roaming at large in the area of collective bargaining, under cover of the antitrust laws, by inquiry into the purpose and motive of the employer and union bargaining on mandatory subjects."[29] One can almost hear baseball's lawyers chuckling as they used Goldberg's own words as a weapon against his client.

Baseball's brief wound up with a short treatment of the state antitrust issue. The brief endorsed both rationales of the Wisconsin Supreme Court—that Congress intended baseball to be exempt from all antitrust law, not just federal law, and that allowing each state to regulate as it saw fit would result in chaos. "In fact," baseball noted, "there has never been any state antitrust regulation of baseball." Wisconsin had been the only state to try, "and that attempt spawned nothing but conflict and disruption." Regulation had to be uniform, baseball's lawyers argued, and the only way to achieve uniformity consistent with the intent of Congress was to exempt baseball completely.[30]

Baseball's labor argument got under Arthur Goldberg's skin. "The realistic view of the matter," he complained to a friend, "is that the Baseball Owners are not willing to bargain on the reserve clause at all but are using the argument in the hope of retaining their immunity under the antitrust laws." He grumbled that "the Owners know full well that the players are unwilling to strike on the issue, and, as a result, collective bargaining on the subject would be futile." His reply brief focused primarily on what it described as "the so-called labor exemption," which Goldberg insisted had no bearing on the legality of the reserve clause. "Could United States Steel, for example, compel the Steelworkers to negotiate over a proposal that open hearth men be forbidden to seek employment with any other steel company, anywhere in the world?" the brief asked. "Could IBM obligate its engineers to negotiate over a proposal that they forego—for life—the alternative of employment with any other employer of engineers anywhere in the world?" Of course not, Goldberg argued, because the reserve clause was without parallel in any other labor context. Nor had the players' union agreed to it, the brief declared; the reserve clause had been imposed on the players long before the union even existed. "The reserve clause is an indentured servitude," Goldberg concluded. Until it was declared unlawful, "it will continue to be a blight upon our national sport."[31]

Oral argument took place at the Supreme Court in late March 1972. The players were preparing for what would be the first work stoppage in baseball history, over the method by which the club owners funded the players' pension. The strike would last throughout the first two weeks of April, causing each team to miss between six and nine games, until the owners capitulated. Curt Flood had retired from baseball. He was working in a bar on the island of Majorca, off the coast of Spain. The argument was Arthur Goldberg's return to the Supreme Court, seven years after stepping down to become U.S. ambassador to the United Nations. Goldberg's presence "presented a little bit of a problem for the Court," Justice Blackmun recalled many years later. "How do we address Mr. Justice Goldberg? Do we call him Mr. Justice, and if we do, is that an act of disfavor to the people on the other side, because it gives him a title. We can't call him Arthur, although, among ourselves, we're always on a first name basis. So I think we all ended up being rather neuter and spoke only of addressing him as counsel, or something like that."[32] Chief Justice Warren Burger used a clipped "Mr. Goldberg" to indicate that the argument should begin.[33]

Goldberg gave one of the worst performances anyone present had ever seen. Like Curt Flood, his best years were behind him. The purpose of oral argument is to provide a succinct statement of why one's side should win and to answer the justices' questions, but Goldberg wasted most of his allotted 30 minutes with a halting, bumbling account of the facts of the case, while the Court looked on in puzzled silence. "Lincolnesque brevity and tight organization are not Goldberg's fortes," joked one journalist. "In the time it took him to wind up and throw the first pitch his half-hour inning was over." Justice Brennan cringed in embarrassment for his friend and former colleague. "Too much time on facts," Justice Blackmun wrote in his notes. When the Court finally began to ask Goldberg questions, as much out of sympathy as a desire to learn the answers, Goldberg was unable to provide coherent responses. "It was one of the worst arguments I'd ever heard—by one of the smartest men I've ever known, in the setting where he should have been a super advocate," recalled his co-counsel Daniel Levitt. "It was like he choked." Goldberg (figure 8.2) knew it. He told Blackmun afterwards that he would never argue in the Supreme Court again.[34]

Baseball's argument, presented by Bowie Kuhn's former law partner Louis Hoynes, was far more professional. Hoynes provided a short summary of baseball's argument, fielded questions from the justices, and sat down. Unlike Goldberg, Hoynes had helped his client's cause.

Figure 8.2: Former Supreme Court justice Arthur Goldberg represented Curt Flood in his antitrust suit against baseball. His appearance before his former colleagues did not go well. A720-5, Lyndon Baines Johnson Library.

When the argument was over, the justices retreated to their conference room to discuss the case. There was nothing left for the lawyers to do but wait for a decision.

A SENTIMENTAL JOURNEY

At their conference, the justices spoke in the traditional order of seniority.[35] Warren Burger declared that *"Toolson* is probably wrong," but he did not indicate whether he thought the Court should overrule it. Burger often annoyed his colleagues by waiting to state his views until the others had spoken, so that he could vote with the majority and keep the prerogative of assigning the majority opinion. (The job of assigning the opinion customarily falls to the senior justice in the majority.) William Douglas was the first to cast a clear vote. In his view the Sherman Act should govern baseball, because "baseball, football, and basketball should be treated alike." Douglas had been part of the *Toolson* majority, but, as he later explained, "I have lived to regret it."[36] William Brennan agreed. He had dissented in *Radovich*, he reminded his colleagues, and was willing to overrule *Toolson* and subject baseball to federal antitrust law. Potter Stewart was the first to side with baseball. "Congress knew about this and did nothing," he argued. The "omission is not inadvertent. This is tantamount to an explicit congressional exception of baseball from the antitrust laws." Stewart wanted to "leave it to Congress to decide." Byron White and Thurgood Marshall quickly agreed with Stewart. After six Justices had spoken, the vote was three for baseball, two for Flood, and one, Burger, still on the fence.

Harry Blackmun, the next to speak, had not yet come to a firm view. Blackmun was only in his second year on the Court. A chronically insecure man, he referred to himself as "old number three" because President Nixon had nominated him only after the Senate rejected Nixon's two previous nominees, Clement Haynsworth and G. Harrold Carswell. Back in 1922, when the Court decided *Federal Baseball Club*, "baseball was a sport, not a business," Blackmun declared. "Today it is a business." He was certain that it would be "intolerable to apply state laws," but he was not sure whether federal antitrust law should apply. He tentatively voted that baseball should retain its antitrust exemption. Lewis Powell then provided a surprise: he announced that he could take no part in the case, because he owned stock in Anheuser-Busch, the company that owned the St. Louis Cardinals.[37] With the vote at four to two in baseball's favor, Powell's recusal created the possibility of a tie, if Warren Burger and William Rehnquist sided with Flood. But Rehnquist voted for baseball. Twenty years earlier, as a law clerk to Justice Robert Jackson when the Court decided *Toolson*, Rehnquist's instinctive preference had been to keep antitrust law out of baseball, and that view had not changed.[38] "Congress has had the chance to act and has not," he explained. He would "affirm on *Toolson*." Rehnquist was the fifth vote to reaffirm baseball's antitrust exemption. With the result no longer in doubt, Burger must have astonished his colleagues when he cast his vote for Flood. The tally was five to three in favor of baseball.

Stewart, the senior justice in the majority, assigned the opinion to Blackmun (figure 8.3). This may have been because Blackmun was the most tentative of the five justices in the majority. If Blackmun were to change his mind, as he might after reading an opinion worded too strongly by another justice, there would no longer be a majority. Then again, the justices all knew Blackmun was a big baseball fan, and Stewart may simply have been doing Blackmun a favor

Figure 8.3: Justice Harry Blackmun, a lifelong baseball fan, began the Supreme Court's opinion in *Flood v. Kuhn* with a long and idiosyncratic history of the game, in a section of the opinion so embarrassing that two of his colleagues refused to join it. LC-USZ62-60137, Prints and Photographs Division, Library of Congress.

by letting him write on a topic in which he had a great interest. Blackmun himself thought so. Many years later he told an interviewer that he had been assigned the opinion "because I had probably talked too much baseball during the discussion." Stewart thought the best way to handle the case was to follow the strategy the Court had used twenty years earlier in *Toolson*. "Harry, do it very briefly," he told Blackmun. "Write a per curiam and we'll get rid of it."[39]

Blackmun did the opposite. After weeks of work, he informed Stewart that he was about to circulate a lengthy opinion. "I must confess to you that I have done more than merely follow *Toolson* with a bare peremptory paragraph," he told Stewart. "The case, for me, proved to be an interesting one, and I have indulged myself by outlining the background somewhat extensively."[40] Blackmun, like the other justices, often delegated the task of writing opinions to his law clerks, but this one he handled himself.

Blackmun's opinion began not with the usual statement of the facts of the case, but rather with a long, rhapsodic, and highly idiosyncratic history of baseball, written in a style rarely seen in judicial opinions. He started with the 1846 game in Hoboken, New Jersey, that is sometimes considered the origin of the sport. He moved on to the first successful professional team, the Cincinnati Red Stockings, in 1869, the formation of the National League in 1876, and a variety of other milestones. In the portion of the opinion that would attract the most criticism, Blackmun recalled "the many names, celebrated for one reason or another, that have sparked the diamond and its environs and that have provided tinder for recaptured thrills, for reminiscence and comparisons, and for conversation and anticipation in-season and off-season." His first draft then listed the names of 74 former players, in no apparent order. Most, like Ty Cobb and Babe Ruth, were well known. Others, including Fred Snodgrass and Hans Lobert, were not. They had been interviewed in Lawrence Ritter's *The Glory of Their Times*, a then-recent bestseller about the early days of baseball. "The list seems endless," Blackmun exclaimed. When it was over, he provided references to some of the literature about baseball. In footnotes, he included parts of a poem by Grantland Rice and all of Franklin Pierce Adams's *Baseball's Sad Lexicon*, the poem with the famous line "Tinker to Evers to Chance." Blackmun concluded this introductory section of the opinion by mentioning "all the other happenings, habits, and superstitions about and around baseball that made it the 'national pastime.'" Most court opinions are straightforward applications of the law to the facts, but the long first part of *Flood v. Kuhn* was an ode to baseball.[41]

The rest of Blackmun's opinion was more conventional. Once he had demonstrated his love for baseball, Blackmun described the facts giving rise to Flood's lawsuit. He marched through the Court's precedents, from *Federal Baseball Club* to *Toolson* to *International Boxing Club* to *Radovich*. He summarized the legislative proposals that had all died in Congress. Finally, after many pages of preliminary material, he reached the legal issue the Court had to decide. "Professional baseball is a business and it is engaged in interstate commerce," Blackmun declared. Its exemption from the antitrust laws was "an exception and an anomaly." Nevertheless, "the aberration is an established one, . . . one that has survived the Court's expanding concept of interstate commerce. It rests on a recognition and an acceptance of baseball's unique characteristics and needs." Congress had repeatedly considered legislation that would have applied antitrust law to baseball, but had not enacted any of it. "Congress as yet has had no intention to subject baseball's reserve system to the reach of the antitrust statute," Blackmun wrote. "This, obviously, has been deemed to be something other than mere congressional silence and passivity."[42]

Blackmun then turned to the crux of the case. "The Court has expressed concern about the confusion and the retroactivity problems that inevitably would result with a judicial overruling of *Federal Baseball*," he noted. "It has voiced a preference that if any change is to be made, it come by legislative action that, by its nature, is only prospective in operation." Baseball's lawyers had convinced Blackmun that it would be unfair to take the antitrust exemption away after team owners had made investments in reliance on it. "The slate with respect to baseball is not clean," Blackmun observed. "Indeed, it has not been clean for half a century. . . . We continue to be loath, 50 years after *Federal Baseball* and almost two decades after *Toolson*, to overturn those cases judicially when Congress, by its positive inaction, has allowed those decisions to stand for so long and, far beyond mere inference and implication, has clearly evinced a desire not to disapprove them legislatively." The Court would accordingly "adhere once again to *Federal Baseball* and *Toolson*." Blackmun acknowledged the oddity that only baseball, but no other sport, was exempt from antitrust law. "If there is any inconsistency or illogic in all this, it is an inconsistency and illogic of long standing that is to be remedied by the Congress and not by this Court," he concluded. "If we were to act otherwise, we would be withdrawing from the conclusion as to congressional intent made in *Toolson* and from the concerns as to retrospectivity therein expressed."[43]

Blackmun's opinion quickly disposed of the remaining issues. He agreed with the lower courts that baseball could not be governed by state antitrust law, because of the need for nationwide uniformity and the policy he had already imputed to Congress of exempting baseball from antitrust scrutiny. The Court's decision to reaffirm the exemption meant that it did not need to consider baseball's argument that the reserve clause was a mandatory subject of collective bargaining and was thus exempt from antitrust law on that ground.[44]

Some of Blackmun's colleagues were appalled—not with the opinion's legal analysis, which was unobjectionable, if plodding and longwinded—but with the paean to baseball that occupied the opinion's first several pages.

Byron White offered what he called a "gentle suggestion that you omit Part I." Blackmun declined. In the final published version of *Flood v. Kuhn*, White pointedly noted that he joined all of Blackmun's opinion except Part I. Warren Burger switched his vote to side with baseball, but he too refused to join Part I. "In part one of that opinion I indulged in a sentimental journey of the history of baseball," Blackmun later recalled. "Two of my colleagues wouldn't join part one. And I think they thought perhaps it was beneath the dignity of the Court to indulge in a sentimental journey about baseball." Other members of the Court had some fun with Blackmun's list of great players of the past. Potter Stewart, who was from Cincinnati, called Blackmun to ask why he had not included the Reds' pitcher Eppa Rixey. "You know what a famous player he was for the Cincinnati Reds," Stewart joked. "If you will add him, I'll join your opinion." Blackmun added Rixey. As a prank, one of Rehnquist's clerks suggested the pitcher Camilo Pascual, who had recently retired after a long career with the Washington Senators and Blackmun's beloved Minnesota Twins. Blackmun decided Pascual was not sufficiently distinguished. The always-polite Lewis Powell told Blackmun that he had "read with fascinated interest your splendid opinion. It is a classic summary of the history of organized baseball which will delight all old fans—as it did me. I had no idea you were such an expert on the game."[45]

William Douglas circulated a sharp dissent a few days later, with some thinly veiled mockery of Blackmun's opinion. "The beneficiaries of the *Federal Baseball Club* decision are not the Babe Ruths, Ty Cobbs, and Lou Gehrigs," Douglas observed, referring to three of the first seven players on Blackmun's list. "Baseball is today big business that is packaged with beer, with broadcasting, and with other industries. . . . The owners, whose records many say reveal a proclivity for predatory practices, do not come to us with equities. The equities are with the victims of the reserve clause." Douglas called *Federal Baseball Club* "a derelict in the stream of the law that we, its creator, should remove. Only a romantic view of a rather dismal business account over the last 50 years would keep that derelict in mid-stream." He did not need to say who he was accusing of holding a "romantic view" of the game.[46]

The author of a proposed majority opinion normally makes changes to it after seeing a draft of a dissenting opinion, but in Blackmun's next draft he made little effort to respond to Douglas's dissent. Instead, he worked on his list of baseball immortals. His first draft had listed 74 players, but his second added 12 more, including Eppa Rixey and 11 others he decided were worthy of inclusion, such as Dizzy Dean and Lefty Grove. Blackmun would further refine his list at each stage of the publication process. The slip opinion published in June would include an eighty-seventh player, the catcher Moe Berg, who had an undistinguished baseball career but a successful record as a spy in the Second World War. Berg had recently died, and Blackmun had read his obituary in the *New York Times*. By the time the official version of the opinion was published, Blackmun added an eighty-eighth player, Jimmie Foxx.[47]

The most widely known story about Blackmun's list of players turns out not to be true. In *The Brethren*, their 1979 behind-the-scenes look at the Supreme Court, Bob Woodward and Scott Armstrong reported that Thurgood Marshall had protested the absence of African-American players, and that Blackmun responded by adding Jackie Robinson, Roy Campanella, and Satchel Paige. In fact, all three were on Blackmun's original list. Long before major league baseball reached Blackmun's home state of Minnesota, he had watched Campanella play for the minor league St. Paul Saints, and he had seen Robinson play for the Brooklyn Dodgers.[48]

Blackmun did have one lifelong regret about an omission from the list. He had forgotten the Giants' great Mel Ott. For the rest of his career, Blackmun kept a gift from his law clerks in his office—a Mel Ott baseball bat, mounted in a glass case, with a small plaque reading "I'll never forgive myself." Blackmun's list of players would be a conversation starter everywhere he went. "I can go to Chicago," he explained, "and somebody will come up and say, 'I read your list of the great heroes of baseball, but why didn't you include Joe Zilch?' And then we'd have a conversation going as to why I didn't include Joe Zilch." When he retired, Blackmun cited *Flood v. Kuhn* as his favorite of the many opinions he authored on the Supreme Court. "That was the most fun in working it up," he recalled. "A lot of fun."[49]

Thurgood Marshall had originally voted in baseball's favor, but he changed his mind after reading the opinions written by Blackmun and Douglas. He circulated a dissenting opinion of his own, in which he emphasized the unfairness of the reserve clause. "To non-athletes it might appear that petitioner [i.e., Flood] was virtually enslaved by the owners of major league baseball clubs who bartered among themselves for his services," Marshall noted. "But athletes know that it was not servitude that bound petitioner to the club owners; it was the reserve clause." Like Douglas,

Marshall took a barely concealed swipe at Blackmun's ode to the game. "Americans love baseball as they love all sports," Marshall wrote. "Perhaps we become so enamored of athletics that we assume they are foremost in the minds of legislators as well as fans. We must not forget, however, that there are only some 600 major league baseball players. Whatever muscle they might have been able to muster by combining forces with other athletes has been greatly impaired by the manner in which this Court has isolated them. It is this Court that has made them impotent, and this Court should correct its error." Marshall would have overruled *Federal Baseball Club* and *Toolson*, but he would not have declared Flood the winner of the case. Rather, he wanted to send the case back to the lower courts, so that they could determine whether the collective bargaining agreement between the players and the owners constituted a new reason for exempting baseball from antitrust scrutiny.[50]

Justice White had also initially voted in baseball's favor, but he too began to waver after seeing Blackmun's draft opinion. Had White changed his mind like Marshall, and had all the other votes stayed the same, White would have provided the fifth vote to overrule *Federal Baseball Club* and subject baseball to the antitrust laws. The other justices waited anxiously throughout May to learn what White would do. Finally, near the end of the month, he announced that he would stick with his original vote.[51]

White's decision resulted in four final votes for baseball and three for Flood, with Burger, whose initial vote was for Flood, yet to declare his final vote. Had Burger stuck with his original vote, Marshall's switch would have yielded a 4–4 tie. In such cases, the Court's practice is to affirm the decision of the lower court but to publish no opinion. A tie in *Flood v. Kuhn* would have been, in effect, an invitation for another player to file an identical suit, in the hope that Powell would sell his Anheuser-Busch stock and provide a fifth vote. Near the end of the Court's term, however, Burger announced that he had changed his mind as well. "I have grave reservations as to the correctness of *Toolson*," he explained in a short concurring opinion. But "the error, if such it be, is one on which the affairs of a great many people have rested for a long time." It would be unfair to the owners, in Burger's view, to change the rules of the game after they had made investments in reliance on those rules. "The least undesirable course now," he concluded, "is to let the matter rest with Congress."[52] With Burger's change of heart, there was a five to three majority in favor of retaining baseball's antitrust exemption.

When the Court published the opinions in *Flood v. Kuhn* in June 1972, much of the press coverage focused on the novelty of Blackmun's paean to the game, which was the easiest part of the opinion for non-lawyers to understand. The reviews were mixed. Blackmun's opinion was "a long recital about The Game, The Game, The Game, and the Apple Pie Americanism of it," complained Shirley Povich, the *Washington Post* sports columnist. "The message should have been coming through to Flood, wherever he was: baseball is a grand game, and the likes of Curt Flood should not be rocking the boat with gripes about the reserve clause and baseball's exemption from the antitrust laws."[53]

The reaction within baseball, from both sides, was far more muted. Commissioner Bowie Kuhn called the decision "constructive in its recognition that baseball has developed its present structure in reliance on past court decisions." But Kuhn knew that in the future, the fate of the reserve clause would depend less on antitrust law than on the outcome of collective bargaining with the newly powerful Players Association. "I am confident," he declared, "that the players and the clubs are in the best position to determine for themselves what the form of the reserve clause should be." Reaction from the players was much the same. "The ruling doesn't make a lot of difference," insisted the pitcher Milt Pappas, who was the union representative for the Chicago Cubs. "What we are still going to seek at the meeting table is an agreement that will give veteran players some freedom in negotiating."[54] Owners and players alike were aware that they were entering a new era. For Curt Flood, tending bar in Majorca, the decision was little more than a reminder of the world he had left behind.

Flood's lawyers were angry; they thought they had deserved better. "The Supreme Court screwed us," Jay Topkis complained to Arthur Goldberg. "I'm afraid that the sad fact is that nothing that today's Court does is terribly likely to surprise me." Goldberg replied that he too "was not surprised at the result in Flood's case although"—here he got in a dig at Blackmun—"I did expect better opinion writing."[55] After almost three years of work, they had not changed the law one bit.

THE BUSINESS AND THE GAME

Flood v. Kuhn did not change the law, but it would have some indirect longer-run effects on the legal climate surrounding professional sports.

With the benefit of hindsight, it is even clearer that Harry Blackmun exercised poor judgment when he let himself get carried away by his love for baseball. His opinion "reads like a catechism of the virtues of baseball," one law professor wrote shortly afterwards, and this kind of criticism has never let up. "The Court seemed to become mired in the cultural mystique of base-ball," another commentator lamented, to the point where the Court treated baseball as "a revered and unique institution that should be beyond judicial tampering." Blackmun's mistake, one critic suggested, was that he "confused the *business* of baseball with the glorious *game* of baseball, the national pas-time wrapped in legend and myth." Judges are often criticized for poor craftsmanship, but the critique of Blackmun's opinion in *Flood* is something more. Blackmun is pilloried, not just for exhibiting poor form, but for letting his exuberance for the game cloud his analytic judgment. The criticism is not merely that Blackmun prefaced a court opinion with an ode to baseball, but rather that he could not keep the ode separate from the rest of the opin-ion. As the sports law specialist Paul Weiler put it, "whatever the legal reasons for the Supreme Court's decision to preserve baseball's unique exemption from antitrust law, a crucial motivating factor was the special place that base-ball has long occupied in American life."[56] The critique is that Blackmun and the other justices in the majority were not applying the normal process of legal reasoning, which would have led them to rule for Flood, but instead chose to reaffirm the antitrust exemption *because* of baseball's special cultural status.

Harry Blackmun's romanticism about baseball's past had a particular cul-tural valence that made this sort of criticism even sharper. Blackmun was an older white man, just like the club owners. His imagined Elysian days of baseball involved no labor strife, no disputes over money, no problems of race relations—just the purity of the game on the field. It was precisely the view of baseball taken by the club owners in their public relations, when they argued that the 1960s generation of players—brasher, blacker, less willing to submit quietly to authority—were pulling the game off its pedes-tal with their crass demands. (This was why it was so easy to believe the untrue story that Blackmun had omitted African-American players from his original list of greats.) This nostalgia for simpler days was no more accurate coming from Blackmun than from the owners. Players and club owners had been fighting over money, sometimes in court, ever since the middle of the nineteenth century. When *Flood v. Kuhn* arrived at the Supreme Court, baseball was in the midst of a half-economic, half-cultural battle between an older generation of white owners and younger generation of players, some of the best of whom were non-white. Blackmun's opinion thus made it appear as if the Court had ruled against Flood because the justices sympathized with the owners in this broader generational struggle.

As a result, the antitrust exemption appeared even more dubious after *Flood v. Kuhn* than before. Normally a court opinion provides justification for a statement of the law, but Blackmun's opinion did the opposite: it provided reasons for doubt. Baseball's antitrust exemption now seemed to rest on the nostalgia of elderly men for the glory days of the national pastime rather than on any defensible legal basis.

Had Blackmun done what Potter Stewart asked him to do and written a short opinion simply explaining why the Court would not overrule its prior cases, the reaction to the case would likely have been very different. Such an opinion would have acknowledged that the exemption rested on an outdated understanding of interstate commerce, but it would have emphasized that large investments had been made over many years in reliance on that understanding and that courts lacked the power to make purely prospective changes in the law. The opinion would have explained that only Congress could change the law in a way that avoided retroactively harming the club owners. Not everyone would have agreed with that conclusion, of course, but it would have been a respectable argument that would not have been open to the same sort of ridicule as the opinion Blackmun actually wrote.

Why did Harry Blackmun exhibit such poor judgment? Perhaps he merely wanted to share with readers his love for baseball, but that seems an insufficient explanation. Other justices have found other avenues for exploring their interests—books, speeches, journal articles, and the like. A more complete answer might take account of Blackmun's insecurity and his aspirations. When he got the assignment in *Flood v. Kuhn*, Blackmun was very early in his career on the Supreme Court. Years later, he still had strong memories of feeling a need to prove himself worthy of the appointment. In *The Brethren*, Woodward and Armstrong report that Potter Stewart was embarrassed by Blackmun's opinion. Blackmun was asked about that in 1995, the year after he retired, and he responded that although Stewart would not admit having said so, "it would not have been out of character for him to make the statement. I think Potter was always critical of me from the very beginning, to a degree. I don't know whether he thought I was incapable of being on the Court or shouldn't be there or what."[57]

Blackmun was likely to have been feeling especially insecure in the spring of 1972, because he was struggling to write the Court's opinion in *Roe v. Wade*, which had been argued the previous December. Things were not going well. When he circulated his first draft in *Flood*, Blackmun had already been wrestling with the *Roe* opinion for nearly five months. A couple of weeks later, when he finally shared his first draft of *Roe* with his colleagues, they were disappointed with the quality of his work. The Court eventually decided to order reargument in *Roe*, so Blackmun had several more months to work on it.[58] *Flood* must have provided Blackmun with a welcome respite from his troubles with the constitutional law of abortion. The case gave him a chance to show himself to be an erudite person who deserved to be a Supreme Court justice. He knew a lot about the history of baseball, certainly more than most judges, and perhaps he saw the case as his opportunity to shine. If that was his aim, however, he fell far short.

At the Players Association meeting a few weeks later, Marvin Miller discussed the case with the assembled players. "We were all aware when the case was filed that it would be a difficult task to have the Court reverse its earlier decisions in baseball," he explained. "If the composition of the Court had not changed so radically since the filing of the case, Flood would almost certainly have won."[59] Miller was probably wrong. While the lawsuit was climbing the ladder of courts, three new justices had joined the Supreme Court. Two of them, Harry Blackmun and William Rehnquist, had been part of the five-justice majority. The third, Lewis Powell, had recused himself. They had replaced Abe Fortas, John Harlan, and Hugo Black. Black had authored the Court's opinion in *Toolson*, so he would have been unlikely to have sided with Flood. Harlan, who joined the Court after *Toolson*, had dissented in *Radovich*, with an opinion declaring that it was up to Congress rather than the Court to alter the antitrust status of baseball. He too would have been unlikely to vote for Flood. Fortas had no record at all in sports antitrust cases, because he served on the Court for only four years before a scandal forced him to resign. Flood would probably have lost even if Richard Nixon had not been able to appoint so many new justices.

Miller found a bright spot in the litigation, however, and here he would be proven right. "It would be a mistake to conclude that nothing was accomplished by the *Flood* case," he told the players. "The case itself and the discussion which has taken place because of it has served to educate not only the public but also many of those in baseball, and has made the situation ripe now for appropriately changing the reserve system." The players nodded in agreement.[60] The law after *Flood v. Kuhn* was just the same as the law before, but the climate of labor relations was not. Before long, the Players Association would mount a new legal challenge to the reserve clause, this time with more success. Curt Flood's ultimate influence would not be due to anything he accomplished himself but rather to what his example inspired others to accomplish.

THE END OF THE RESERVE CLAUSE

The saddest aspect of Curt Flood's quest for free agency is that only three years after he lost in the Supreme Court, baseball players obtained exactly what Flood had been denied—the right to choose their employers. Free agency came to baseball, not because a court declared the reserve clause unlawful, but because an arbitrator determined that the clause meant something different from the way players and owners alike had understood it for a century. Rather than binding players to their clubs for life, the arbitrator decided, the clause bound players only for the season after their contracts expired. The decision revolutionized baseball. When players gained the power to sell their services to the highest bidder, their salaries skyrocketed. Curt Flood never enjoyed the benefit of these changes. He was a few years too old.

The primary function served by baseball's antitrust exemption, for nearly a century, had been to insulate the reserve clause from antitrust attack. All three of the Supreme Court cases involving the exemption, and most of the debates over the exemption in Congress, had been about the reserve clause and whether it should be held up to the standards of antitrust law. To understand how the meaning of the antitrust exemption changed in the late twentieth century, one first has to understand how the reserve clause could disappear with the exemption still in place.

A LIFE SENTENCE

The decline of the reserve system had its origin in a seemingly innocuous provision of the 1970 collective bargaining agreement between the owners and the Players Association. Before then, disputes between teams and players had always been resolved by the commissioner, who was appointed by the owners and could be expected to take their side. The 1970 collective bargaining agreement established a new grievance procedure in which the final decision-maker would be a panel of three arbitrators, one chosen by the owners, one by the Players Association, and the third by the agreement of the first two arbitrators. This sort of impartial arbitration had long been the norm in agreements between big employers and large labor unions. Marvin Miller, the executive director of the Players Association, was familiar with it from his many years with the steelworkers' union. In sports, though, arbitration was a novelty. "I reluctantly went along," Commissioner Bowie Kuhn recalled in his memoirs. "Provisions of this kind were commonplace in American collective bargaining agreements and could not realistically be resisted by sports managements."[1]

The opportunity to present grievances to an impartial arbitrator opened a new route for attacking the reserve system. The precise language of the reserve clause in player contracts had changed many times over the years, but the gist of it was always the same. It was a one-year club option to renew the player's contract for the following year. The clause did not explicitly give the club further options to renew the contract again in succeeding years. Both sides had always assumed, however, that the renewed contract would include all the same provisions as the original one, including the one-year club option to renew. The effect of this assumption was to make the reserve clause one that would repeat perpetually, year after year, for the duration of a player's career. It took the fresh eyes of an outsider like Marvin Miller, with a background in labor unions rather than in baseball, to wonder whether it would be possible to challenge this assumption and to argue that the clause should instead be interpreted as a single one-year option that did not repeat in subsequent years. Such a challenge would have been pointless before 1970, because the final authority to interpret the terms of player contracts rested with the commissioner, and the commissioner would have been certain to take the view that the reserve clause was perpetual. But with the chance to present the argument to an arbitrator, there was a possibility of change.

Miller began advising players who were having salary disputes with their clubs to refrain from signing contracts. Instead, he suggested, they should force the clubs to exercise the one-year option to renew, and then, at the end of that year, attempt to persuade an arbitrator that the clubs no longer had any right to prevent them from playing elsewhere. Over the next few years, several players pursued this strategy part of the way, but then signed contracts at salaries considerably higher than their clubs had originally been willing to pay. The first was the Oakland pitcher Vida Blue, who had earned $14,500 in 1971, when he had been named Most Valuable Player in the American League. Blue threatened to sit out the 1972 season unless the A's paid him more than their final offer of $50,000. His lawyer argued that this tactic would make Blue a free agent, capable of signing with any club, when he returned to baseball in 1973. In May 1972, more than a month into the season, the A's finally capitulated and agreed to a package totaling $63,000.[2]

Similar cases followed soon after. The St. Louis catcher Ted Simmons played half the 1972 season without a contract before the Cardinals acceded to his demands for 1972 as well as a substantial increase in salary for 1973. Stan Bahnsen, a pitcher for the White Sox, did not sign a 1973 contract until June. Nine players began the 1974 season without contracts for that year, including stars like Sparky Lyle of the Yankees and Bobby Tolan of the Padres. Lyle pitched nearly all of 1974 under the renewal of his contract for the previous year. The Yankees avoided a test case of the reserve clause by signing Lyle to a two-year contract on the very last day of the season. Tolan did the same: on the final day of the 1974 season he signed a contract for 1974 and 1975 at a much higher salary than he had received in 1973.[3]

The owners' repeated concessions suggest that they were nervous that an arbitrator might adopt the Players Association's view of the reserve clause as a single one-year option rather than a perpetually repeating series of options. They were willing to pay higher salaries to a handful of players in order to avoid the risk of losing lifetime control of all players. It bears emphasizing, though, how sharply the Players Association's new interpretation of the reserve clause diverged from established practice. For a century, players and owners alike had understood the clause as a perpetually renewing series of options that bound players to their teams for their entire careers. In *Flood v. Kuhn*, the most prominent recent example, all of Flood's arguments had been based on this assumption. The Supreme Court's opinions, both the majority opinion and the dissents, had likewise assumed that the reserve clause lasted for Flood's entire career. After all, why would Flood have gone to the trouble of filing an antitrust suit if he could have become a free agent simply by playing for one season without a contract? If the reserve clause was merely a single one-year club option, why was it that no player in the history of the game had ever played out his option year and become a free agent? The owners may have been nervous about how an arbitrator would interpret the reserve clause, but Marvin Miller and the Players Association could not have had as much confidence in their interpretation as their public comments suggested, because they knew how big a change it represented.

The owners might have been able to put off a decision on the issue for several more years by continuing to reach settlements, one by one, with players who declined to sign new contracts. But the first dent in the reserve system came in 1974 from an unexpected direction. It was not due to any deliberate action on the part of a player, but rather to the incompetence of an owner. Charlie Finley, the longtime owner of the Oakland A's, had a well-deserved reputation for cheapness and irrationality. "He had few redeeming features as far as I was concerned," Kuhn recalled. "One more like him and I would have gone to work for Marvin Miller."[4] One of Finley's players was the pitcher Jim "Catfish" Hunter, who was midway through a career that would end in the Hall of Fame. In 1974, Hunter would win the Cy Young award as the American League's best pitcher. His contract that year called for him to be paid $50,000 in current salary and, for tax reasons, an additional $50,000 in payments to an insurance company for the purchase of an annuity that would begin paying out several years later. It was not until the middle of the 1974 season that Finley first realized that the payments to the insurance company would not be a deductible business expense for the A's until Hunter began receiving payments from the annuity, and that the A's would not have the use of the money in the interim. Finley refused to buy the annuity. The Players Association filed a grievance on Hunter's behalf, in which it asserted that Hunter's contract was terminated by the A's breach and that Hunter had accordingly become a free agent.

Finley had clearly breached his contract with Hunter. The only real point in contention was the consequence of that breach. Did it terminate Hunter's contract, as the Players Association contended, or did it merely obligate

Finley to pay to the insurance company the $50,000 he had wrongly with-held, as baseball argued? Before 1970, a grievance of this nature would have been decided by the commissioner. If Kuhn still had had that power in 1974, he would have ordered Finley to buy the annuity, but he believed that termi-nating Hunter's contract was too harsh a punishment. "To forfeit the con-tract," he insisted, "was like giving a life sentence to a pickpocket."[5] But the owners had bargained away Kuhn's authority four years earlier.

Hunter's case went to an arbitration panel composed of Marvin Miller for the players, baseball's chief negotiator John Gaherin for the owners, and Peter Seitz as the neutral third arbitrator. The same three arbitrators would decide all the baseball grievances of 1974 and 1975. Although their decisions were nominally taken as a group, Miller always sided with the players and Gaherin with the owners, so in practice Seitz was the sole decision-maker. He was an experienced labor arbitrator, nearly 70 years old, who had de-cided cases in a wide range of industries, including professional baseball and professional basketball. The question of the appropriate remedy for an employer's breach of a contract was not a new one to him. In fact, the issue had arisen in another baseball case Seitz heard only ten days before the Hunter case, a grievance filed by the Players Association on behalf of Mike Corkins, a relief pitcher for the Padres. In Corkins's case, the Players Associ-ation alleged that the Padres had failed to reimburse Corkins for approxi-mately $300 in travel expenses and that as a result Corkins had the right to terminate his contract and become a free agent. Seitz agreed that the Padres had breached Corkins's contract, and he recognized that the standard player contract provided for the termination of the contract in the event of a breach, but he concluded that terminating the contract would be too drastic a remedy for such a minor mistake. "Where the parties, as in this case, ex-pressly provide for forfeiture, it is the duty of the decision-makers to respect and apply such provision," Seitz acknowledged. "However, in doing so it seems appropriate and desirable to apply the forfeiture provisions strictly rather than liberally. Surely, it was not intended that a forfeiture of contract rights would result from trivial or insignificant violations." Seitz ordered the Padres to reimburse Corkins for his travel expenses, but he refused to declare the contract terminated. Before he even heard Catfish Hunter's case, Seitz had already drawn a distinction between trivial and important breaches of contract, and he had made clear that he would find contracts terminated when breaches were important enough.[6]

In the Hunter case, Seitz began by noting that the terms of the standard player contract were very clear. The contract provided that when a club defaulted on one of its obligations, the player was to give the club written notice of the default, and if the club failed to cure the default within 10 days, "the Player may terminate this contract." Hunter's lawyer had given Finley the required written notice, and Finley had not purchased the annuity he was supposed to buy. "Faced with such clear and unequivocal provisions," Seitz concluded, "the Arbitration Panel has no alternative but to enforce them." Seitz had some doubts about the wisdom of this provision, he explained. "The remedy afforded may be too radical and oppressive," he noted, especially in a case where the two sides genuinely disagreed over the meaning of a complex contractual term. "It is not for the Chairman of the Panel, however, to rewrite the provisions which the parties agreed to place in the Player's Contract," Seitz held. "He has no franchise to administer his personal brand of industrial justice." Because Charlie Finley had breached an important term of Catfish Hunter's contract, Hunter had the right to terminate the contract.[7]

No longer under contract with the A's, Catfish Hunter became baseball's first free agent. Two weeks later, after 20 clubs submitted bids, he signed a five-year contract with the Yankees worth approximately $3.5 million, by far the most lucrative contract in the history of the game to that point. Much of the money was deferred, so Hunter's annual salary could not be directly compared with the salaries of players who had simpler contracts, but even by the most conservative estimate Hunter was earning at least twice as much per year as any other player.

The players had always suspected that the reserve system was keeping their salaries down, but Hunter's contract was the first clear proof of just how much they were losing. As American League president Lee MacPhail put it, "this had shown everybody exactly what free agency could amount to."[8] Miller's strategy of playing out the reserve year in order to test the meaning of the reserve clause began to look much more attractive. Nine more players began the 1975 season under the renewal terms of their 1974 contracts. Seven of them signed new contracts in the middle of the season. Two did not: the Dodgers' pitcher Andy Messersmith and the Expos' pitcher Dave McNally. Miller finally had the cases he had been waiting for. On the last day of the 1975 season, the Players' Association filed grievances on behalf of Messersmith and McNally, seeking to have them declared free agents.

VISIONS OF THE EMANCIPATION PROCLAMATION

Andy Messersmith was at the peak of his career. He had been an all-star in 1974, when he led the National League in wins, and again in 1975, when he led the league in shutouts and complete games. His refusal to sign a contract for 1975 was not motivated by the desire to become a free agent. It was the opposite: Messersmith wanted a no-trade clause so he could be sure of remaining with the Dodgers, but the Dodgers refused to give him one. Dave McNally's career, by contrast, was over. After 13 seasons with the Baltimore Orioles, he had been traded to the Expos for 1975, but he injured his arm and retired halfway through the season. He was working at a car dealership in Billings, Montana, when Miller called and asked if he would join the grievance. In principle, McNally was still covered by the reserve clause; if he ever returned to baseball, he would belong to the Expos. Unlike Messersmith, however, McNally had nothing to gain from adding his name to the grievance. He was done with baseball. He participated in the grievance simply to help the other players. McNally had been the Orioles' player representative, and he was still "a good union man," as Miller put it. Miller needed McNally just in case the Dodgers, at the last minute, complied with Messersmith's request for a no-trade clause and signed him to a contract. "McNally had been a starter for fourteen years," Miller recalled, "but the last act of his career was to serve in arbitration as a reliever."[9]

The case very nearly did not make it to arbitration. The owners' first move was to file a lawsuit seeking a declaration that the arbitration panel had no jurisdiction over the grievance. They lost, but only temporarily: the judge ordered the arbitration to proceed, on the understanding that the jurisdictional question could be presented to the court once the arbitration was over. The owners then met to decide whether to replace Peter Seitz as the neutral arbitrator. The collective bargaining agreement allowed either side to withdraw its support for the neutral arbitrator at any time. It was a difficult strategic decision from the owners' point of view. On one hand, Seitz had ruled against them in the Catfish Hunter case. On the other, he was a respected veteran of arbitration, with a reputation for intelligence and fairness. The owners believed their interpretation of the reserve clause was the correct one and that their lawyers could demonstrate that to Seitz. To fire Seitz on the eve of arbitration in the highly publicized Messersmith case, moreover, would be very poor public relations. The owners accordingly voted to retain him as the third arbitrator. The Expos offered a contract to McNally for the following season, including a $25,000 signing bonus, even though there was little chance he could play, as an inducement to drop the grievance before it reached the arbitrators. McNally sacrificed his own interests for the players' cause: he turned down the money. Meanwhile the Dodgers, fearing the loss of Messersmith, were prepared to offer him a no-trade contract to end his participation in the grievance. It took the pleading of the other owners, who worried that other players would demand similar contracts, to make the Dodgers relent.[10] After all these obstacles were cleared, the arbitration took place in New York in November and December of 1975.

In a small conference room in the Barbizon Plaza Hotel, Richard Moss presented the Players Association's arguments to Peter Seitz, while baseball countered with a team of four lawyers led by Louis Hoynes, who had represented baseball for years. Three years before, Hoynes had been the lawyer who bested Arthur Goldberg at the Supreme Court in *Flood v. Kuhn*. Only a handful of spectators looked on, including Andy Messersmith and Peter O'Malley, the president of the Dodgers.

Moss made four main points on behalf of the players. The reason no player in the history of the game had ever tried to claim free agency by playing out his option year, he argued, was that the players had never been aware of their rights and that they had been afraid to make any such claim, because it would have meant the sacrifice of their careers. Before the advent of arbitration, Moss pointed out, such a claim would have been fruitless, because all decisions were made by the commissioner, "and that was hardly the kind of issue any player would think of taking to the commissioner."[11]

Moss then turned to the language of the reserve clause itself. The clause simply said that "the club shall have the right to renew this contract for the period of one year under the same terms." That phrase "means precisely what it says," Moss argued. "If it meant the club could renew it again and again in succeeding years, that could have been said." It would have been very easy to draft a reserve clause that specified that the club's option would be repeated in subsequent years, but baseball had never done so. "What the contract says," Moss concluded, "is that the club can renew for one year, and we submit that is exactly what it means."[12]

Even if the language of the reserve clause were ambiguous, Moss continued, the players' interpretation should prevail. He cited a well-established doctrine of contract interpretation, under which, when a contract drafted by one party includes a term capable of more than one reasonable meaning, the term should be interpreted in favor of the other party, the one who had not drafted the contract. The rationale for this doctrine, as Moss explained, is that the party drafting the contract can prevent mistakes or ambiguities from arising more easily than the other party can. The reserve clause, he reminded Seitz, had been written entirely by the owners. When it was first instituted, there had been no players union and no collective bargaining. He urged Seitz to "apply the basic tenet of contract law that ambiguities are to be resolved against the draftsman."[13]

Finally, Moss cited precedents in basketball. The National Basketball Association used a reserve clause that was worded similarly to baseball's, and it had been at issue in two recent cases. Both involved NBA stars who had signed contracts to play for teams in a new league, the American Basketball Association. Rick Barry of the San Francisco Warriors had left for the ABA's Oakland Oaks, while Billy Cunningham had left the Philadelphia 76ers to join the ABA's Carolina Cougars. In both cases, courts interpreted the reserve clause as a single one-year option, not a perpetually renewing option. Baseball's reserve clause, Moss suggested, should be construed the same way.[14]

Baseball's lawyers responded by emphasizing that the Players Association's interpretation was "wholly inconsistent with the history and meaning and effect of the reserve system as it has existed in baseball for decades and decades." Louis Hoynes reminded Seitz that it wasn't just the owners who had understood the reserve clause to bind a player to a team for the player's entire career. Even those who attacked the reserve clause had the same understanding. "Hundreds of thousands of dollars have been spent on all sides litigating this question," Hoynes exclaimed, "and the Association really comes here today to tell us that all of that activity and all of that money and all of that fuss and bother, in my personal case sweat, blood and tears, was pointless." If, all this time, the reserve clause had been only a one-year option, what had been the purpose of "all the threats of congressional action, all the questions about antitrust restraints, claims of peonage and involuntary servitude"? Hoynes pointed out that even Marvin Miller, in his public statements deploring the reserve clause, had characterized it as a lifelong obligation on the part of players. During collective bargaining, Hoynes added, the Players Association had repeatedly asked for the reserve clause to be modified to become something less than perpetual—for example, to last only for the first seven years of a player's career. That negotiating position was unreconcilable with the view the association was taking in the Messersmith case. "Where is the Association's current theory evident in any of this collective bargaining history?" Hoynes wondered. The Association was asking an arbitrator to give it the very thing it had been unable to obtain in collective bargaining.[15]

Hoynes hardly needed to add that he too had a hoary principle of contract interpretation on his side. When the words of a contract were ambiguous, it was standard practice to examine the course of dealing between the parties, to see if they had acted according to one interpretation or the other. Peter Seitz himself had explained, only a few years before, that "agreement can be evidenced and proved by conduct over time, as well as by the written or spoken word. Thus, a history of a single accepted way of meeting a problem could mature into a usage binding on the parties."[16] Using this method of interpretation, the owners' view of the reserve clause as perpetual was the correct one, because owners and players had acted in accordance with that view for nearly a century.

The Messersmith-McNally arbitration thus posed a difficult question of contract interpretation, one with plausible arguments on both sides. It also posed a difficult question of whether the arbitration panel even had jurisdiction to decide the case. The 1973 collective bargaining agreement that was in effect at the time, like its 1970 predecessor, specified that "this agreement does not deal with the reserve system." The owners contended that this provision deprived the arbitrators of jurisdiction to resolve disputes over the reserve system. The Players Association responded that the provision was intended only to clarify that the players had not agreed to the reserve system during collective bargaining, and thus to preserve the ability of the union or any individual player to file a lawsuit alleging that the reserve clause was illegal. In the association's view, this provision did not prevent arbitrators from trying to figure out how long the reserve clause bound a player to his team.

Soon after the hearing ended, Seitz announced that he had concluded that the panel did have jurisdiction, but that he had not yet come to a decision on the merits. He urged both sides to reach a settlement. "It is my deep conviction," he explained, "that questions as to the scope and operation of a Reserve System—so critical to the interests of the clubs and players—are much better answered by the parties affected, by pursuing the national policy of collective bargaining, than by a tribunal performing the quasi-judicial function of arbitration." Coincidentally, the two sides were already engaged in negotiations for a new collective bargaining agreement to replace the 1973 agreement, which was scheduled to expire at the end of 1975, just a few weeks later. Seitz encouraged them to include the reserve clause in these negotiations. He announced that he would delay his decision in the Messersmith-McNally case for two weeks, until December 24, to give the parties time to reach a settlement.[17]

In deferring his decision, Seitz was motivated by a deeply felt belief, acquired over the course of almost three decades as an arbitrator, that major labor-management disputes over the terms of employment were best resolved by the parties themselves. "A negotiated settlement is almost always better than one made by a fiat, bull, ukase or award, no matter how well-intentioned the decision-maker may be," he observed a few years later.[18] Arbitration, as Seitz saw it, worked well for individual grievances—for disputes over whether a rule had been violated in a particular case—but not when the question to be decided was what the rule should be in the first place. In the lingo of arbitrators, Seitz favored "grievance arbitration" but not "interest arbitration." The Messersmith-McNally case was somewhere in the middle. As a formal matter, it was a grievance over the application of a particular rule in two individual cases. As a practical matter, however, it was a dispute over the content of the rule itself.

The Players Association was willing to negotiate over the reserve clause, but the owners were not. Seitz was baffled at the owners' stubbornness. "I shall go to eternal rest wondering why the Leagues gave a negative response to my suggestion," he later told Bowie Kuhn. He could not understand why baseball failed "to seize the opportunity to bargain for a less rigid reserve system in advance of the date when I should have to wield the surgical knife in arbitration." From a greater distance, the owners' reluctance to negotiate over the reserve clause is more readily comprehended. The status quo favored the owners. Any negotiated settlement over the reserve clause would yield an outcome less favorable for the owners than what they already had. A negotiated settlement might be better than a ruling against them by Peter Seitz, of course, because negotiation might result in a reserve clause lasting several years, while if they lost before Seitz, it would be because Seitz agreed with the players that the reserve clause lasted only one year. But baseball's lawyers believed they had presented a persuasive case. "After all," Kuhn recalled, "no one had ever seriously imagined that the reserve system had a large, heretofore undiscovered ocean of free agency floating in its midst." And if Seitz erroneously ruled against them, the lawyers reasoned, they had a good chance of persuading a court to reverse his decision.[19] Baseball informed Seitz that it would not negotiate over the reserve clause.

Seitz ruled in favor of the players. He found decisive the fact that the reserve clause did not explicitly state that it would be perpetually renewing. In cases involving real estate leases, he observed, courts had enforced perpetually renewing contracts only where it was clear that this was what the parties intended. In ambiguous cases, courts interpreted the leases to renew once only. Seitz determined that the rule should be the same in labor contracts. "There is nothing in" the reserve clause "which, explicitly, expresses agreement that the Player Contract can be renewed for any period beyond the first renewal year," he pointed out. "I find great difficulties, in so implying or assuming, in respect of personal services in which one would expect a more explicit expression of intention." Messersmith and McNally were thus no longer under contract when the 1975 baseball season ended. Seitz acknowledged that baseball officials predicted chaos from such a result, but he insisted that the consequences of the decision were none of his business. "The Panel's sole duty is to interpret and apply the agreements and undertakings of the parties," he concluded. "If any of the expressed apprehensions and fears are soundly based, I am confident that the dislocations and damage to the reserve system can be avoided or minimized through good faith collective bargaining between the parties."[20] Three times the Supreme Court had upheld the perpetual reserve clause against claims that it violated federal antitrust law, but in the end the clause was undone by a single arbitrator interpreting the player contract.

"I am enormously disturbed," Bowie Kuhn (figure 9.1) complained. "It is just inconceivable that after nearly 100 years of developing this system for the over-all good of the game, it should be obliterated in this way." Chub Feeney and Lee MacPhail, presidents of the National and American Leagues, issued a joint statement predicting that the decision "would do irreparable harm to baseball, allowing every player currently in the major leagues to turn his back on his club and move at will from team to team." (Red Smith, the veteran *New York Times* sports columnist, smirked that "whoever is writing their stuff makes them sound like boobs.") The owners appealed Seitz's ruling, but courts review the work of arbitrators by an extremely

Figure 9.1: Baseball Commissioner Bowie Kuhn enjoys a light moment with President Gerald Ford, in a period when baseball's century-old system of labor relations changed dramatically. BL-1356.96, National Baseball Hall of Fame.

deferential standard. The decision was upheld by the courts within a few months, in time for the 1976 season.[21]

Andy Messersmith, now a free agent, signed a three-year contract with the Atlanta Braves for a total of $1 million, which gave him an annual salary more than three times what he had earned with the Dodgers. After a successful 1976 season with the Braves, however, Messersmith was never the same pitcher again. He struggled through injuries in 1977. The Braves sold him to the Yankees in 1978, the last year of his contract, but he appeared in only six games that season, and the Yankees released him at the end of the year. Messersmith ended his career back with the Dodgers in 1979. He retired with a career earned run average of 2.86, still the fourth lowest among starting pitchers whose careers began after 1920, behind only Whitey Ford, Sandy Koufax, and Jim Palmer.

As for Peter Seitz, the owners fired him within hours of his decision. He continued working as an arbitrator in other industries, including professional basketball, for the next several years, almost until his death in 1983, but he never heard a baseball case again. He became, as he put it, "a resident of the Gulag Archipelago of baseball." In his later years he would look back on the episode with considerable bitterness. "I was dismissed unceremoniously with the conventional pink slip without a word of kindness," he complained to Bowie Kuhn. "The dismissal was ignominious and shameless in character and took no account of my professional career and general acceptance as an arbitrator. . . . At the time, the brutality and rudeness of the action hurt deeply." Kuhn replied politely. "There is no excuse for bad manners," he wrote, "and I am truly sorry that you were subjected to that."[22]

After Seitz's death, however, Kuhn took the gloves off. In his memoirs he accused Seitz of harboring "a barely concealed, antimanagement bias. Kindly and well-intentioned, he was a prisoner of his own philosophy and would rationalize his way to the destruction of the reserve system." As he heard the Messersmith-McNally case, Kuhn charged, Seitz had "visions of the Emancipation Proclamation dancing in his eyes." Regardless of one's opinion of the merits of Seitz's decision, there can be no doubt that the decision made Seitz famous as the man who freed professional baseball players from the reserve clause. Before December 1975, Seitz was known only within the small community of labor arbitrators, but afterward he was mentioned in the sports pages nearly as often as the star players. For the rest of his life, whenever there was labor conflict in one of the major professional sports, reporters would call Seitz for a quote. "I am constantly being told that this is the most important arbitration case decided in the last few decades," he declared in 1982. "As a result of this decision it is said that I freed the slaves like A. Lincoln or, alternatively, I killed the game of baseball." Even the headline in Seitz's obituary in the *New York Times* referred to him as "the arbitrator in baseball free-agent case."[23] Had Seitz decided the case the other way, baseball would have gone on as before, and Seitz would not have become well known in the world beyond labor arbitration. Baseball officials could hardly be blamed for wondering whether this consideration influenced his decision.

Five years after the Messersmith-McNally case, Peter Seitz sat down for an interview with the baseball historian Lee Lowenfish. His decision had been "a leap," Seitz admitted, "but a justifiable one."[24] He knew as well as anyone that his interpretation of the reserve clause was contrary to a century of practice, and that it would cause major changes in the structure of professional baseball. But he also believed those changes would be good ones and that he was doing the right thing by setting them in motion. In that sense,

Seitz's decision was of a piece with other controversial judicial decisions of the period. Three years earlier the Supreme Court had outlawed the death penalty. Two years earlier it had legalized abortion (in an opinion that would eclipse *Flood v. Kuhn* in the public image of Harry Blackmun). The idea that judges should promote legal change was still at its high-water mark in the mid-1970s. Peter Seitz was not a judge, much less a justice of the Supreme Court. He was an arbitrator, down near the bottom of the judicial hierarchy. But the attitude toward judicial decision-making that lay behind the big Supreme Court cases was spread widely throughout the American legal culture, well beyond the Supreme Court. "A leap, but a justifiable one"—those were words that lawyers might have used to describe any number of the high-profile decisions of the era. In more recent times, as the profession's conventional view of the proper role of a judge has narrowed, Seitz's description of his decision has come to sound almost like an oxymoron. When leaps are not for judges to make, no leap is justifiable.

BILLIONS AND BILLIONS OF DOLLARS

When Peter Seitz announced his decision in the Messersmith-McNally case, the players and the owners were in the midst of negotiating a new collective bargaining agreement. The decision shifted the terrain of negotiations in favor of the players. Now the status quo was a rule according to which all players could become free agents one year after the expiration of their contracts. The owners had a fresh incentive to agree to some plan that would tamp down the annual bidding wars that loomed on the horizon. Marvin Miller calculated that the players had the same incentive. Rather than flooding the market with hundreds of players each year, he reasoned, it would be better to find some way of constricting the annual supply of free agents, in order to boost their salaries.[25] After protracted negotiations lasting halfway through the 1976 season, the two sides finally agreed to a reserve clause that would apply only to players who were in their first six years in the major leagues. After six years of service, a player would become a free agent upon the expiration of his contract. This six-year provision, with some tinkering around the edges, would remain a part of all subsequent collective bargaining agreements up to the present.

With the onset of free agency, player salaries ballooned. In 1970, the minimum major league salary was $12,000, and the average was only a bit over

$29,000. By 1980, the minimum was $30,000, more than the average had been a decade earlier, and the average was nearly $144,000. In 1990, the minimum was $100,000, and the average had reached $579,000. By 2000, the minimum was $200,000, and the average was almost $1.9 million.[26] Even when one adjusts these numbers for inflation, average salaries nearly tripled each decade.[27] These gains were especially pronounced at the top. Messersmith's salary of $333,000 had been enormous in 1976, but in 1988, the Mets' catcher, Gary Carter, made $2.4 million. By 2011, the highest paid was the Yankees' Alex Rodriguez, at $32 million.[28] Few labor unions have ever succeeded so spectacularly.

While the players were growing richer, the owners were too. Professional baseball enjoyed considerable commercial success during the period, producing gains that flowed to owners and players alike. Between 1971 and 1990, for example, baseball's revenue from national television contracts grew by a factor of approximately 17, almost exactly matching the growth in player salaries.[29] Free agency was not the only factor causing salaries to rise.

On the twenty-fifth anniversary of the Messersmith-McNally ruling, Richard Moss, the lawyer who had won the case for the Players Association, looked back on his work with understandable pride. "The difference between winning and losing can be stated in billions and billions of dollars," Moss declared. "I don't think you can find another labor arbitration case that can say that."[30] But this seems too strong a claim. The decision clearly played a big part in the onset of free agency, but baseball players would almost certainly have attained some form of free agency even without it, eventually, simply because of the clout they could wield in collective bargaining. There can be little doubt, however, that Seitz's decision accelerated the process. Before the decision, when players and owners negotiated, the owners held tightly to the reserve clause in its classic form, a guarantee of lifetime control over players. It might have taken years of negotiation, and perhaps even a player strike, for the owners to budge. After the decision, the owners capitulated within a few months.

By the time Curt Flood died of cancer in 1997, labor relations in baseball and other professional sports looked nothing like they had when Flood lost his case in the Supreme Court 25 years earlier. Free agency had come to all four of the major sports. The best players were millionaires. Curt Flood had lost his suit, but professional athletes gained so much afterward that Flood was often remembered incorrectly as the winner. Even people who realized

Flood had lost nevertheless credited him with helping to pave the way for the transformation of professional sports. At his funeral, George Will compared Flood with Rosa Parks. *Time* magazine put him on its list of the ten most influential athletes of the century. "How can anyone drawing a paycheck in sports today not know about Curt Flood?" wondered the basketball player Charles Barkley.[31] A year after Flood died, when Congress enacted its first and only statute modifying baseball's antitrust exemption, it named the law the Curt Flood Act of 1998.

The development of free agency had important consequences for baseball's antitrust exemption. For decades, the exemption's primary function had been to insulate the reserve clause from antitrust attack, but now the reserve clause was partially gone. It still applied to players in their first six years in the major leagues, but now that the players had agreed to it in collective bargaining, they could not challenge it as illegal under the antitrust laws. The antitrust exemption was no longer as valuable to organized baseball as it had once been.

But the exemption had not lost its value completely. There were people other than major league baseball players who still had reasons to hold baseball to the standards of antitrust law, and there were still aspects of the game that might be deemed unlawful if antitrust law were to apply. In the late twentieth and early twenty-first centuries, baseball would continue to cling to its antitrust exemption.

A SHRUNKEN EXEMPTION

Even without the old reserve system to protect, baseball's antitrust exemption continued to serve the club owners well. They only had to glance over at the other major professional sports to see the value of not being governed by the Sherman Act. In the late twentieth and early twenty-first centuries, the National Football League, the National Basketball Association, and the National Hockey League faced a barrage of antitrust suits from players, from teams, and from competing leagues. The leagues lost most of them. The owners of baseball teams enjoyed a legal status that their counterparts in other sports could only envy.

An easy mark

The other three sports each had their own versions of a reserve clause, and courts found that all three violated the Sherman Act. Football had been governed since 1963 by the so-called "Rozelle Rule," named for Commissioner Pete Rozelle. Under this provision of the NFL's bylaws, the reserve clause was a one-year club option to renew, after which a player would become a free agent. When a free agent left his old team and signed with a new one, however, the commissioner could designate one or more players to be transferred from the new team back to the old as compensation. The Rozelle Rule was intended to discourage clubs from signing free agents, and it had that effect in practice. It was challenged as an antitrust violation in two lawsuits, one filed by the quarterback Joe Kapp and the other by a group of players led by the tight end John Mackey. In both cases, courts determined that the Rozelle Rule was illegal. Eventually, collective bargaining between the owners and the players' union yielded a system of free agency similar to baseball's, in which players with enough years of service can become free agents after the expiration of their contracts. The NBA had a similar practice of requiring a team signing a free agent to compensate the player's former team. This practice was likewise found to be a violation of the Sherman Act, after a class action suit brought on behalf of all NBA players. As in football, this outcome eventually led to a collective bargaining agreement allowing veteran players to become free agents. In hockey, the NHL's reserve clause was invalidated after a suit brought by a new rival league, the World Hockey Association. The outcome was the same as in football and basketball: a collective bargaining agreement including a reserve clause for newer players and free agency for veterans.[1]

The NFL and NBA player drafts were also attacked as antitrust violations, and the leagues lost these suits as well. In 1979 a federal court of appeals found that the NFL's draft robbed new football players "of any real bargaining power" with respect to their employers. The effect, the court held, was "to suppress or even destroy competition in the market for players' services." The NBA's player draft suffered the same fate.[2] Both leagues quickly reached collective bargaining agreements in which the players' unions agreed to reinstate the draft. The player draft became part of the NHL's collective bargaining agreement as well. After all, the draft depressed the salaries only of incoming players, none of whom were yet union members. The more money that was paid out to new players, the less would be available for existing players, and the unions were made up entirely of existing players. They had no incentive to sacrifice their own incomes for the benefit of their future colleagues.

Football, basketball, and hockey lacked an antitrust exemption, but through collective bargaining they reached virtually the same outcome as baseball regarding free agency and the player draft. This was legally possible because of a different exemption from the antitrust laws, the one that applied to arrangements that had been secured by collective bargaining. In the *Flood* case, baseball had made what was then a novel argument that this exemption covered the reserve clause, but the argument turned out to be unnecessary, because the Supreme Court chose instead to preserve baseball's own antitrust exemption. In the other sports, the argument *was* necessary, and it was put to immediate use. It soon became known as the "nonstatutory" labor exemption, to distinguish it from the explicit statutory exemption for the activities of labor unions. "As a matter of logic," Justice Stephen Breyer explained, "it would be difficult, if not impossible, to require groups of employers and employees to bargain together, but at the same time to forbid them to make among themselves or with each other *any* of the competition-reducing agreements potentially necessary to make the process work."[3] So long as a particular practice, like the reserve clause or the player draft, was a subject of collective bargaining, it was effectively immune from antitrust attacks on the part of union members. This was why the NFL players had to dissolve their union in order to file antitrust suits against the league in 1989 and 2011.

For the aspects of the sports business that did not involve labor relations between owners and players, by contrast, baseball's antitrust exemption gave club owners a significant advantage over their counterparts in other sports. This edge was at its clearest when leagues tried to prevent teams from changing cities. The major professional leagues all required some form of league consent before teams could move. In 1980, when the NFL owners voted unanimously to prevent the Oakland Raiders from moving to Los Angeles, the Raiders brought an antitrust suit against the league. They won, and moved to Los Angeles in 1982. (They would move back to Oakland in 1995). Emboldened by the Raiders' victory, five more NFL teams moved in the next fifteen years: the Colts from Baltimore to Indianapolis, the Cardinals from St. Louis to Phoenix, the Rams from Los Angeles to St. Louis, the Browns from Cleveland to Baltimore, and the Oilers from Houston to Nashville. When the Rams moved despite almost unanimous opposition from the other clubs, NFL commissioner (and former league attorney) Paul Tagliabue complained that it was the fear of an antitrust suit that caused the league to back down. "Even though we believed that we should have prevailed in any lawsuit," Tagliabue lamented, "the NFL members were unwilling to endure years of antitrust litigation in a St. Louis court, not to mention the punitive nature of any errant treble damage judgment." Antitrust law rendered the NBA and the NHL equally powerless to prevent franchises from moving to new cities. Basketball and hockey teams moved even more often than football teams did. By 2002, no major league baseball franchise had relocated in 30 years, while in that period the other three sports had seen a total of 22 moves. "It is not a coincidence," explained Robert Dupuy, baseball's chief legal officer, "that baseball is the only sport with an exemption."[4]

The NFL's antitrust troubles did not end there. The league prohibited club owners from also owning teams in other sports. This rule was challenged as an antitrust violation by the North American Soccer League. The NFL lost once again. The most well known of the antitrust suits against the NFL was brought by a competing league, the United States Football League, which argued that the NFL had tried to monopolize the markets for players and television coverage. The NFL lost yet again, although in a way that was tantamount to winning: the jury found that the USFL had not been harmed by the NFL's antitrust violations and so only awarded the USFL nominal damages of one dollar. Antitrust law "affects everything we do," observed Dan Rooney, the owner of the Pittsburgh Steelers. Art Modell, owner of the Cleveland Browns, put it more bluntly. "We're an easy mark," he said, just before the USFL trial. "As long as we have such a hold on the viewing public . . . we're going to be a target, from players, agents and leagues."[5] A few years later, Modell himself would take advantage of the NFL's vulnerability to antitrust suits by moving the Browns to Baltimore.

Throughout the 1980s and 1990s, the NFL repeatedly lobbied Congress for an antitrust exemption like baseball's, but to no avail. In 1982, Commissioner Pete Rozelle complained to the Senate Judiciary Committee that without the ability to restrict teams from moving, "you will have the auctioning of franchises," as "the owners will call in the mayors and say, 'What do you have to offer.'" In 1985, Rozelle could be found outside the Senate chamber, shaking hands with the senators walking in and out, in order to garner support for an antitrust exemption. Rozelle's successor Paul Tagliabue was just as active. "The very things that we are trying to do in professional sports today to ensure franchise stability are the measures that are subject to antitrust challenge," he testified before a congressional committee in 1996. "Our internal decision-making process should not be subject to antitrust challenges."[6] But Tagliabue was no more successful than Rozelle had been. Football had more political muscle than basketball or hockey, but even football could not persuade Congress to grant it an exemption from the antitrust laws. Only baseball could prevent its teams from moving to new cities.

Baseball's exemption also allowed it to operate its elaborate system of minor leagues. There are more than 200 minor league teams, currently organized into 20 leagues at 5 levels. Most minor league teams have contractual arrangements with major league clubs, under which the major league clubs pay the players and decide the level at which they will play. Minor league players are typically paid low salaries, on a fixed scale. They are initially allocated to major league organizations in a player draft, and they are subject to a six-year reserve clause that prevents other organizations from bidding for their services. Minor league players are not members of the Major League Baseball Players Association, or indeed any labor union. Because their salaries and other terms of employment are not determined by collective bargaining, the nonstatutory labor exemption from the antitrust laws does not apply to them. (Hockey also has minor leagues, but minor league hockey players are unionized, so their employment conditions are set in collective bargaining and are thus exempt from antitrust scrutiny.) Baseball's exemption protects the minor league structure from being challenged as a violation of the antitrust laws. If major league clubs were no longer able to control minor league players, they would almost certainly stop subsidizing the minor leagues by paying salaries, and many minor league teams would likely go out of business. For this reason, the minor leagues have been ardent lobbyists against any legislation that would weaken baseball's antitrust exemption. As in their prior efforts to defeat adverse legislation, the minor leagues have had a powerful weapon at their disposal: the fact that minor league teams are scattered throughout congressional districts all over the country and are often beloved local institutions. In 1993, Representative Sherwood Boehlert, whose New York district included three minor league teams plus the Baseball Hall of Fame, even formed a Minor League Baseball Caucus, made up of the approximately 125 representatives with minor league teams in their districts.[7]

THE BUSINESS OF BASEBALL

While baseball continued to enjoy its antitrust exemption, the game's officials could never rest, because the exemption was constantly in peril of being diminished in the courts or abolished entirely by Congress. By the 1990s, baseball was engaged in nearly continuous lobbying and litigation to preserve its freedom from the antitrust laws.

Although the exemption had been around since the 1920s, its outer limits had never been completely clear. Certainly the reserve clause could not be challenged as an antitrust violation, but what about other aspects of the game? Baseball teams engaged in all kinds of transactions. They sold food, they purchased advertising, they rented office space, and so on. Activities like these were ultimately for the purpose of putting on baseball games, but otherwise they had little to do with the sport itself. Were they nevertheless exempt from antitrust scrutiny? Organized baseball itself likewise did all sorts of things in addition to employing players. It restricted the movement of teams from one city to another. It disciplined players and owners for various infractions. Were these activities protected by the umbrella of the antitrust exemption? Before the 1980s, there was little litigation over questions like these, so there were no definitive answers.

To the extent there was a conventional view, it was that the antitrust exemption covered "the business of baseball." This ambiguous phrase came from *Toolson*, in which the Court had held that "Congress had no intention of including the business of baseball within the scope of the federal antitrust laws." While there was room for argument about whether particular activities were encompassed within the business of baseball, some activities clearly were. In 1976, for example, A's owner Charlie Finley attempted to sell the contracts of three of his best players to other teams. Baseball's rules authorized the commissioner to disallow player transactions that he found "not in the best interests of baseball," and Bowie Kuhn exercised that authority to nullify the three sales on the ground that the A's would be left too weak to compete. Finley sued Kuhn on a variety of grounds, one of which was that Kuhn was violating the antitrust laws. When Kuhn defended against this claim by citing baseball's antitrust exemption, Finley argued that the exemption covered only the reserve clause, not other aspects of the game. The court disagreed with Finley's narrow interpretation of the exemption. Although the *Flood* case had only involved the reserve clause, the court noted, it seemed clear "that the Supreme Court intended to exempt the business of baseball, not any particular facet of that business, from the federal antitrust laws." As the commissioner's authority to approve trades was part of the business of baseball, it could not be challenged on antitrust grounds.[8]

In the 1990s, however, a few judges began to reduce the scope of the exemption. The first of the important cases involved Pam Postema, the first woman ever to umpire a professional game above the class A minor league level.

She rose through the ranks to the AAA Pacific Coast League, and she umpired major league spring training games, but she was never promoted to the majors. Postema filed a lawsuit alleging gender discrimination and a violation of the antitrust laws. Baseball defended against the latter claim by invoking the antitrust exemption. The hiring of umpires was surely part of the business of baseball. Indeed, shortly before *Flood v. Kuhn*, a federal court of appeals had used the exemption to dismiss a suit brought by umpires who alleged that they had been wrongfully discharged. In Postema's case, however, Judge Robert Patterson interpreted the exemption more narrowly to encompass only baseball's "league structure and its reserve system." In *Flood*, he reasoned, the Supreme Court had explained that the exemption was useful to protect baseball's "unique characteristics and needs." Unlike the reserve system, Patterson concluded, "baseball's relations with non-players are not a unique characteristic or need of the game. Anti-competitive conduct toward umpires is not an essential part of baseball and in no way enhances its vitality or viability." Postema's antitrust suit could accordingly proceed.[9] The parties settled before the suit reached a conclusion, but the antitrust exemption had suffered its first blow.

A more serious blow came just a year later. In 1992, a group of investors led by Vince Piazza (the father of catcher Mike Piazza) reached a preliminary agreement to purchase the San Francisco Giants and move them to Tampa. When baseball denied permission, Piazza sued on a variety of grounds, including antitrust. Baseball once again defended the antitrust claim by invoking its antitrust exemption, but Judge John Padova viewed the exemption even more narrowly than in *Postema*. In *Flood*, Padova reasoned, the Supreme Court had spoken only of the reserve clause as exempt from antitrust scrutiny. It had not repeated the broader claim of *Toolson* that the entire business of baseball was exempt. Padova concluded that after *Flood*, the only aspect of baseball covered by the antitrust exemption was thus the reserve clause. All other facets of the game, including the restrictions on franchise relocation, were open to antitrust challenge. The following year, in another lawsuit growing out of the Giants' frustrated move to Tampa—this one filed by Florida attorney general Robert Butterworth—the Florida Supreme Court agreed. "There is no question that *Piazza* is against the great weight of federal cases regarding the scope of the exemption," the court acknowledged. "However, none of the other cases have engaged in such a comprehensive analysis of *Flood* and its implications." The court accordingly concluded that "baseball's antitrust exemption extends only to the reserve system."[10]

The *Piazza* and *Butterworth* decisions rested on a not-very-plausible reading of *Flood v. Kuhn*, one that may have stemmed (in *Piazza*) from Judge Padova's sense that the exemption was so absurd that it ought to be confined as narrowly as possible, and (in *Butterworth*) from the Florida's Supreme Court's dissatisfaction with the power of the commissioner's office to stymie the state's efforts to attract a major league team. These were nevertheless troubling developments for organized baseball. As one contemporary observer put it, the two decisions "could signify the first note of the death knell for baseball's antitrust exemption." Baseball promptly settled the cases and announced that a new franchise would be located in Tampa. "Once the Florida Supreme Court issued that decision, Major League Baseball caved in and, boom, Tampa Bay got baseball," remarked the law professor Stephen Ross. Thomas Ostertag, baseball's general counsel, worried that "a legal trend might be developing," under which "baseball's exemption had been greatly narrowed."[11]

In the subsequent cases, however, courts have returned to the older view that the exemption covers the entire business of baseball, not just the reserve system. *Piazza* and *Butterworth* were erroneous interpretations of the Supreme Court's opinion in *Flood v. Kuhn*, a Seattle judge concluded in dismissing a lawsuit brought by fans deprived of baseball by the 1994–1995 players' strike. "This Court rejects the reasoning and results of *Piazza* and *Butterworth*," the judge declared. "In essence, the plaintiffs invite this Court to invalidate a rule that was established by the Supreme Court over seventy years ago and that has been reaffirmed by the Supreme Court twice since its inception." When the state of Minnesota sued to block the Twins' prospective move to North Carolina, the Minnesota Supreme Court likewise held that the exemption protected every aspect of the baseball business, including decisions about the sale and relocation of franchises.[12]

The strongest statement of this view came in a 2001 decision that barred the state of Florida from investigating baseball's plan to contract by eliminating two teams. (Baseball did not announce which teams would be the ones to go, but two of the likely candidates were the new teams in Florida, the Marlins and the Devil Rays, who were both losing money.) After an exhaustive analysis of the Supreme Court's opinions in *Federal Baseball Club*, *Toolson*, and *Flood*, Judge Robert Hinkle concluded that "*Flood* constitutes an unequivocal, binding decision of the United States Supreme Court, establishing that the business of baseball is exempt from the antitrust laws, as it has been since 1922, and as it will remain unless and until Congress decides otherwise. Period." On appeal, the court of appeals agreed emphatically. Hinkle "forcefully destroyed the notion that the antitrust exemption should be narrowly cabined to the reserve system," the court noted. The court of appeals drove the point home by repeatedly referring to the exemption as "the business-of-baseball exemption." Indeed, Hinkle's opinion was so thorough and persuasive that when the state appealed, it completely abandoned the argument that the exemption applied only to the reserve clause and contended instead that the determination to eliminate teams was in fact not part of the business of baseball, a claim the court of appeals had little trouble rejecting.[13] After a few years of uncertainty in the courts, baseball had succeeded in beating back the effort to narrow the exemption to the reserve clause.

Meanwhile, baseball had to fight similar battles in Congress. Whenever there was political advantage in publicly chastising baseball, some member of Congress could be depended upon to introduce a bill modifying or eliminating the antitrust exemption, and baseball officials could count on having to testify before a House or Senate committee. After a two-month player strike in the middle of the 1981 season, the House held hearings on a bill to repeal baseball's antitrust exemption. Similar hearings on similar bills took place after the shorter work stoppages of 1985 and 1990. The 1994–1995 strike, the longest in baseball history, produced several bills to repeal the exemption, one of which was even approved by the Senate Judiciary Committee and sent to the full Senate. Repealing baseball's antitrust exemption would hardly have brought any of these strikes closer to an end, but these bills were more about theater than pragmatism. Members of Congress were engaging in symbolic politics by trying to ensure that the public saw them punishing baseball for not providing games for the fans. (The 1994–1995 strike ended, not because of anything Congress had done, but because a young trial judge named Sonia Sotomayor enjoined the owners from unilaterally changing the free agency and salary arbitration rules while negotiating a new collective bargaining agreement.[14] Fourteen years later, the retired pitcher David Cone, who had been the American League's player representative during the strike, testified in favor of Sotomayor's confirmation as a Supreme Court justice.)

The sporadic controversies over the relocation or elimination of franchises also spawned bills to limit or end baseball's antitrust exemption.

These efforts had their element of theater as well, but they also had a practical purpose in that the antitrust exemption was what allowed baseball to control the location of its teams. When the Giants were not permitted to move to Florida, the state's two senators supported legislation to repeal the exemption. One of them was Connie Mack, whose views were of special interest because his grandfather, also named Connie Mack, had been the owner and manager of the Philadelphia A's for half a century. These efforts lost steam when baseball promised to add an expansion team in Florida. In 2001, when baseball planned to contract by disbanding two teams, the idea elicited a proposed "Fairness in Antitrust in National Sports Act of 2001" (the initials spelled "FANS"), which would have made the antitrust laws applicable to the elimination or relocation of major league baseball franchises. The House sponsors of the bill included representatives from Florida and Minnesota, the states with teams on the chopping block.[15]

Because of all this legislative activity, baseball opened a full-time office in Washington in 1993. In the first half of 1996 alone, the owners spent $630,000 on lobbyists. They also made considerable campaign contributions.[16] The antitrust exemption was not the only baseball issue before Congress, but it was the most important one. Baseball's political expenditures were a form of insurance against the possibility that the exemption would be revoked.

The only fruit of all these legislative battles was the Curt Flood Act of 1998. The law had an unusual origin. The collective bargaining agreement reached in December 1996, the first such agreement after the strike of 1994–1995, included a clause requiring the players and the owners to cooperate in asking Congress to pass a law clarifying that major league baseball players are covered under the antitrust laws to the same extent as professional athletes in other sports. This legislation was important to the players, one of their lobbyists explained, because without it, free agency would be at risk whenever a collective bargaining agreement expired. In other sports, athletes could rely on antitrust law to secure free agency, even without a collective bargaining agreement, but baseball's antitrust exemption meant that free agency in baseball depended entirely on the existence of a collective bargaining agreement providing for it, and the strike had demonstrated to the players that they could not necessarily count on bargaining to succeed.[17]

The club owners were willing to relinquish this one part of the antitrust exemption, because it had no practical effect so long as there was a collective bargaining agreement providing for free agency, and it was extremely unlikely that the players would ever agree to give up free agency. By contrast, it was important to the owners to retain the antitrust exemption as it applied to all other parts of the game, especially franchise relocation, where it still insulated baseball from being sued on antitrust grounds. The minor leagues likewise clung to the exemption, because they would be on treacherous ground without it. This political configuration gave the Curt Flood Act a very unusual structure for a statute. Most statutes are made up entirely of provisions that state what the law is to be. A few statutes also include language specifying a particular way in which prior law is not to change, but such provisions are typically very short. The Flood Act is exactly the opposite. It includes a brief section stating that the antitrust laws apply to the employment of major league players, and then a considerably longer section listing the ways in which the law is not changing at all. This latter section specifies that the act does not apply the antitrust laws to aspects of the game other than the employment of major league players, including matters relating to broadcasting, to the minor leagues, to the relationship among teams, to the location and ownership of franchises, and to the employment of umpires.[18]

The ink was barely dry before lawyers began arguing about the Flood Act's implications. By abolishing the antitrust exemption for one aspect of the game, was Congress implying that there *was* an exemption for all the other aspects? If so, it would be the first intimation of approval from Congress in the 76 years since the exemption had been recognized in *Federal Baseball Club*. The sports law professor Gary Roberts concluded the act did imply a recognition of the exemption. The ironic result, he suggested, was that "legislation that started out to apply antitrust more broadly to baseball has probably caused exactly the opposite effect." Steven Fehr, who represented the Players Association, disagreed. He argued that the Flood Act had been carefully drafted to avoid taking any position on how antitrust law should apply to aspects of the game other than the employment of major league players, and that courts would thus not recognize any implied approval of the exemption in these other areas. There have not yet been any cases interpreting the act, so we don't yet know who is right.[19]

Explaining the exemption

When one looks closely at the history of baseball's antitrust exemption, it becomes clear that baseball's unique cultural status has played only a small part in the story. In 1922, when the Supreme Court held in *Federal Baseball Club* that baseball was not governed by federal antitrust law because it was not a form of interstate commerce, the decision had little to do with baseball's cultural status. Baseball was the only commercially successful professional team sport in the United States in 1922, so it happened to be the one challenged under the antitrust laws, but the result would have been the same with any other sport. If a professional football or basketball league had been sued under the antitrust laws in 1922, football or basketball would have been treated just the same as baseball. If *Federal Baseball Club* had come to the Supreme Court in 1942 rather than 1922, the Court would have deemed baseball a form of interstate commerce. Baseball's antitrust exemption originated in the constitutional law of the 1920s and the fortuity that baseball happened to get sued early, not in any special solicitude for baseball on the part of judges.

The perpetuation of baseball's exemption, long after its supporting structure of constitutional law crumbled to the ground, likewise had little to do with romanticism about baseball. Antitrust suits against baseball were rare events. It took 30 years for another baseball antitrust case to reach the Supreme Court, in part because of strategic litigation decisions made by baseball officials and their lawyers. By then, baseball could point to decades of investments club owners had made in reliance on their immunity from antitrust law. For the Court to overrule *Federal Baseball Club* would have been to declare that all along baseball actually *had* been governed by antitrust law. There was a substantial risk that such a decision would have subjected owners to massive retroactive liability, because thousands of players in the majors and minors might have had plausible antitrust suits. In *Toolson v. New York Yankees*, the Court accordingly shied away from overruling *Federal Baseball Club*. The Court acknowledged that baseball's antitrust exemption rested on an outdated view of interstate commerce, but it held that any change in the law should come from Congress, because only Congress had the power to make a change with only prospective effect. Two decades later, when the issue came up in again in *Flood v. Kuhn*, the Court said the same thing.

Some of the justices involved in these cases were baseball fans, and some, especially Harry Blackmun, wore their hearts on their sleeves. Baseball could turn some sharp analytic minds to mush, but that was not the primary reason the Supreme Court refused to overrule *Federal Baseball Club*. The same justices who gushed over the sport were perfectly happy for Congress to declare that baseball would be governed by antitrust law. The persistence of the exemption, in the courts, has distinctly legal roots: the unwillingness of judges to impose retroactive liability for conduct that was lawful at the time it took place.

Why, then, did Congress not step in and treat all sports equally, especially in light of the Supreme Court's repeated invitations that it do so? The answer is that Congress did step in; the difficult thing was to step out. The question of how to apply antitrust law to sports was before Congress almost continuously between 1957 and 1966 and has been back intermittently ever since. Nearly everyone has agreed that all sports should be treated equally, but there has been no agreement over exactly how that should be done, so Congress has never been able to pass a uniform sports antitrust law. Meanwhile, as other sports grew to rival baseball in commercial success—and then even, in the case of football, to surpass baseball—the other sports were able to obtain statutory antitrust immunity for broadcasting and league mergers, the issues that mattered most to them. Finally, with the emergence of powerful labor unions in professional sports beginning in the 1970s, baseball's exemption became less significant, because the terms of player contracts came to be set by collective bargaining rather than unilaterally by club owners. Baseball's antitrust exemption was thus able to survive several decades of congressional attempts to abolish it.

The exemption is just as anomalous as it ever was. It shows no signs of weakening. As of 2012, there does not appear to be any significant chance that either Congress or the Supreme Court will abolish it. Then again, both institutions have confounded expectations in the past. There have been times when knowledgeable lawyers—sometimes even baseball's own lawyers—have predicted that Congress or the Supreme Court would set things straight. Maybe one day one of them will. For now, though, baseball's antitrust exemption looks set to reach its centenary in 2022. One of the strangest doctrines in our legal system is also becoming one of the oldest.

NOTES

INTRODUCTION

1. Gary R. Roberts, "The Case for Baseball's Special Antitrust Immunity," *Journal of Sports Economics* 4 (2003): 307. As the title of Roberts's article suggests, he is one of the very few defenders of baseball's unique status who is not employed in the baseball business.
2. The only previous sustained historical treatment of baseball's antitrust exemption is Jerold J. Duquette, *Regulating the National Pastime: Baseball and Antitrust* (Westport, Conn.: Praeger, 1999). Duquette relies on what he calls "an historical-institutionalist methodology" to divide the twentieth century into four successive "regimes," each characterized by a particular approach to regulation, and to identify the factors associated with each regime that were conducive to the exemption. In my view, this method is not helpful in explaining either the exemption's origin or its persistence, because the "regimes" are so stylized that one could use them to account for just about anything that took place during the period.
3. G. Edward White, *Creating the National Pastime: Baseball Transforms Itself, 1903–1953* (Princeton, N.J.: Princeton University Press, 1996), 83; Paul Finkelman, "Baseball and the Rule of Law," *Cleveland State Law Review* 46 (1998): 248; Larry G. Bumgardner, "Baseball's Antitrust Exemption," in Paul D. Staudohar, ed., *Diamond Mines: Baseball & Labor* (Syracuse, N.Y.: Syracuse University Press, 2000), 83.
4. A. Bartlett Giamatti, *Take Time for Paradise: Americans and Their Games* (New York: Summit Books, 1989), 67; Stephen R. Lowe, *The Kid on the Sandlot: Congress and Professional Sports, 1910–1992* (Bowling Green, Ohio: Bowling Green State University Popular Press, 1995), 27.

CHAPTER 1

1. John Thorn, *Baseball in the Garden of Eden: The Secret History of the Early Game* (New York: Simon & Schuster, 2011), 164–171; Harold Seymour, *Baseball: The Early Years* (New York: Oxford University Press, 1960), 86–93.
2. *Buffalo Commercial Advertiser*, September 30 and October 3, 1879, reproduced in Dean A. Sullivan, ed., *Early Innings: A Documentary History of Baseball, 1825–1908* (Lincoln: University of Nebraska Press, 1995), 114.

3. "The First Reserve Agreement," Clipping File: Economics-Reserve Clause, BHF.

4. Alfred H. Spink, *The National Game*, 2nd ed. (1911; Carbondale: Southern Illinois University Press, 2000), 14; *Organized Baseball: Report of the Subcommittee on Study of Monopoly Power of the Committee on the Judiciary* (Washington, D.C.: Government Printing Office, 1952), 23–25; David Nemec, *The Beer and Whisky League: The Illustrated History of the American Association—Baseball's Renegade Major League* (Guilford, Conn.: Lyons Press, 2004), 46.

5. *Organized Baseball*, 23.

6. *New York Times*, October 21, 1913, 7; *Life*, July 28, 1887, 2; Remarks of Charles H. Lichtman, appended to James R. Burnet, "Critical Opinions Upon Recent Employers' Liability Legislation in the United States," *Journal of Social Science* 40 (1902): 80.

7. Bryan Di Salvatore, *A Clever Base-Ballist: The Life and Times of John Montgomery Ward* (New York: Pantheon Books, 1999).

8. John Montgomery Ward, "Is the Base-Ball Player a Chattel?" *Lippincott's Monthly Magazine* 40 (1887): 310–319.

9. Steven A. Riess, *Touching Base: Professional Baseball and American Culture in the Progressive Era*, rev. ed. (Urbana: University of Illinois Press, 1999), 158; Robert F. Burk, *Never Just a Game: Players, Owners, and American Baseball to 1920* (Chapel Hill: University of North Carolina Press, 1994), 243; *New-York Tribune*, April 15, 1888, 14; "Base-Ball Slavery," *Puck*, September 15, 1886, 37; *Los Angeles Times*, July 14, 1912, VII7; A. G. Mills to Thomas J. Lynch, May 31, 1910, A.G. Mills papers, box 1, folder 3, BHF.

10. Jennifer K. Ashcraft and Craig A. Depken, II, "The Introduction of the Reserve Clause in Major League Baseball: Evidence of its Impact on Select Player Salaries During the 1880s" (2007), http://ssrn.com/abstract=899390; E. Woodrow Eckard, "The Origin of the Reserve Clause: Owner Collusion Versus 'Public Interest,'" *Journal of Sports Economics* 2 (2001): 113–130; "Baseball Law," *Law Notes* 17 (1914): 208; Hugh S. Fullerton, "The Baseball Primer," *American Magazine* 74 (1912): 204; Affidavit of August Herrmann, 11, Chicago Case, box 2, folder 6.

11. Adrian C. Anson, *A Ball Player's Career* (Chicago: Era Publishing Co., 1900), 120; Seymour, *Baseball: The Early Years*, 51–52; Affidavit of A. G. Mills, 1, Chicago Case, box 6, folder 21; Francis C. Richter, *Richter's History and Records of Base Ball, the American Nation's Chief Sport* (1914; Jefferson, N.C.: McFarland & Co., 2005), 280.

12. Charles Jacobson, "The Supreme Court of Baseball," *Case and Comment* 23 (1917): 667; Charles D. Stewart, "The United States of Baseball," *Century Illustrated Monthly Magazine* 74 (1907): 317.

13. Albert G. Spalding, *America's National Game: Historic Facts Concerning the Beginning, Evolution, Development and Popularity of Base Ball* (1911; San Francisco: Halo Books, 1991), 142; F.C. Lane, "A Rising Menace to the National Game," *Baseball Magazine*, August 1918, 345; "Editorials," *Baseball Magazine*, May 1914, 12.

14. John J. Evers and Hugh S. Fullerton, *Touching Second: The Science of Baseball* (Chicago: Reilly & Britton Co., 1910), 42, 45; David L. Fultz, "The Reserve Clause: The Greatest Problem in the Baseball World Today," *Baseball Magazine*, March 1913, 31.

15. *Salt Lake Herald*, February 15, 1890, 6.

16. An earlier case, *Allegheny Base-Ball Club v. Bennett*, 14 F. 257 (W.D. Pa. 1882), is sometimes said to be the first legal challenge to the reserve clause, but this is true only in an indirect sense. The catcher Charlie Bennett, who played for the Detroit Wolverines of the National League, signed an agreement with the Pittsburgh Alleghenys of the American Association toward the end of the 1882 season in which, in exchange for $100, he promised to sign a contract for the 1883 season with the Alleghenys. When Bennett instead signed with Detroit for 1883, the Alleghenys sued. The court refused to enforce the Alleghenys' agreement with Bennett. The judge did not issue a written opinion, so the grounds of his decision are not clear, but Bennett's primary argument was that the agreement was too uncertain to be enforced, because it did not specify what Bennett's salary would be. Courts would later refuse to enforce the reserve clause for the same reason, and perhaps the judges in these cases had Bennett's case in mind, although they did not cite it as precedent. Strictly speaking, however, this was not a case involving the reserve clause. Neither the Wolverines nor the Alleghenys were claiming Bennett on the ground that he had been reserved for the 1883 season.

17. George V. Tuohey, *A History of the Boston Base Ball Club* (Boston: M.F. Quinn & Co., 1897), 101; Henry Chadwick, "The Secession Movement in the Professional Baseball Arena," *Outing* 15 (1890): 313.

18. National League Minutes: Scrapbook, 1881–1891, 63, BHF.

19. "Hub Happenings," *Sporting Life*, December 11, 1889, 2; F. J. Stimson, *Handbook to the Labor Law of the United States* (New York: Charles Scribner's Sons, 1896), 30.

20. *Lumley v. Wagner*, 42 Eng. Rep. 687 (1852); *Daly v. Smith*, 38 N.Y. Super. 158 (1874); "Hub Happenings," 2.

21. "The Law Suit," *Sporting Life*, December 25, 1889, 5; "That Law Suit," *Sporting Life*, January 5, 1890, 1.

22. *Metropolitan Exhibition Co. v. Ward*, 9 N.Y.S. 779 (N.Y. Sup. 1890).

23. *New York Times*, January 29, 1890, 2; "Beginning to Reap the Whirlwind," *Sporting Life*, February 5, 1890, 4; National League Minutes: Scrapbook, 1881–1891, 66.

24. *Philadelphia Ball Club, Ltd. v. Hallman*, 8 Pa. Co. Ct. Rep. 57 (1890).

25. *New York Times*, March 17, 1890, 4; Rogers quoted in David Quentin Voigt, *American Baseball* (University Park: Pennsylvania State University Press, 1983), 1:163.

26. *Metropolitan Exhibition Co. v. Ewing*, 42 F. 198 (C.C.S.D.N.Y. 1890).

27. *Harrisburg Base-Ball Club v. Athletic Association*, 8 Pa. Co. Ct. Rep. 337 (1890); *Columbus Base Ball Club v. Reiley* [sic], 11 Ohio Dec. 272 (1891); *American Association Base-Ball Club of Kansas City v. Pickett*, 8 Pa. Co. Ct. Rep. 232 (1890).

28. *American Base Ball & Athletic Exhibition Co. v. Harper* (1902), reported in *Central Law Journal* 54 (1902): 449–451; *Brooklyn Baseball Club v. McGuire*, 116 F. 782 (C.C.E.D. Pa. 1902).

29. This form of reserve clause was instituted in some contracts after the Players' League litigation, in order to make the contracts seem less one-sided. In practice, no players became free agents when their reserve clauses ostensibly expired. Clubs simply required them to sign new contracts with identical reserve provisions. Peter S. Craig, "Monopsony in Manpower: Organized Baseball Meets the Antitrust Laws," *Yale Law Journal* 62 (1953): 588 n.67.

30. *Philadelphia Base-Ball Club, Ltd. v. Lajoie*, 10 Pa. Dist. Rep. 309 (1901).

31. *Philadelphia Ball Club, Ltd. v. Lajoie*, 51 A. 973 (Pa. 1902).

32. *Washington Evening Times*, April 22, 1902, 3; *New York Times*, April 22, 1902, 6; *New York Times*, April 23, 1902, 5; Eugene C. Murdock, *Ban Johnson: Czar of Baseball* (Westport, Conn.: Greenwood Press, 1982), 54; *Philadelphia Baseball Club Co. v. Lajoie*, 13 Ohio Dec. 504 (1902); Seymour, *Baseball: The Early Years*, 315.

33. John W. Stayton, "Baseball Jurisprudence," *American Law Review* 44 (1910): 393; "Base-Ball and the Bench," *Canada Law Journal* 38 (1902): 482; Editorial, *Columbia Jurist* 2 (1885): 146.

34. *New York Times*, November 2, 1913, S1; *New York Times*, December 29, 1913, 5.

35. August Herrmann, "The National Commission and Its Helpful Relationship to the National Game" (1913), Chicago Case, box 1, folder 1; Barry Gilbert, "Some Old Problems in a Modern Guise," *California Law Review* 4 (1915): 118 and n.22.

36. John C. Bell to John K. Tener, February 3, 1914, AH, box 108, folder 15; Ellis G. Kinkead and John Galvin to August Herrmann, February 25, 1914, AH, box 108, folder 15; Paul B. Moody to Frank J. Navin, February 20, 1914, AH, box 108, folder 15; "More Baseball Law," *Law Notes* 18 (1914): 23.

37. John Galvin and Ellis G. Kinkead to August Herrmann, April 20, 1914, AH, box 110, folder 7.

38. John Galvin and Ellis G. Kinkead to August Herrmann, June 19, 1914, AH, box 104, folder 1; August Herrmann to B. B. Johnson and John K. Tener, December 19, 1914, AH, box 104, folder 1.

39. Joe Tinker, "Putting Across the Federal League," *Everybody's Magazine* 30 (1914): 587; *New York Times*, January 6, 1914, 11; *New York Times*, April 5, 1914, S1.

40. Harold Seymour, *Baseball: The Golden Age* (New York: Oxford University Press, 1971), 206; *Cincinnati Exhibition Co. v. Marsans*, 216 F. 269 (E.D. Mo. 1914); Peter T. Toot, *Armando Marsans: A Cuban Pioneer in the Major Leagues* (Jefferson, N.C.: McFarland & Co., 2004), 77–124.

41. "Release Clause in Baseball Contracts," *Law Notes* 18 (1914): 82–83; *Cincinnati Exhibition Co. v. Johnson*, 190 Ill. App. 630 (1914); *American League Baseball Club of Chicago v. Chase*, 86 Misc. 441 (N.Y. Sup. 1914).

42. Brad Snyder, *Beyond the Shadow of the Senators: The Untold Story of the Homestead Grays and the Integration of Baseball* (Chicago: Contemporary Books, 2003), 66; Jeffrey Powers-Beck, *The American Indian Integration of Baseball* (Lincoln: University of Nebraska Press, 2004), 120–142; Martin Donell Kohout, *Hal Chase: The Defiant Life and Turbulent Times of Baseball's Biggest Crook* (Jefferson, N.C.: McFarland & Co., 2001); Donald Dewey and Nicholas Acocella, *The Black Prince of Baseball: Hal Chase and the Mythology of Baseball* (Toronto: Sport Classic Books, 2004).

43. Affidavit of Charles Weeghman and W. M. Walker, 4, Affidavit of William M. Killefer, Jr., 3, both in *Weeghman v. Killefer* (W.D. Mich. 1914), Equity Case 1789, RG21, NA-C.

44. *Weeghman v. Killefer*, 215 F. 168 (W.D. Mich. 1914); *Weeghman v. Killefer*, 215 F. 289 (6th Cir. 1914).

45. *New York Times*, April 11, 1914, 12; Ellis G. Kinkead to August Herrmann, April 13, 1914, AH, box 110, folder 7.

46. Charles Weeghman, "What the Federal League is Fighting For," *Baseball Magazine*, March 1915, 22; *New York Times*, April 12, 1914, S1.

47. Ward, "Is the Base-Ball Player a Chattel?" 311; John Montgomery Ward, "Our National Game," *Cosmopolitan* 5 (1888): 445; *Deseret Evening News*, March 4, 1890, 1; *New York Sun*, quoted in "Editor v. Player," *Sporting Life*, May 31, 1890, 8; "Three-tee's Thoughts," *Sporting Life*, August 9, 1890, 9.

48. "Comments from the Press," *Baseball Magazine*, April 1915, 87; Lee Lowenfish and Tony Lupien, *The Imperfect Diamond: The Story of Baseball's Reserve System and the Men Who Fought to Change It* (New York: Stein & Day, 1980), 27–84.

CHAPTER 2

1. *Salt Lake Herald*, March 27, 1892, 2; Ralph D. Paine, "The Reign of Baseball," *Munsey's Magazine* 37 (1907): 333; *Hopkinsville Kentuckian*, October 15, 1908, 2; *Sporting Life*, December 28, 1907, 5; *Evening Times* [Washington, D.C.], March 28, 1901, 2.

2. Adam Smith, *The Wealth of Nations* (1776; Hartford: Oliver D. Cooke, 1804), 1:109; William Blackstone, *Commentaries on the Laws of England*, 4th ed. (Oxford: Clarendon Press, 1770), 4:159; Tony Freyer, *Regulating Big Business: Antitrust in Great Britain and America, 1880–1990* (Cambridge: Cambridge University Press, 1992), 24–25; James May, "Antitrust Practice and Procedure in the Formative Era: The Constitutional and Conceptual Reach of State Antitrust Law, 1880–1918," *University of Pennsylvania Law Review* 135 (1987): 497–501.

3. Business combinations were called "trusts" because some of the early ones took that legal form. The term quickly became a misnomer when the trust was superseded by other merger techniques, but it nevertheless persisted in popular speech, and lawyers still refer to this area of law as "antitrust."

4. 26 Stat. 209 (1890); Martin J. Sklar, *The Corporate Reconstruction of American Capitalism, 1890–1916* (Cambridge: Cambridge University Press, 1988), 86–154; Rudolph J. R. Peritz, *Competition Policy in America, 1888–1992* (New York: Oxford University Press, 1996).

5. "Come, Let Us Reason Together!" *Sporting Life*, December 5, 1891, 2; "Level Headed Ward," *Sporting Life*, April 23, 1892, 1; John B. Foster, "Brooklyn Budget," *Sporting Life*, November 5, 1910, 6.

6. A. G. Mills to John Tener, April 14, 1914, A. G. Mills papers, box 1, folder 4, BHF; "National Agreement and Legality" (February 18, 1916), A. G. Mills papers, box 2, folder 8, BHF.

7. *American Base Ball & Athletic Exhibition Co. v. Harper* (1902), reported in *Central Law Journal* 54 (1902): 450–451.

8. *New York Times*, November 4, 1906, 11; *Los Angeles Herald*, November 10, 1906, 8; "Callahan's Suit," *Sporting Life*, November 24, 1906, 5.

9. *Washington Herald*, December 18, 1907, 8; *Washington Times*, December 24, 1907, 8; Lyell D. Henry, Jr., *Zig-Zag-and-Swirl: Alfred W. Lawson's Quest for Greatness* (Iowa City: University of Iowa Press, 1991).

10. *San Francisco Call*, January 15, 1910, 20; *New-York Tribune*, February 7, 1910, 8.

11. *Times Dispatch* [Richmond, Va.], September 28, 1910, 3; *New York Times*, January 20, 1912, 11.

12. *Sporting Life*, November 27, 1909, 4; *Sporting Life*, June 28, 1913, 4.

13. H. Res. 450, 62nd Cong., 2nd Sess. (March 11, 1912).

14. *New York Times*, March 12, 1912, 10; "Have No Fear," *Sporting Life*, March 23, 1912, 2.
15. Nicholas Longworth to August Herrmann, March 13, 1912 and March 16, 1912, AH, box 114, folder 1; Charles Comiskey to August Herrmann, March 14, 1912, AH, box 114, folder 1.
16. Charles W. Murphy to August Herrmann, March 15, 1912, AH, box 114, folder 1; Charles W. Murphy, "Taft, the Fan," *Baseball Magazine*, July 1912, 7; *Wall Street Journal*, March 13, 1912, 1; *New York Times*, March 17, 1912, C7.
17. "One Understandable Trust," *Munsey's Magazine* 47 (1912): 195; *New York Times*, March 13, 1912, 10; "Charles Barnard," *Baseball Magazine*, April 1912, 17.
18. "It's Necessary," *Sporting Life*, January 11, 1913, 13; "At the Capital," *Sporting Life*, April 19, 1913, 3.
19. One of those batting titles, from 1910, is now generally credited to Napoleon Lajoie, due to a statistical error that came to light many years later.
20. Ty Cobb, with Al Stump, *My Life in Baseball: The True Record* (Garden City, N.Y.: Doubleday, 1961), 105–106; *New York Times*, April 20, 1913, 1; Charles Comiskey to F. J. Navin, April 22, 1913, AH, box 114, folder 2; Charles Comiskey to August Herrmann, April 22, 1913, AH, box 114, folder 2; Charles C. Alexander, *Ty Cobb* (New York: Oxford University Press, 1984), 109–113.
21. "More Progress in Georgia," *Life* 61 (1913): 1036; "The Return of Tyrus," *Outing* 62 (1913): 381; "Ready for Issue When it Arises," *Sporting Life*, May 3, 1913, 4.
22. H. Res. 64, 63rd Cong., 1st Sess. (April 22, 1913); *New York Times*, April 24, 1913, 9; "Down with the Base-Ball Trust," *Puck*, May 14, 1913, 2.
23. Illegible correspondent to August Herrmann, April 29, 1913, AH, box 114, folder 2; F. C. Lane, "Horace Fogel, the Man Who Is Trying to Wreck Baseball," *Baseball Magazine*, June 1913, 21–32; *Los Angeles Times*, June 6, 1913, III2.
24. Daniel R. Levitt, *The Battle That Forged Modern Baseball: The Federal League Challenge and Its Legacy* (Lanham, Md.: Ivan R. Dee, 2012); Robert Peyton Wiggins, *The Federal League of Base Ball Clubs: The History of an Outlaw Major League, 1914–1915* (Jefferson, N.C.: McFarland & Co., 2009), 9–17; John Conway Toole to Thomas J. Lynch, June 17, 1913, AH, box 114, folder 3; *New York Times*, June 16, 1913, 7; Francis Richter to August Herrmann, June 10, 1913, AH, box 114, folder 3.
25. Benjamin Minor to John E. Bruce, April 26, 1913, AH, box 114, folder 2; Alfred G. Allen to John E. Bruce, April 25, 1913, AH, box 114, folder 2; William Alden Smith to F. J. Navin, May 12, 1913, AH, box 114, folder 3; Frank E. Doremus to Frank J. Navin, May 12, 1913, AH, box 114, folder 3; James M. Curley to Herman Nickerson, May 14, 1913, AH, box 114, folder 3.
26. National Commission to "Presidents and Club-owners," n.d. (1913), AH, box 114, folder 2; Oscar W. Underwood to A. H. Woodward, May 12, 1913, AH, box 114, folder 3; O. B. Andrews to Gordon Lee, May 8, 1913, AH, box 114, folder 3; Claude G. Bowers to Sol Myer, May 15, 1913, AH, box 114, folder 3; J. Cal Ewing to Joseph R. Knowland, May 14, 1913, AH, box 114, folder 3.
27. August Herrmann to A. H. Woodward, April 24, 1913, AH, box 114, folder 2; O. B. Andrews to August Herrmann, May 8, 1913, AH, box 114, folder 3; C. F. Curry to J. Cal Ewing, May 20, 1913, AH, box 114, folder 2; John A. Moon to O. B. Andrews, May 12, 1913, AH, box 114, folder 3.

28. Clark Griffith to C. T. Chapin, April 16, 1913, AH, box 114, folder 3; Charles Comiskey to August Herrmann, May 23, 1913, AH, box 114, folder 3; *Congressional Record* 50 (1913): 4623; *Saturday Evening Post*, May 24, 1912, in AH, box 114, folder 3.
29. *New York Times*, April 25, 1913, 9.
30. "Law Dangers Reduced," *Sporting Life*, July 5, 1913, 4.
31. *New York Times*, December 31, 1913, 12; *Sporting Life*, January 10, 1914, 14.
32. *New York Times*, January 26, 1914, 8; *Sporting Life*, January 10, 1914, 13.
33. John C. Bell to John K. Tener, February 3, 1914, AH, box 108, folder 15; Ellis G. Kinkead and John Galvin to August Herrmann, February 25, 1914, AH, box 108, folder 15; Paul B. Moody to Frank J. Navin, February 20, 1914, AH, box 108, folder 15.
34. *New York Times*, June 13, 1913, 10; "Reserve Rule," *Sporting Life*, June 21, 1913, 1; "Dreyfuss Wins His Case," *Sporting Life*, April 11, 1914, 13; "The Law and Baseball," *Sporting Life*, August 1, 1914, 2; *Cincinnati Exhibition Co. v. Marsans*, 216 F. 269 (E.D. Mo. 1914); *Los Angeles Times*, October 17, 1914, 11; "More Trouble for Base Ball," *Sporting Life*, October 31, 1914, 1.
35. "That Chase for Chase," *Sporting Life*, July 18, 1914, 2; Ellis G. Kinkead to August Herrmann, July 14, 1914, AH, box 108, folder 24; Memorandum for Plaintiff in Reply, AH, box 108, folder 24.
36. *American League Baseball Club of Chicago v. Chase*, 86 Misc. 441 (N.Y. Sup. 1914).
37. "Whither Goest Thou?" *Sporting Life*, August 1, 1914, 4; Watson & Freeman to Pittsburgh Athletic Company, January 5, 1915, AH, box 110, folder 30; August Herrmann to Barney Dreyfuss, January 6, 1915, AH, box 110, folder 30.
38. Wiggins, *Federal League*, 160.
39. Bill of Complaint, Chicago Case, box 1, folder 3. In requesting injunctive relief, the Federal League was taking advantage of the recently enacted Clayton Act of 1914, which authorized such relief for violations of the antitrust laws, a remedy not available under the Sherman Act.
40. *United States v. Standard Oil Co. of Indiana*, 155 F. 305 (N.D. Ill. 1907); Shayna M. Sigman, "The Jurisprudence of Judge Kenesaw Mountain Landis," *Marquette Sports Law Review* 15 (2005): 292–295; David Pietrusza, *Judge and Jury: The Life and Times of Judge Kenesaw Mountain Landis* (South Bend, Ind.: Diamond Communications, 1998), 47–78. Strictly speaking, *Standard Oil* was not an antitrust case but a conviction of violating the Elkins Act of 1903, which barred shippers from accepting rebates from railroads. Landis's judgment was reversed on appeal.
41. Charles Thomas to August Herrmann, January 11, 1915, AH, box 105, folder 7; Benjamin Minor to August Herrmann, January 8, 1915, AH, box 105, folder 7; Clark Griffith to August Herrmann, January 8, 1915, AH, box 105, folder 7.
42. "The Famous Federal Suit," *Baseball Magazine*, March 1915, 65; "Famous Magnates of the Federal League," *Baseball Magazine*, October 1915, 70–71; *New York Times*, January 8, 1915, 9.
43. August Herrmann to "all major league club owners," January 6, 1915, AH, box 105, folder 7; August Herrmann to John K. Tener, January 6, 1915, AH, box 104, folder 1.

44. *Evening Public Ledger* [Philadelphia], January 20, 1915, 12; James Gilmore to Baseball Magazine, February 24, 1915, F.C. Lane papers, box 2, folder 13, BHF; Affidavit of Joseph B. Tinker, 2–3, Chicago Case, box 1, folder 1; Affidavit of Otto Knabe, 3, Chicago Case, box 1, folder 2; Affidavit of Mordecai Brown, 6, Chicago Case, box 1, folder 2.

45. *New York Times,* January 17, 1915, S1; Affidavit of Clark C. Griffith, 2–3, Chicago Case, box 2, folder 5; Affidavit of Roger Bresnahan, Chicago Case, box 3, folder 10; Affidavit of Charles H. Ebbets, 3, Chicago Case, box 5, folder 19.

46. *New York Times,* January 21, 1915, 10; *New Republic,* January 30, 1915, 5; *New York Times,* January 22, 1915, 12.

47. Transcript, vol. 1, *Federal League of Professional Baseball Clubs v. National League of Professional Base Ball Clubs* (January 20–23, 1915), 32, 203, 209–213 AH, box 105, folder 5.

48. Ibid., vol. 1, 231–232, 238.

49. Brief, 18, Chicago Case, box 6, folder 23.

50. Transcript, vol. 1, 247, 248, AH, box 105, folder 5; Transcript, vol. 2, 273, AH, box 105, folder 6.

51. Samuel Lichtenstein to August Herrmann, January 29, 1915, AH, box 106, folder 1; *Evening Public Ledger* [Philadelphia], January 13, 1915, 12; "If Feds Bust the Trust—What Then?" *Sporting News,* January 21, 1915, in AH, box 106, folder 1; *Chicago Tribune,* February 14, 1915, in AH, box 106, folder 1.

52. *Baseball Magazine,* April 1915, 13; J. G. Taylor Spink, *Judge Landis and Twenty-Five Years of Baseball* (New York: Thomas Y. Crowell Co., 1947), 37; *Baseball Magazine,* September 1915, 18; August Herrmann to John K. Tener, November 15, 1915, FLS, box 1, folder 1.

53. Wiggins, *Federal League,* 276; George Wharton Pepper to John K. Tener, October 29, 1915, FLS, box 1, folder 1; George Wharton Pepper to John K. Tener, November 3, 1915, FLS, box 1, folder 1; John K. Tener to George Wharton Pepper, November 6, 1915, FLS, box 1, folder 1; George Wharton Pepper to John K. Tener, November 8, 1915, FLS, box 1, folder 1; Barney Dreyfuss to John K. Tener, November 10, 1915, FLS, box 1, folder 1; August Herrmann to John K. Tener, November 9, 1915, FLS, box 1, folder 1.

54. *Baseball Magazine,* January 1916, 14; Agreement, December 22, 1915, AH, box 104, folder 1; Transcript of Record, 336–338, *Federal Baseball Club of Baltimore v. National League of Professional Baseball Clubs,* 259 U.S. 200 (1922).

55. Wiggins, *Federal League,* 23; Appendix to Brief of Defendants in Error, 145, 147, 155–156, *Federal Baseball Club of Baltimore v. National League of Professional Baseball Clubs,* 259 U.S. 200 (1922).

56. Transcript of dismissal proceedings, February 7, 1916, AH, box 104, folder 1.

57. Ibid.

CHAPTER 3

1. *Federal Baseball Club of Baltimore, Inc. v. National League of Professional Baseball Clubs,* 259 U.S. 200 (1922); Spencer Weber Waller, Neil B. Cohen, and Paul Finkelman, eds., *Baseball and the American Legal Mind* (New York: Garland Publishing, 1995), 75; G. Edward White, *Creating the National Pastime: Baseball Transforms Itself, 1903–1953*

(Princeton, N.J.: Princeton University Press, 1996), 70; Kent M. Krause, "Regulating the Baseball Cartel: A Reassessment of the National Commission, Judge Landis and the Anti-Trust Exemption," *International Journal of the History of Sport* 14 (1997): 72; *Salerno v. American League of Professional Baseball Clubs*, 429 F.2d 1003, 1005 (2d Cir. 1970). For some recent revisionism on the subject, see Samuel A. Alito, Jr., "The Origin of the Baseball Antitrust Exemption: *Federal Baseball Club of Baltimore, Inc. v. National League of Professional Baseball Clubs*," *Journal of Supreme Court History* 34 (2009): 183–195; Kevin McDonald, "Antitrust and Baseball: Stealing Holmes," *Journal of Supreme Court History* 1998 (1998): 89–128.

2. *New York Times*, January 11, 1916, 12.

3. Plaintiff's Statement of Claim, *Federal League Baseball Club of Baltimore, Inc. v. National League of Professional Baseball Clubs* (E.D. Pa., March 24, 1916), AH, box 106, folder 2.

4. "Baltimore Suit Postponed," *Sporting Life*, February 3, 1917, 3; "Organized Ball in Full Power Again," *Sporting Life*, February 24, 1917, 2; "Baltimore Suit Again Postponed," *Sporting Life*, April 7, 1917, 7; *New York Times*, June 12, 1917, 10; *New York Times*, June 16, 1917, 13.

5. Trial transcript, *Federal League Base-Ball Club of Baltimore, Inc. v. National League of Professional Base Ball Clubs* (E.D. Pa., June 11, 1917), 473–474, FLS, box 8; George Wharton Pepper to John Conway Toole, July 5, 1917, AH, box 107, folder 1; *New York Times*, July 26, 1917, 14; George Wharton Pepper to John K. Tener, August 28, 1917, AH, box 107, folder 1.

6. Transcript of Record, 2–36, *Federal Baseball Club of Baltimore, Inc. v. National League of Professional Baseball Clubs*, 259 U.S. 200 (1922); *New York Times*, October 31, 1917, 10; Ban Johnson to August Herrmann, November 3, 1917, AH, box 107, folder 1; August Herrmann to Ban Johnson, November 5, 1917, AH, box 107, folder 1.

7. John K. Tener to James A. Gilmore, May 18, 1916, FLS, box 3, folder 8; *New York Times*, January 14, 1918, 13; *New York Times*, February 13, 1919, 12.

8. Ban Johnson to August Herrmann, February 17, 1919, AH, box 107, folder 1; John Heydler to "all club presidents," February 19, 1919, AH, box 107, folder 1.

9. Wendell Phillips Stafford, *Dorian Days* (New York: Macmillan, 1909); "A Book of Verses," *Green Bag* 22 (1910): 306; Wendell Phillips Stafford, *Speeches of Wendell Phillips Stafford* (St. Johnsbury, Vt.: A.F. Stone, 1913).

10. John Heydler to "all club presidents," March 29, 1919, AH, box 107, folder 3; Trial transcript, *Federal Base Ball Club of Baltimore v. National League of Professional Base Ball Clubs* (D.C. Sup. Ct., April 2, 1919), 1131, 1140, 1144, FLS, box 6; George Wharton Pepper, *Philadelphia Lawyer: An Autobiography* (Philadelphia: J.B. Lippincott Co., 1944), 357.

11. Transcript of Record, 495–497.

12. August Herrmann to George Wharton Pepper, April 21, 1919, FLS, box 4, folder 5; Ban Johnson to August Herrmann, May 19, 1919, AH, box 107, folder 5; John Heydler to all club presidents, April 14, 1919, AH, box 107, folder 4; George Wharton Pepper to August Herrmann, April 28, 1919, AH, box 107, folder 4.

13. George Wharton Pepper to John Heydler, November 8, 1919, AH, box 107, folder 5; Paul W. Eaton, "Baseball's Great Legal Victory," *Baseball Magazine*, February 1921, 426; John Conway Toole to B. B. Johnson, September 24, 1920, FLS, box 5, folder 1; August Herrmann to George Wharton Pepper, December 31, 1919, AH, box 107, folder 6.

14. This court was the federal court of appeals in Washington, the predecessor to today's D.C. Circuit. Today's D.C. Court of Appeals was not created until 1970.

15. "Prominent Lawyers," *Lawyer and Banker and Southern Bench and Bar Review* 8 (1915): 223; *Smyth v. Ames*, 169 U.S. 466 (1898); Jeffrey Brandon Morris, *Calmly to Poise the Scales of Justice: A History of the Courts of the District of Columbia Circuit* (Durham, N.C.: Carolina Academic Press, 2001), 71.

16. George Wharton Pepper to John A. Heydler, October 15, 1920, FLS, box 4, folder 3; Robert C. Cottrell, *Blackball, the Black Sox, and the Babe: Baseball's Crucial 1920 Season* (Jefferson, N.C.: McFarland & Co., 2002); Mike Sowell, *The Pitch That Killed* (New York: Macmillan, 1989); Gene Carney, *Burying the Black Sox: How Baseball's Cover-Up of the 1919 World Series Fix Almost Succeeded* (Washington, D.C.: Potomac Books, 2006).

17. Brief on Behalf of Appellants, 11–12, FLS, box 9.

18. *National League of Professional Baseball Clubs v. Federal Baseball Club of Baltimore, Inc.*, 269 F. 681, 684–685 (D.C. App. 1920).

19. Ibid., 685.

20. "Recent Cases," *Harvard Law Review* 34 (1921): 559; "Recent Important Decisions," *Michigan Law Review* 19 (1921): 868–869; "Baseball Law," *Law Notes*, May 1921, 24.

21. *National League of Professional Baseball Clubs*, 688.

22. *Paul v. Virginia*, 75 U.S. 168, 183 (1869); *Hooper v. California*, 155 U.S. 648, 655 (1895).

23. *United States v. E.C. Knight Co.*, 156 U.S. 1, 12–13 (1895); *Kidd v. Pearson*, 128 U.S. 1, 21 (1888).

24. *Standard Oil Co. of New Jersey v. United States*, 221 U.S. 1, 68–69 (1911); *United States v. American Tobacco Co.*, 221 U.S. 106, 183–184 (1911); *Swift & Co. v. United States*, 196 U.S. 375, 397 (1905).

25. *International Textbook Co. v. Pigg*, 217 U.S. 91 (1910).

26. *Hoke v. United States*, 227 U.S. 308, 320 (1913).

27. *Metropolitan Opera Co. v. Hammerstein*, 147 N.Y.S. 532 (App. Div. 1914).

28. Gerald Gunther, *Learned Hand: The Man and the Judge* (New York: Alfred A. Knopf, 1994), 448; *New York Times*, November 12, 1913, 7; *Marienelli v. United Booking Offices of America*, 227 F. 165 (S.D.N.Y. 1914).

29. Edward A. Hartnett, "Questioning Certiorari: Some Reflections Seventy-Five Years After the Judges' Bill," *Columbia Law Review* 100 (2000): 1643–1738.

30. G. Edward White, *Justice Oliver Wendell Holmes: Law and the Inner Self* (New York: Oxford University Press, 1993), 469; Ross E. Davies, "A Crank on the Court: The Passion of Justice William R. Day," *Baseball Research Journal* 38(2) (2009): 94–107.

31. George Wharton Pepper to John A. Heydler, December 9, 1922, FLS, box 4, folder 13; Brief on Behalf of Plaintiff in Error, *Federal Baseball Club of Baltimore, Inc. v. National League*, 259 U.S. 200 (1922), 12, 14, 120, 145.

32. Brief on Behalf of Defendants in Error, *Federal Baseball Club of Baltimore, Inc. v. National League*, 259 U.S. 200 (1922), 47–48, 11.

33. Ibid., 70.

34. Alexander M. Bickel and Benno C. Schmidt, Jr., *History of the Supreme Court of the United States*, vol. 9: *The Judiciary and Responsible Government, 1910–21* (New York: Macmillan, 1984), 238.

35. *Federal Baseball Club of Baltimore, Inc. v. National League*, 259 U.S. 200, 208–209 (1922).

36. John A. Heydler to George Wharton Pepper, June 1, 1922, FLS, box 5, folder 2; John A. Heydler to Julian Curtis, June 3, 1922, FLS, box 5, folder 2; Julian Curtis to John A. Heydler, May 31, 1922, FLS, box 5, folder 2.

37. "Memorandum of Costs to National League Account Federal League" (December 12, 1922), FLS, box 4, folder 12; *Study of Monopoly Power: Hearings Before the Subcommittee on Study of Monopoly Power of the Committee on the Judiciary, House of Representatives*, 82nd Cong., 1st Sess., Serial No. 1, Part 6: Organized Baseball (1951), 1599.

38. G. F. F., "The Effect of the Sherman Act Upon Monopolies in Amusement Enterprises," *University of Pennsylvania Law Review* 72 (1924): 293–296; "Federal Control of Baseball," *Law Notes* 28 (1925): 202–203; "Baseball and Vaudeville as Interstate Commerce," *Central Law Journal* 96 (1923): 237.

39. Bill Veeck with Ed Linn, *The Hustler's Handbook* (Chicago: Ivan R. Dee, 1965), 77; *Fairness in Antitrust in National Sports (FANS) Act of 2001: Hearing Before the Committee on the Judiciary, House of Representatives*, 107th Cong., 1st Sess. (2001), 1. For another recent example, see George F. Will, *Men at Work: The Craft of Baseball* (New York: Macmillan, 1990), 307.

CHAPTER 4

1. Roger I. Abrams, *Legal Bases: Baseball and the Law* (Philadelphia: Temple University Press, 1998), 62.

2. *Hart v. B.F. Keith Vaudeville Exchange*, 262 U.S. 271 (1923).

3. *Hart v. B.F. Keith Vaudeville Exchange*, 12 F.2d 341 (2d Cir. 1926).

4. *New York World*, December 13, 1923, 15.

5. *New York Times*, October 7, 1924, 17; December 28, 1926, 14; January 1, 1927, 16.

6. *New York Times*, April 3, 1937, 1; April 8, 1937, 3; April 15, 1937, 25; *Chicago Times*, January 22, 1947, clipping in ABC, box 152.

7. *Wickard v. Filburn*, 317 U.S. 111 (1942); Barry Cushman, *Rethinking the New Deal Court: The Structure of a Constitutional Revolution* (New York: Oxford University Press, 1998), 221; *United States v. South-Eastern Underwriters Association*, 322 U.S. 533 (1944).

8. John W. Neville, "Baseball and the Antitrust Laws," *Fordham Law Review* 16 (1947): 208–230; M. L. C., "Baseball and the Law—Yesterday and Today," *Virginia Law Review* 32 (1946): 1164–1176; *Niemiec v. Seattle Rainier Baseball Club*, 67 F. Supp. 705, 712 (W.D. Wash. 1946); John Eckler, "Baseball—Sport or Commerce?" *University of Chicago Law Review* 17 (1949): 56–78; John Eckler, "The Reserve Clause and the Law," *Baseball Digest*, June 1951, 85–88.

9. Jules Tygiel, *Baseball's Great Experiment: Jackie Robinson and His Legacy* (New York: Oxford University Press, 1983), 82–83; "Report for Submission to National and American Leagues on August 27, 1946," ABC, box 162; *American League Baseball Club of New York, Inc. v. Pasquel*, 66 N.Y.S.2d 743, 744 (N.Y. Sup. 1946).

10. G. Richard McKelvey, *Mexican Raiders in the Major Leagues: The Pasquel Brothers vs. Organized Baseball, 1946* (Jefferson, N.C.: McFarland & Co., 2006); John Virtue, *South of the Color Barrier: How Jorge Pasquel and the Mexican League Pushed Baseball Toward Racial Integration* (Jefferson, N.C.: McFarland & Co., 2008); Happy Chandler, *Heroes, Plain Folks, and Skunks: The Life and Times of Happy Chandler* (Chicago: Bonus Books, 1989), 181.

11. "Mexican Hayride," *Time*, March 11, 1946; McKelvey, *Mexican Raiders*, 85–93. The most thorough account of Gardella and his litigation is in William Marshall, *Baseball's Pivotal Era, 1945–1951* (Lexington: University Press of Kentucky, 1999), 45–47, 231–249.

12. Frank Graham, Jr., "The Great Mexican War of 1946," *Sports Illustrated*, September 19, 1966.

13. *Gardella v. Chandler*, 79 F. Supp. 260, 263 (S.D.N.Y. 1948). The dilemma posed by Gardella's case is inherent in a precedent-based legal system and thus persists to this day. See *Rodriguez de Quijas v. Shearson/American Express, Inc.*, 490 U.S. 477, 484 (1989); Evan H. Caminker, "Precedent and Prediction: The Forward-Looking Aspects of Inferior Court Decisionmaking," *Texas Law Review* 73 (1994): 1–82.

14. Chase memorandum, December 3, 1948, *Gardella v. Chandler*, LH, box 211, folder 9.

15. Frank memorandum, December 10, 1948, *Gardella v. Chandler*, LH, box 211, folder 9.

16. Hand memorandum, December 6, 1948, *Gardella v. Chandler*, LH, box 211, folder 9.

17. *Gardella v. Chandler*, 172 F.2d 402, 404–405, 409–410 (2d Cir. 1949).

18. Ibid., 407–408.

19. Quoted in A. J. Liebling, "The Wayward Press: The Doldrums: George and Danny," *New Yorker*, March 12, 1949, 61–62.

20. *Los Angeles Times*, February 16, 1949, 11; Minutes, March 7, 1949, BR, box 33, folder 6; *New York Times*, March 20, 1949, S3.

21. *Study of Monopoly Power: Hearings Before the Subcommittee on Study of Monopoly Power of the Committee on the Judiciary, House of Representatives*, 82nd Cong., 1st Sess., Serial No. 1, Part 6: Organized Baseball (1951), 290–291.

22. *New York Times*, March 8, 1949, 32; March 9, 1949, 34; March 23, 1949, 39; *Los Angeles Times*, March 7, 1949, C1; Mickey Owen to Branch Rickey, February 25, 1949, BR, box 34, folder 2.

23. *New York Times*, June 6, 1949, 24; *Martin v. National League Baseball Club*, 174 F.2d 917 (2d Cir. 1949).

24. *New York Times*, April 20, 1949, 36; September 20, 1949, 39.

25. *New York Times*, October 8, 1949, 17; "Sport: I'm So Happy," *Time*, October 24, 1949.

26. *New York Times*, June 21, 1950, 38; *Los Angeles Times*, February 27, 1966, H4; October 22, 1994, 1.

27. *New York Times*, February 11, 1949, 30; April 6, 1949, 40.

28. "Memorandum for the Commissioner of Baseball" (November 30, 1949), ABC, box 162; Graham Claytor to Albert B. Chandler, December 20, 1949, and Albert B. Chandler to Graham Claytor, February 20, 1950, ABC, box 154.

29. *New York Times*, April 11, 1950, 35; April 26, 1951, 49.

30. *New York Times*, May 5, 1951, 30; Emanuel Celler, *You Never Leave Brooklyn: The Autobiography of Emanuel Celler* (New York: John Day Co., 1953), 155–167.

31. *Study of Monopoly Power*, 3; Emanuel Celler to A. B. Chandler, May 11, 1951, CAH, box 1, folder 2; Statement by Representative Emanuel Celler, August 3, 1951, EC, box 1, folder 2; *Study of Monopoly Power*, 1024.

32. Albert B. Chandler to Emanuel Celler, July 19, 1951, ABC, box 154; Albert B. Chandler to Tyrus R. Cobb, July 23, 1951, ABC, box 154; Emanuel Celler to Clark Griffith, August 3, 1951, EC, box 1, folder 2.

33. "Minutes of Meeting of Subcommittee on Study of Monopoly Power" (July 25, 1951), EC, box 52; Bill Barnhart and Gene Schlickman, *John Paul Stevens: An Independent Life* (DeKalb: Northern Illinois University Press, 2010), 89–92. In private practice many years later, Stevens would be retained by Charlie Finley, the owner of the Kansas City A's, to advise on antitrust issues surrounding the team's move to Oakland and to smooth labor relations with players. John Paul Stevens, "A Judge's Use of History—Thomas E. Fairchild Inaugural Lecture," *Wisconsin Law Review* (1989): 225; Tony Mauro, "Stevens' Influential Inning: Marvin Miller Recalls Justice's Role in the History of Ballplayers' Rights," *National Law Journal*, August 1, 2011, 1.

34. *New York Times*, August 5, 1951, 122; *Study of Monopoly Power*, 31, 853; Vincent X. Flaherty to Emanuel Celler, October 15, 1951, CAH, box 1, folder 2.

35. Unidentified correspondent to Emanuel Celler, July 24, 1951, EC, box 1, folder 2; Fred H. Delano to Emanuel Celler, August 2, 1951, EC, box 1, folder 2; Howard Osterhout to Emanuel Celler, August 2, 1951, EC, box 1, folder 2.

36. "Minutes of Meeting of Antitrust Subcommittee: Subcommittee No. 5" (May 7, 1952), and "Minutes of Meeting of Antitrust Subcommittee: Subcommittee No. 5" (May 15, 1952), EC, box 52.

37. *Organized Baseball: Report of the Subcommittee on Study of Monopoly Power of the Committee on the Judiciary*, H. Rep. No. 2002, 82nd Cong., 2nd Sess. (Washington, D.C.: Government Printing Office, 1952), 228–232.

38. Ford Frick, Press release (May 23, 1952), CAH, box 1, folder 10; E. Ernest Goldstein to Emanuel Celler, June 3, 1952, EC, box 1, folder 2.

39. Transcript of Record, 3–19, *Toolson v. New York Yankees*, 346 U.S. 356 (1953).

40. *Toolson v. New York Yankees*, 101 F. Supp. 93, 94–95 (C.D. Cal. 1951); *New York Times*, November 8, 1951, 37.

41. Transcript of Record, 25–26, *Kowalski v. Chandler*, 346 U.S. 356 (1953).

42. *Toolson v. New York Yankees*, 200 F.2d 198 (2d Cir. 1952); *Kowalski v. Chandler*, 202 F.2d 413, 414 (6th Cir. 1953); *Corbett v. Chandler*, 202 F.2d 428 (6th Cir. 1953).

43. Petition for Writ of Certiorari, *Toolson v. New York Yankees*, 346 U.S. 356 (1953); Petition for Writ of Certiorari, *Kowalski v. Chandler*, 346 U.S. 356 (1953).

44. Brief for Respondents in Opposition to Petition for Certiorari, *Toolson v. New York Yankees*, 346 U.S. 356 (1953); Brief for Respondents in Opposition to Petition for Certiorari, *Kowalski v. Chandler*, 346 U.S. 356 (1953); William H. Rehnquist to Robert Jackson, undated (ca. May 1953), RHJ, box 185, folder 8; Bowie Kuhn, *Hardball: The Education of a Baseball Commissioner* (New York: Times Books, 1987), 19.

45. *New York Times*, May 26, 1953, 25.
46. Shirley Povich, "The Supreme Court Takes the Mound," *Baseball Digest*, August 1953, 30; *New York Times*, May 26, 1953, 37; Craig, "Monopsony in Manpower," 576–639; "Baseball Players and the Antitrust Laws," *Columbia Law Review* 53 (1953): 242–258; *New York Times*, February 22, 1953, S3; Sherman Minton to Albert B. Chandler, September 19, 1949, Tom Clark to Albert B. Chandler, September 12, 1949, ABC, box 161.
47. Ford Frick to Emanuel Celler, July 17, 1953, EC, box 1, folder 4; J. G. Taylor Spink to Emanuel Celler, September 11, 1953, EC, box 1, folder 4.
48. Brief for Respondents, 22–23, *Kowalski v. Chandler*, 346 U.S. 356 (1953); Brief for Respondents, 42, *Toolson v. New York Yankees*, 346 U.S. 356 (1953).
49. Brief for Boston American League Base Ball Company as Amicus Curiae, 15–16, *Toolson v. New York Yankees*, 346 U.S. 356 (1953).
50. Brief for Respondents, 68–69, *Kowalski v. Chandler*, 346 U.S. 356 (1953).
51. *New York Times*, October 11, 1953, E10; October 15, 1953, 46; October 14, 1953, 37.
52. Conference notes, *Toolson v. New York Yankees*, October 17, 1953, WOD, box 1147, folder 2.
53. Robert Jackson, handwritten notes on William H. Rehnquist to Robert Jackson, undated (ca. May 1953), RHJ, box 185, folder 8.
54. Black is identified as the author in a handwritten note by Frances Lamb, his secretary, on the folder holding Black's records of the case. HLB, box 321, folder 11.
55. Earl Warren to Hugo Black, October 23, 1953, HLB, box 321, folder 11.
56. Stanley Reed to Harold Burton, October 26, 1953, HHB, box 245, folder 3, LC; *Toolson v. New York Yankees*, 346 U.S. 356, 357, 360 (1953).
57. *Toolson* is sometimes criticized on the ground that the Court drew the incorrect inference from Congress's failure to enact antitrust legislation in 1951–1952. The bills before Congress would have created an antitrust exemption for professional sports, the argument goes, and since the bills did not pass, we should infer that Congress did not intend sports to have such an exemption. See, for example, Lionel S. Sobel, *Professional Sports and the Law* (New York: Law-Arts Publishers, 1977), 28. In the hearings, however, the subcommittee members all expressed the desire to protect baseball from antitrust suits, as well as the knowledge that baseball was already exempt under *Federal Baseball Club*.
58. See, for example, Neil J. Sullivan, *The Dodgers Move West* (New York: Oxford University Press, 1987), 121–122; Andrew Zimbalist, *May the Best Team Win: Baseball Economics and Public Policy* (Washington, D.C.: Brookings Institution Press, 2003), 19.
59. *Organized Baseball*, 192; J. Gordon Hylton, "Why Baseball's Antitrust Exemption Still Survives," *Marquette Sports Law Journal* 9 (1999): 399.
60. *New York Times*, November 22, 1953, E4.

CHAPTER 5

1. *Organized Professional Team Sports: Hearings Before the Antitrust Subcommittee of the Committee on the Judiciary, House of Representatives*, 85th Cong., 1st Sess. (1957), 2498; Jay H. Topkis, "Monopoly in Professional Sports," *Yale Law Journal* 58 (1949): 702–704; "Soundtrack," *Sports Illustrated*, November 22, 1954.

2. *Study of Monopoly Power: Hearings Before the Subcommittee on Study of Monopoly Power of the Committee on the Judiciary, House of Representatives,* 82nd Cong., 1st Sess., Serial No. 1, Part 6: Organized Baseball (1951), 1454–1455, 1505.

3. *Cleveland Plain Dealer,* November 10, 1953, BB.

4. *Subjecting Professional Baseball Clubs to the Antitrust Laws: Hearings Before a Subcommittee of the Committee on the Judiciary, United States Senate,* 83rd Cong., 2nd Sess. (1954), 4; *The Attorney General's National Committee to Study the Antitrust Laws* (Washington, D.C.: Government Printing Office, 1955), 63–64.

5. *United States v. Shubert,* 120 F. Supp. 15, 16 (S.D.N.Y. 1953); *Subjecting Professional Baseball Clubs to the Antitrust Laws,* 3–4.

6. Robert C. Bonges, "The Antitrust Expediting Act: A Critical Reappraisal," *Michigan Law Review* 63 (1965): 1240–1257.

7. Elliott J. Gorn, *The Manly Art: Bare-Knuckle Prize Fighting in America* (Ithaca, N.Y.: Cornell University Press, 1986), 220–221; Jeffrey T. Sammons, *Beyond the Ring: The Role of Boxing in American Society* (Urbana: University of Illinois Press, 1988), 71, 78, 149.

8. The government's complaint is reproduced as Appendix A in Statement as to Jurisdiction, *United States v. International Boxing Club of New York, Inc.,* 348 U.S. 236 (1955).

9. *New York Times,* February 5, 1954, 27; *Shall v. Henry,* 211 F.2d 226, 229 (7th Cir. 1954).

10. Brief for the United States, 7–9, *United States v. International Boxing Club of New York, Inc.,* 348 U.S. 236 (1955).

11. *United States v. Paramount Pictures, Inc.,* 334 U.S. 131 (1948).

12. Brief for Appellees, *United States v. International Boxing Club of New York, Inc.,* 348 U.S. 236 (1955).

13. *United States v. International Boxing Club of New York, Inc.,* 348 U.S. 236, 240–244 (1955).

14. *United States v. Shubert,* 348 U.S. 222, 228, 230 (1955).

15. *International Boxing Club,* 348 U.S. at 248–249, 251.

16. Charles Gromley, "Baseball and the Anti-Trust Laws," *Nebraska Law Review* 34 (1955): 609; Samuel S. McKenney, "Baseball—An Exception to the Antitrust Laws," *University of Pittsburgh Law Review* 18 (1956): 147; *Washington Post,* February 2, 1955, 19; *International Boxing Club,* 348 U.S. at 251, 249.

17. *New York Times,* March 9, 1957, 22; *International Boxing Club of New York, Inc. v. United States,* 358 U.S. 242 (1959).

18. *New York Times,* February 26, 1957, 36.

19. Dan Daly and Bob O'Donnell, *The Pro Football Chronicle* (New York: Collier Books, 1990), 92; *New York Times,* October 2, 1994, S13; Transcript of Record, 3–18, *Radovich v. National Football League,* 352 U.S. 445 (1957).

20. David Harris, *The League: The Rise and Decline of the NFL* (New York: Bantam Books, 1986), 333.

21. Brief of Appellees National Football League et al., 28, *Radovich v. National Football League,* No. 14394, RG276, box 1252, NA-SF ("*Radovich* Court of Appeals Record").

22. Executive Session Meeting, November 7, 1949, NFL Meeting Minutes, PFHF.

23. Ibid.
24. Memorandum in Opposition to the Defendants' Memorandum of Points and Authorities in Support of Motions to Dismiss (October 10, 1950), 4–5, *Radovich v. National Football League*, No. 28988, RG21, box 773, NA-SF ("*Radovich* Trial Record").
25. Deposition of William Radovich, 63, *Radovich* Trial Record, box 774; Meeting, January 18, 1952, NFL Meeting Minutes, PFHF.
26. Defendants' Reply Memorandum of Points and Authorities (April 27, 1954), 6–9, *Radovich* Trial Record, box 774; Transcript of Record, 64, *Radovich v. National Football League*, 352 U.S. 445 (1957).
27. Opening Brief for Appellant, 15, *Radovich* Court of Appeals Record, box 1252; Reply Brief of Appellant, 2, *Radovich* Court of Appeals Record, box 1252.
28. *Radovich v. National Football League*, 231 F.2d 620, 622 (9th Cir. 1956).
29. Ibid.
30. Memorandum for the United States as Amicus Curiae in Support of the Petition for a Writ of Certiorari, 2, *Radovich v. National Football League*, 352 U.S. 445 (1957).
31. Petitioner's Opening Brief, 13–14, Brief for the United States of America as Amicus Curiae, 7, Brief for Respondents, 21, 34, *Radovich v. National Football League*, 352 U.S. 445 (1957).
32. *Radovich v. National Football League*, 352 U.S. 445, 456, 455 (1957).
33. John Marshall Harlan to William Brennan, February 1, 1957, FF, part 2, reel 24, frame 81.
34. *Radovich*, 352 U.S. at 451–452.
35. *Los Angeles Times*, February 26, 1957, C1; *New York Times*, February 26, 1957, 36; *Detroit News*, February 26, 1957, BB.
36. *New York World Telegram*, unidentified date, *Philadelphia Evening Bulletin*, February 27, 1957, *New York World Telegram*, February 26, 1957, all BB.
37. *Wall Street Journal*, February 27, 1957, 12; *New York Times*, February 28, 1957, 26; February 27, 1957, 25.
38. Philip B. Kurland, "The Supreme Court and the Attrition of State Power," *Stanford Law Review* 10 (1958): 279; "The Supreme Court, 1956 Term," *Harvard Law Review* 71 (1957): 173; Roger C. Cramton to Harold Burton, March 31, 1957, HHB, box 281, folder 3.
39. *New York Tribune*, February 26, 1957, BB.
40. *Organized Professional Team Sports*, 41, 10.
41. *New York Tribune*, February 26, 1957, *Pittsburgh Press*, February 26, 1957, *Cleveland Plain Dealer*, March 5, 1957, *Los Angeles Times*, March 17, 1957, *Sporting News*, May 1, 1957, *New York World Telegram*, February 27, 1957, *New York Mirror*, February 27, 1957, all BB; Gerald Holland, "Baseball Forecast: Rain," *Sports Illustrated*, March 11, 1957.
42. *Los Angeles Times*, February 26, 1957, C1; *Los Angeles Times*, April 16, 1958, Bill Radovich clipping file, PFHF; *New York Times*, October 2, 1994, S13; *Los Angeles Times*, March 12, 2002, B10.

CHAPTER 6

1. *Organized Professional Team Sports: Hearings Before the Antitrust Subcommittee of the Committee on the Judiciary, House of Representatives*, 85th Cong., 1st Sess. (1957) ("1957 hearings"), 1–5.

2. *Organized Professional Team Sports: Hearings Before the Subcommittee on Antitrust and Monopoly of the Committee on the Judiciary, United States Senate*, 85th Cong., 2nd Sess. (1958) ("1958 hearings"), 1–6. The 1958 hearings are best remembered for the rambling testimony of the first witness, Yankees' manager Casey Stengel, who elicited several outbursts of laughter with his characteristically spirited but nonsensical responses. Stengel was followed by the Yankees' star player Mickey Mantle, who brought down the house by dead-panning "My views are just about the same as Casey's." Ibid., 11–24.

3. *Relating to Exemption of Certain Professional Sports Enterprises from Antitrust Laws* (unpublished typescript, 1959) ("1959 House hearings"), 5–6; *Organized Professional Team Sports: Hearings Before the Subcommittee on Antitrust and Monopoly of the Committee on the Judiciary, United States Senate*, 86th Cong., 1st Sess. (1959) ("1959 Senate hearings"), 1–5; *Organized Professional Team Sports—1960: Hearings Before the Subcommittee on Antitrust and Monopoly of the Committee on the Judiciary, United States Senate*, 86th Cong., 2nd Sess. (1960), 1–6; Paul Porter, *Organized Baseball and the Congress: A Review and Chronological Summary of the Past Ten Years* (unpublished, 1961), 39; *Professional Sports Antitrust Bill—1964: Hearings Before the Subcommittee on Antitrust and Monopoly of the Committee on the Judiciary, United States Senate*, 88th Cong., 2nd Sess. (1964) ("1964 hearings"); *Professional Sports Antitrust Bill—1965: Hearings Before the Subcommittee on Antitrust and Monopoly of the Committee on the Judiciary, United States Senate*, 89th Cong., 1st Sess. (1965).

4. 1964 hearings, 1, 12, 125; *Professional Sports Act of 1965*, S. Rep. No. 462, 89th Cong., 1st Sess (1965), 6.

5. *Congressional Record* 106 (1960): 14732; 1959 House hearings, 29.

6. *New York Times*, April 20, 1957, 13; Torbert H. Macdonald to Ernest J. Lanigan, June 19, 1957, Clipping File: Economics-Antitrust Exemption, BHF.

7. "'Sports'—But Businesses, Too," *Philadelphia Inquirer*, March 3, 1957, B24; John Davenport, "Rhubarb at Home Plate," *Town and Country*, April 1958, reprinted in 1958 hearings, 680; "Not Sporting," *New Republic*, January 18, 1964, 7.

8. 1957 hearings, 7; Kenneth B. Keating, "A Bill to Grant 'a Square Deal for Sports',"
Sports Illustrated, June 17, 1957.

9. 1957 hearings, 92–93; 1958 hearings, 149; 1959 Senate hearings, 52.

10. *Wall Street Journal*, April 3, 1957, 1; 1957 hearings, 1344.

11. R. G. Utley and Tim Peeler, *Outlaw Ballplayers: Interviews and Profiles from the Independent Carolina Baseball League* (Jefferson, N.C.: McFarland & Co., 2006), 64–65; Bobby Hipps to George Trautman, n.d. (handwritten notation on George Trautman to "all National Association leagues and clubs," May 2, 1958), CAH, box 1, folder 12; George Trautman to Ford C. Frick, June 4, 1958, CAH, box 1, folder 12; George Docking to Errett P. Scrivner, May 28, 1958, CAH, box 1, folder 12; George Trautman "to all National Association clubs and leagues," June 18, 1958, Clipping File: Economics-Antitrust Exemption, BHF.

12. Veeck and Linn, *Hustler's Handbook*, 78; Ford C. Frick "to all clubs," December 19, 1963, Clipping File: Economics-Antitrust Exemption, BHF; Joseph F. Cairnes to Alvin E. O'Konski, May 26, 1958, CAH, box 1, folder 12; Alvin E. O'Konski to Joseph F. Cairnes, May 22, 1958, CAH, box 1, folder 12; *Statement of Organized Baseball on Antitrust Sports Bill* (1958), Clipping File: Economics-Antitrust Exemption, BHF; Porter, *Organized Baseball and the Congress*; Ford Frick "to all owners and/or club presidents," September 1, 1965, Clipping File: Economics: Antitrust Exemption, BHF.

13. Meeting, January 29, 1958, NFL Meeting Minutes, PFHF; *New York Times*, March 21, 1957, 38; Meeting, January 22, 1959, NFL Meeting Minutes, PFHF; *New York Times*, May 7, 1957, 45.

14. 1957 hearings, 2497–2498, 2697; 1958 hearings, 389–390.

15. 1957 hearings, 2874, 2855, 2986.

16. *New York Times*, November 22, 1957, 39; December 3, 1957, 58; Meeting, January 22, 1959, NFL Meeting Minutes, PFHF; *Sports Illustrated*, October 28, 1957; *New York Times*, June 5, 1958, 41; July 31, 1959, 15.

17. 1957 Hearings, 40, 1233, 1306, 1207; 1958 Hearings, 294.

18. 1957 Hearings, 2594, 2676; 1958 Hearings, 328–329, 342, 453, 428.

19. R. R. M. Carpenter, Jr., to Emanuel Celler, April 9, 1958, folder 1:69:16, KBK; Ford Frick to unidentified recipients, May 21, 1958, folder 1:69:12, KBK; *Statement of Organized Baseball on Antitrust Sports Bill*, 13, folder 2:477:4, KBK.

20. *Applicability of Antitrust Laws to Organized Professional Team Sports*, H.R. Rep. No. 1720, 85th Cong., 2nd Sess. (1958), 10–11; *Congressional Record* 104 (1958): 12073–12105; Walter O'Malley to Kenneth B. Keating, June 25, 1958, folder 1:69:12, KBK.

21. 1959 Senate Hearings, 4–5, 33, 197.

22. *Broadcasting and Televising Baseball Games: Hearings Before a Subcommittee of the Committee on Interstate and Foreign Commerce, United States Senate*, 83rd Cong., 1st Sess. (1953) ("1953 Hearings"), 11; Benjamin G. Rader, *In Its Own Image: How Television Has Transformed Sports* (New York: Free Press, 1984), 26; *Sporting News* quoted in G. Edward White, *Creating the National Pastime: Baseball Transforms Itself, 1903–1953* (Princeton, N.J.: Princeton University Press, 1996), 215.

23. 1953 Hearings, 11.

24. W. Graham Claytor, Jr., to Albert B. Chandler, July 20, 1949, ABC, box 154; 1953 Hearings, 13, 29.

25. 1953 Hearings, 4.

26. 1958 Hearings, 692–695.

27. *New York Times*, April 3, 1951, 35; April 19, 1951, 52; April 29, 1951, S7; May 22, 1951, 55; October 17, 1951, 54; November 24, 1951, 21.

28. Executive session meeting, January 21, 1951, PFHF; Complaint, *United States v. National Football League* (October 9, 1951), Clipping File, Economics-Reserve Clause-1879–1968, BHF; *New York Times*, October 10, 1951, 1.

29. *United States v. National Football League*, 116 F. Supp. 319 (E.D. Pa. 1953).

30. Ibid.

31. Meeting, January 27, 1954, NFL Meeting Minutes, PFHF; *New York Herald Tribune*, November 13, 1953, BB.

32. Frank J. Shaughnessy to Emanuel Celler, January 9, 1958, folder 1:69:12, KBK; 1958 hearings, 158.

33. 1958 hearings, 116; 1959 House hearings, 117–118.

34. 1957 hearings, 1359, 1367; Sullivan, *Dodgers Move West*, 120–130; "Celler States New York Victim of Baseball Monopolists" (April 12, 1958), folder 2:347:1, KBK.

35. 1959 House hearings, no page number (from prepared statement inserted after page 12); 1958 hearings, 169, 84, 316, 314, 313.

36. Lee Lowenfish, *Branch Rickey: Baseball's Ferocious Gentleman* (Lincoln: University of Nebraska Press, 2007), 565–575; *Statement of Organized Baseball on (S. 3483) "Professional Sports Antitrust Act of 1960,"* Clipping File: Economics-Antitrust Exemption, BHF.

37. *New York Times,* January 29, 1960, 18; Joe Foss to Frank L. McNamee et al., January 6, 1960, Minutes of AFL Meetings, PFHF; AFL meeting, January 28, 1960, Minutes of AFL Meetings, PFHF; *Sporting News,* January 20, 1960, folder 2:477:6, KBK.

38. *New York Times,* March 10, 1960, 42; Telegram, Ralph C. Wilson to Kenneth B. Keating, April 13, 1960, Kenneth B. Keating to Ralph C. Wilson, April 25, 1960, Ralph C. Wilson to Kenneth B. Keating, June 1, 1960, all in folder 2:386:1, KBK; *American Football League v. National Football League,* 205 F. Supp. 60 (D. Md. 1962).

39. *United States v. National Football League,* 196 F. Supp. 445 (E.D. Pa. 1961); *Telecasting of Professional Sports Contests: Hearing Before the Antitrust Subcommittee of the Committee on the Judiciary, House of Representatives,* 87th Cong., 1st Sess. (1961), 1, 52–53, 69; 75 Stat. 732 (1961); Michael MacCambridge, *America's Game: The Epic Story of How Pro Football Captured a Nation* (New York: Anchor Books, 2004), 173–174.

40. James Edward Miller, *The Baseball Business: Pursuing Pennants and Profits in Baltimore* (Chapel Hill: University of North Carolina Press, 1990), 84; S. Rep. No. 1654, 89th Cong., 2nd Sess. (1966); *Professional Football League Merger: Hearings Before Antitrust Subcommittee of the Committee on the Judiciary, House of Representatives,* 89th Cong., 2nd Sess. (1966), 1–3; 80 Stat. 1515 (1966).

CHAPTER 7

1. John T. Soma, "Enforcement Under the Illinois Antitrust Act," *Loyola University of Chicago Law Journal* 5 (1974): 27; Edwin A. Matto et al., "Antitrust Enforcement in Ohio," *Ohio State Law Journal* 37 (1976): 561, 563; Stanley M. Lipnick and Janis M. Gibbs, "An Overview of the Last Decade of State Antitrust Law, Including 'Little FTC Acts,' Unfair Trade Practice Legislation, Franchise and Business Opportunity Legislation, RICO and the Rejection of *Illinois Brick,*" *University of Toledo Law Review* 16 (1985): 929–930.

2. The story of the Braves' move to Atlanta is well told in Glen Gendzel, "Competitive Boosterism: How Milwaukee Lost the Braves," *Business History Review* 69 (1995): 530–566.

3. Richard S. Falk to Albert B. Chandler, November 27, 1953, Walter Henry Bender papers, box 6, folder 5, WHS.

4. Walter Bingham, "No More Joy in Beertown," *Sports Illustrated,* July 23, 1962.

5. "Number of TV Homes in Major League Baseball Markets" (March 1964), Ralph L. Andreano papers, box 2, folder 4, WHS.

6. Press release, November 16, 1962, SRRH, box 4, folder 3; Joseph W. Simpson, Jr., to William G. Brunder, October 23, 1964, SRRH, box 3, folder 2; *New York Times,* July 3, 1964, 15; "Presentation to National League" (undated), SRRH, box 3, folder 4.

7. "The Laughing Indian," *Milwaukee Commerce*, November 1964, 7; Warren G. Giles to E. B. Fitzgerald, February 8, 1965, SRRH, box 4, folder 1; Richard W. Cutler to William C. Bartholomay, September 30, 1964, SRRH, box 4, folder 1; Richard W. Cutler to Ford C. Frick, October 15, 1964, SRRH, box 4, folder 1; Richard W. Cutler to Charles O. Finley, October 15, 1964, SRRH, box 3, folder 5; Charles O. Finley to Richard W. Cutler, October 30, 1964, SRRH, box 3, folder 5.

8. William Proxmire to Ford Frick, July 10, 1964, SRRH, box 3, folder 6; Henry Reuss to Ford Frick, July 13, 1964, SRRH, box 3, folder 6; Henry Reuss to Warren Giles, August 4, 1964, SRRH, box 4, folder 1; William Proxmire to Warren Giles, October 22, 1964, SRRH, box 4, folder 1.

9. Huston Horn, "Bravura Battle for the Braves," *Sports Illustrated*, November 2, 1964; National League meeting minutes, October 22, 1964, SRRH, box 3, folder 4; National League meeting minutes, November 7, 1964, SRRH, box 3, folder 3.

10. Eugene H. Grosschmidt to Warren Giles, October 22, 1964, SRRH, box 3, folder 2. "Separate but equal" was of course a reference to *Brown v. Board of Education* (1954), "reapportionment" was a reference to *Baker v. Carr* (1962) and *Reynolds v. Sims* (1964), and "due process" may have been a reference to the Court's then-recent cases recognizing new rights for criminal defendants, cases such as *Gideon v. Wainwright* (1963).

11. John K. MacIver to Edmund B. Fitzgerald, February 9, 1965, SRRH, box 3, folder 4; Rudolph A. Schoenecker to E. B. Fitzgerald et al., March 16, 1965, SRRH, box 3, folder 4; Rudolph A. Schoenecker to E. B. Fitzgerald, February 4, 1965, SRRH, box 3, folder 4; James Edward Held to John L. Doyne, May 27, 1965, SRRH, box 3, folder 4.

12. National League meeting minutes, July 21, 1965, SRRH, box 3, folder 4.

13. Ibid.

14. Trial transcript, 4652, SRRH, box 10, folder 1.

15. Veeck and Linn, *Hustler's Handbook*, 335.

16. Kuhn, *Hardball*, 21; Order, *City of Atlanta v. Atlanta Braves, Inc.* (February 8, 1966) (referring to the court's earlier temporary restraining order of December 17, 1965), SRRH, box 3, folder 5; Memorandum Decision and Order, *State of Wisconsin v. Milwaukee Braves* (January 26, 1966), SRRH, box 2, folder 5; *New York Times*, January 28, 1966, 25; *Wall Street Journal*, March 22, 1966, 18.

17. The decision was never published. It can be found in SRRH, box 12, folder 3. The most important parts are reproduced in *State v. Milwaukee Braves, Inc.*, 144 N.W.2d 1 (Wis. 1966).

18. *New York Times*, April 15, 1966, 24; April 16, 1966, 51.

19. Robert R. Nathan to Willard Stafford, April 20, 1966, SRRH, box 1, folder 2; Willard Stafford to Robert R. Nathan, May 27, 1966, Walter Henry Bender papers, box 6, folder 7, WHS.

20. Brief of Appellants, *Wisconsin v. Milwaukee Braves, Inc.*, 24–29, SRRH, box 12, folder 9.

21. Respondent's Brief, *Wisconsin v. Milwaukee Braves, Inc.*, 22–36, SRRH, box 12, folder 10.

22. *State v. Milwaukee Braves, Inc.*, 144 N.W.2d 1 (Wis. 1966).

23. Ibid.

24. Ibid.

25. Ibid.

26. Michael Koehler, "Baseball, Apple Pie and Judicial Elections: An Analysis of the 1967 Wisconsin Supreme Court Race," *Marquette Law Review* 85 (2001): 223–250.

27. Bronson C. La Follette to Donald F. Turner, August 25, 1966, SRRH, box 1, folder 2; unidentified writer (probably La Follette) to Donald F. Turner, October 18, 1966, SRRH, box 1, folder 2; Brief of the State of Illinois as Amicus Curiae, *Wisconsin v. Milwaukee Braves, Inc.*, 385 U.S. 990 (1966).

28. Petition for a Writ of Certiorari, *Wisconsin v. Milwaukee Braves, Inc.*, 385 U.S. 990 (1966).

29. *Wisconsin v. Milwaukee Braves, Inc.*, 385 U.S. 990 (1966); Timothy B. Dyk to Louis F. Oberdorfer, December 20, 1966, SRRH, box 13, folder 9; Petition for Rehearing, *Wisconsin v. Milwaukee Braves, Inc.*, 385 U.S. 990 (1966).

30. Mike Fuller has compiled a great deal of information about the case, including interviews with lawyers and deposition transcripts, at http://seattlepilots.com.

CHAPTER 8

1. Of the several books about *Flood v. Kuhn*, the best by a wide margin is Brad Snyder, *A Well-Paid Slave: Curt Flood's Fight for Free Agency in Professional Sports* (New York: Plume, 2007). See also Robert M. Goldman, *One Man Out: Curt Flood versus Baseball* (Lawrence: University Press of Kansas, 2008); Stuart L. Weiss, *The Curt Flood Story: The Man Behind the Myth* (Columbia: University of Missouri Press, 2007); Alex Beith, *Stepping Up: The Story of Curt Flood and His Fight for Baseball Players' Rights* (New York: Persea, 2006).

2. *New York Times*, June 21, 1972, 33; Abrams, *Legal Bases*, 69; William Eskridge, "Overruling Statutory Precedents," *Georgetown Law Review* 76 (1988): 1381.

3. Snyder, *Well-Paid Slave*, 82–91; Marvin Miller, *A Whole Different Ball Game: The Sport and Business of Baseball* (New York: Birch Lane Press, 1991), 189.

4. Appendix, 37, 38, *Flood v. Kuhn*, 407 U.S. 258 (1972).

5. Curt Flood with Richard Carter, *The Way It Is* (New York: Trident Press, 1971), 16.

6. Gerald L. Early, *A Level Playing Field: African American Athletes and the Republic of Sports* (Cambridge, Mass.: Harvard University Press, 2011), 70–109; David Remnick, *King of the World: Muhammad Ali and the Rise of an American Hero* (New York: Vintage, 1999), 221.

7. Charles P. Korr, *The End of Baseball As We Knew It: The Players Union, 1960–1981* (Urbana: University of Illinois Press, 2002); Jon Krister Swanson, *The Rise of the MLBPA: One Craft Guild's Safe Path Home* (University of California–Santa Barbara, Ph.D. dissertation, 2008).

8. Carl Yastrzemski to Marvin Miller, January 15, 1970, MM, box 8, folder 20; Jim Bunning to Marvin Miller, May 20, 1970, MM, box 3, folder 10.

9. Appendix, 6–19, *Flood v. Kuhn*, 407 U.S. 258 (1972).

10. *Flood v. Kuhn*, 312 F. Supp. 404 (S.D.N.Y. 1970).

11. "The Judiciary: Day in Court," *Time*, March 30, 1962; Snyder, *Well-Paid Slave*, 137–139.

12. Excerpts of the testimony can be found in Appendix, 142–406, *Flood v. Kuhn*, 407 U.S. 258 (1972).

13. *Salerno v. American League of Professional Baseball Clubs*, 429 F.2d 1003, 1005 (2d Cir. 1970).

14. *Flood v. Kuhn*, 316 F. Supp. 271, 278 (S.D.N.Y. 1970).

15. *Flood v. Kuhn*, 443 F.2d 264 (2d Cir. 1971).

16. Docket sheet, *Flood v. Kuhn*, No. 71–32, WJB, box I:253, folder 8. I am inferring the initial vote from the erasures of check marks in the "deny" column for White and Burger.

17. Draft dissent from denial of certiorari, October 14, 1971, HAB, box 145, folder 2.

18. *Salerno v. Kuhn*, 400 U.S. 1001 (1971) (Douglas, J., dissenting from the denial of certiorari); *Haywood v. National Basketball Association*, 401 U.S. 1204 (1971).

19. "The Justice Harry A. Blackmun Oral History Project," 4, LC.

20. Brief for Petitioner, 24–25, *Flood v. Kuhn*, 407 U.S. 258 (1972).

21. Ibid., 26–29.

22. Ibid., 30–32.

23. William Blackstone, *Commentaries on the Laws of England* (Oxford: Clarendon Press, 1765–1769), 1:69–70; *Kuhn v. Fairmont Coal Co.*, 215 U.S. 349, 372 (1910) (Holmes, J., dissenting).

24. *Cipriano v. City of Houma*, 395 U.S. 701, 706 (1969) (internal quotation marks omitted); *Johnson v. New Jersey*, 394 U.S. 719 (1966).

25. For a then-recent discussion of the problem, see "Prospective Overruling and Retroactive Application in the Federal Courts," *Yale Law Journal* 71 (1962): 930–933.

26. Brief for Petitioner, 32–38, *Flood v. Kuhn*, 407 U.S. 258 (1972).

27. Ibid., 45.

28. Brief for Respondents, 24–44, *Flood v. Kuhn*, 407 U.S. 258 (1972).

29. Ibid., 45–52; Michael S. Jacobs and Ralph K. Winter, Jr., "Antitrust Principles and Collective Bargaining by Athletes: Of Superstars in Peonage," *Yale Law Journal* 81 (1971): 1–29; *United Mine Workers of America v. Pennington*, 381 U.S. 676, 710, 716 (1965) (Goldberg, J., concurring).

30. Brief for Respondents, 53–59, *Flood v. Kuhn*, 407 U.S. 258 (1972).

31. Arthur Goldberg to David Fuller, December 31, 1971, AJG, box I:94, folder 11; Petitioner's Reply Brief, 8–17, *Flood v. Kuhn*, 407 U.S. 258 (1972).

32. "Blackmun Oral History Project," 184–185.

33. A recording of the argument is at http://www.oyez.org/cases/1970-1979/1971/ 1971_71_32/argument.

34. *Washington Evening Star*, March 21, 1972, clipping in HAB, box 145, folder 3; Oral argument notes, *Flood v. Kuhn*, HAB, box 145, folder 2; Snyder, *Well-Paid Slave*, 268–281; "Blackmun Oral History Project," 185.

35. I have reconstructed the conference from Justice Douglas's notes, at WOD, box 1561, folder 11, and Justice Brennan's notes, at WJB, box I:253, folder 8. In some cases this required filling in words to make full sentences.

36. *Flood v. Kuhn*, 407 U.S. at 286 n.1 (Douglas, J., dissenting).

37. Powell would have sided with Flood. "Congressional inaction," he argued, "only means they won't act unless we force them to by reversing." At the conference he was uncertain whether the Cardinals were in fact owned by Anheuser-Busch, but he later confirmed that they were and accordingly recused himself. Powell memorandum to conference, March 21, 1972, HAB, box 145, folder 2.

38. William H. Rehnquist to Robert Jackson, undated (ca. May 1953), RHJ, box 185, folder 8.

39. "Blackmun Oral History Project," 185, 473; Stewart to Burger, March 20, 1972, WOD, box 1561, folder 11.
40. Harry Blackmun to Potter Stewart, May 4, 1972, HAB, box 145, folder 2.
41. Draft opinion, May 5, 1972, 4–5, HAB, box 145, folder 3; Roger I. Abrams, "Blackmun's List," *Virginia Sports & Entertainment Law Journal* 6 (2007): 181–207; *Flood v. Kuhn*, 407 U.S. 258, 260–264.
42. *Flood*, 407 U.S. at 264–283.
43. Ibid., 283–284.
44. Ibid., 284–285.
45. Byron White to Harry Blackmun, May 26, 1972, WJB, box I:268, folder 2; "Blackmun Oral History Project," 18, 184; Bob Woodward and Scott Armstrong, *The Brethren: Inside the Supreme Court* (New York: Simon & Schuster, 1979), 190; Lewis Powell to Harry Blackmun, May 8, 1972, HAB, box 145, folder 2.
46. *Flood v. Kuhn*, 407 U.S. at 286–288 (Douglas, J., dissenting).
47. Blackmun's drafts and the obituary of Moe Berg are in HAB, box 145, folder 2.
48. Woodward and Armstrong, *Brethren*, 191; Draft opinion, May 5, 1972, 4–5, HAB, box 145, folder 3; Harry Blackmun to Daniel Crystal, October 9, 1980, HAB, box 145, folder 3; "Blackmun Oral History Project," 106.
49. "Blackmun Oral History Project," 1–2, 18, 473.
50. *Flood v. Kuhn*, 407 U.S. at 288–296 (Marshall, J., dissenting).
51. Kenneth R. Reed to William Douglas, May 11 and May 21, 1972, WOD, box 1561, folder 8; Byron White to Harry Blackmun, May 26, 1972, HAB, box 145, folder 2.
52. Warren Burger to Harry Blackmun, June 13, 1972, HAB, box 145, folder 2; *Flood v. Kuhn*, 407 U.S. at 285–286 (Burger, C.J., concurring).
53. *Washington Post*, June 20, 1972, clipping in HAB, box 145, folder 3.
54. *New York Times*, June 20, 1972, 45.
55. Jay H. Topkis to Arthur J. Goldberg, June 30, 1972, AJG, box I:94, folder 12; Arthur J. Goldberg to Jay H. Topkis, July 12, 1972, AJG, box I:94, folder 12.
56. John P. Morris, "In the Wake of the *Flood*," *Law and Contemporary Problems* 38 (1973): 85; Morgen A. Sullivan, "'A Derelict in the Stream of the Law': Overruling Baseball's Antitrust Exemption," *Duke Law Journal* 48 (1999): 1273 n.57; Abrams, *Legal Bases*, 67; Paul Weiler, *Leveling the Playing Field: How the Law Can Make Sports Better for Fans* (Cambridge, Mass.: Harvard University Press, 2000), 170.
57. Tinsley E. Yarbrough, *Harry A. Blackmun: The Outsider Justice* (New York: Oxford University Press, 2008), vii–xi, 346–348; "Blackmun Oral History Project," 292.
58. David J. Garrow, *Liberty and Sexuality: The Right to Privacy and the Making of* Roe v. Wade (Berkeley: University of California Press, 1994), 547–555.
59. "Minutes of Executive Board Meeting" (July 24, 1972), PS, box 2, folder 4.
60. Ibid.

CHAPTER 9

1. Kuhn, *Hardball*, 141.
2. Ed Edmonds, "At the Brink of Free Agency: Creating the Foundation for the Messersmith-McNally Decision—1968–1975," *Southern Illinois University Law Journal* 34 (2010): 581–582.
3. Ibid., 584–586, 589, 600, 606, 608.

4. Kuhn, *Hardball*, 126.

5. Ibid., 140.

6. Opinion, *In re Michael Corkins*, December 3, 1974, PS, box 1, folder 19.

7. Opinion, *In re James A. Hunter*, December 13, 1974, PS, box 1, folder 21. The arbitration award was upheld in *American and National League of Professional Baseball Clubs v. Major League Baseball Players Association*, 59 Cal. App. 3d 493 (1976).

8. John Helyar, *Lords of the Realm: The Real History of Baseball* (New York: Villard, 1994), 149.

9. Miller, *Whole Different Ball Game*, 243.

10. *Kansas City Royals Baseball Corp. v. Major League Baseball Players Association*, 409 F. Supp. 233, 236 (W.D. Mo. 1976); Miller, *Whole Different Ball Game*, 245; Kuhn, *Hardball*, 155–158.

11. Transcript, *In re Arbitration Between the Major League Baseball Players Association and the 24 Major League Clubs* ("Messersmith transcript"), 54–55, PS, box 2, folder 1.

12. Ibid., 105.

13. Ibid., 105–107.

14. Ibid., 108–121; *Lemat Corp. v. Barry*, 275 Cal. App. 2d 671 (1969); *Munchak Corp. v. Cunningham*, 457 F.2d 721 (4th Cir. 1972).

15. Messersmith transcript, 150–153, 503–505, 833–834.

16. Peter Seitz, "Value Judgments in the Decisions of Labor Arbitrators," *Industrial and Labor Relations Review* 21 (1968): 428.

17. "Statement by Chairman of Arbitration Panel" (December 8, 1975), PS, box 2, folder 2.

18. Peter Seitz to Editor, *Wall Street Journal*, November 5, 1981, PS, box 21, folder 33.

19. Peter Seitz to Robert H. Avery, October 15, 1981, PS, box 21, folder 32; Peter Seitz to Bowie Kuhn, November 23, 1982, PS, box 21, folder 39; Kuhn, *Hardball*, 159.

20. *In re The Twelve Clubs Comprising the National League of Professional Baseball Clubs*, 66 Lab. Arb. Rep. 101 (1975).

21. *New York Times*, December 24, 1975, 1; December 28, 1975, 139; *Kansas City Royals Baseball Corp. v. Major League Baseball Players Association*, 409 F. Supp. 233 (W.D. Mo. 1976), aff'd, 532 F.2d 615 (8th Cir. 1976).

22. John J. Gaherin to Peter Seitz, December 23, 1975, PS, box 2, folder 3; Peter Seitz to Columbia Journalism Review, January 8, 1981, PS, box 21, folder 28; Peter Seitz to Bowie Kuhn, November 8, 1982, PS, box 21, folder 39; Bowie Kuhn to Peter Seitz, November 16, 1982, PS, box 21, folder 39.

23. Kuhn, *Hardball*, 157, 158; Peter Seitz to Columbia Journalism Review, October 23, 1980, PS, box 21, folder 26; Peter Seitz to Russell L. Greenman, December 9, 1982, PS, box 21, folder 40; *New York Times*, October 19, 1983.

24. Lee Lowenfish to Peter Seitz, May 9, 1980, PS, box 21, folder 23.

25. Miller, *Whole Different Ball Game*, 267.

26. "Silver Anniversary: Baseball Salaries Have Skyrocketed Since 1975 Ruling," Associated Press, December 23, 2000, available at http://sportsillustrated.cnn.com/baseball/mlb/news/2000/12/22/free_agency_ap/.

27. Michael J. Haupert, "The Economic History of Major League Baseball" (2007), http://eh.net/encyclopedia/article/haupert.mlb.

28. Salary information for 1988 and 2011 is from the *USA Today* salary database, at http://content.usatoday.com/sportsdata/baseball/mlb/salaries/team.
29. Helyar, *Lords of the Realm*, 364.
30. *New York Times*, December 23, 2000, D1.
31. Snyder, *Well-Paid Slave*, 347, 351.

CHAPTER 10

1. *Mackey v. National Football League*, 543 F.2d 606 (8th Cir. 1976); *Kapp v. National Football League*, 586 F.2d 644 (9th Cir. 1978); Scott E. Backman, "NFL Players Fight for Their Freedom: The History of Free Agency in the NFL," *Sports Law Journal* 9 (2002): 1–56; *Robertson v. National Basketball Association*, 389 F. Supp. 867 (S.D.N.Y. 1975); *Wood v. National Basketball Association*, 809 F.2d 964 (2d Cir. 1987); *Philadelphia World Hockey Club, Inc. v. Philadelphia Hockey Club, Inc.*, 351 F. Supp. 462 (E.D. Pa. 1972); *McCourt v. California Sports, Inc.*, 600 F.2d 1193 (6th Cir. 1979).
2. *Smith v. Pro Football, Inc.*, 593 F.2d 1173, 1185–1186 (D.C. Cir. 1979); *Robertson v. National Basketball Association*, 389 F. Supp. 867 (S.D.N.Y. 1975).
3. *Brown v. Pro Football, Inc.*, 518 U.S. 231, 237 (1996).
4. *Los Angeles Memorial Coliseum Commission v. National Football League*, 726 F.2d 1381 (9th Cir. 1984); *Houston Chronicle*, March 8, 1996, in Anti-Trust File, PFHF; *The Application of Federal Antitrust Laws to Major League Baseball: Hearing Before the Committee on the Judiciary, United States Senate*, 107th Cong., 2nd Sess. (2002), 24.
5. *North American Soccer League v. National Football League*, 670 F.2d 1249 (2d Cir. 1982); *United States Football League v. National Football League*, 842 F.2d 1335 (2d Cir. 1988); *Yale Daily News*, October 26, 1990, in Anti-Trust File, PFHF; *Sporting News*, August 11, 1986, in Court Cases: USFL v. NFL Antitrust File, PFHF.
6. *Cleveland Plain Dealer*, August 17, 1982, *Wall Street Journal*, July 16, 1985, Associated Press, January 23, 1996, all in Anti-Trust File, PFHF.
7. J. Gordon Hylton, "Why Baseball's Antitrust Exemption Still Survives," *Marquette Sports Law Journal* 9 (1999): 391–402; Stanley M. Brand, "The Case for the Minor League Baseball Antitrust Exemption," *Antitrust* 14 (2000): 31–32; David M. Szuchman, "Step Up to the Bargaining Table: A Call for the Unionization of Minor League Baseball," *Hofstra Labor Law Journal* 14 (1996): 265–312; Jerold J. Duquette, *Regulating the National Pastime: Baseball and Antitrust* (Westport, Conn.: Praeger, 1999), 99.
8. *Toolson v. New York Yankees*, 346 U.S. 356, 357 (1953); *Charles O. Finley & Co., Inc. v. Kuhn*, 569 F.2d 527, 541 (7th Cir. 1978).
9. *Salerno v. American League of Professional Baseball Clubs*, 429 F.2d 1003 (2d Cir. 1970); *Postema v. National League of Professional Baseball Clubs*, 799 F. Supp. 1475, 1489 (S.D.N.Y. 1992).
10. *Piazza v. Major League Baseball*, 831 F. Supp. 420, 436–438 (E.D. Pa. 1993); *Butterworth v. National League of Professional Baseball Clubs*, 644 So. 2d 1021, 1025 (Fla. 1994).

11. Brian J. Duff, "Antitrust—Exemption—Baseball's Antitrust Exemption Does Not Extend to Decisions Involving Sale and Location of Baseball Franchises," *Seton Hall Journal of Sports Law* 5 (1995): 660; John Gibeaut, "Skybox Shakedown," *ABA Journal*, June 1998, 71; Thomas J. Ostertag, "Baseball's Antitrust Exemption: Its History and Continuing Importance," *Virginia Sports and Entertainment Law Journal* 4 (2004): 63.

12. *McCoy v. Major League Baseball*, 911 F. Supp. 454, 457 (W.D. Wash. 1995); *Minnesota Twins Partnership v. Minnesota*, 592 N.W.2d 847, 856 (Minn. 1999).

13. *Major League Baseball v. Butterworth*, 181 F. Supp. 2d 1316, 1331 (N.D. Fla. 2001); *Major League Baseball v. Crist*, 331 F.3d 1177 (11th Cir. 2003).

14. Duquette, *Regulating the National Pastime*, 93–115; *Silverman v. Major League Baseball Players Relations Committee*, 880 F. Supp. 246 (S.D.N.Y. 1995), aff'd, 67 F.3d 1054 (2d Cir. 1995).

15. H.R. 3288, 107th Cong., 1st Sess. (2001).

16. Ed Henry, "Baseball Lobbying Hits Major League on Hill," *Roll Call*, October 21, 1996.

17. Marianne McGettigan, "The Curt Flood Act of 1998: The Players' Perspective," *Marquette Sports Law Journal* 9 (1999): 380–381.

18. 15 U.S.C. § 26b.

19. Gary R. Roberts, "A Brief Appraisal of the Curt Flood Act of 1998 from the Minor League Perspective," *Marquette Sports Law Journal* 9 (1999): 437; Steven A. Fehr, "The Curt Flood Act and Its Effect on the Future of the Baseball Antitrust Exemption," *Antitrust* 14 (2000): 25–30.

INDEX